New Labour

D1324302

Also by Stuart White

OPTIONS FOR BRITAIN (*co-editor with David Halpern, Stewart Wood and Gavin Cameron*)

New Labour

The Progressive Future?

Edited by

Stuart White
Jesus College
Oxford

Editorial matter, selection and Chapter 1 © Stuart White 2001
Chapter 16 © Susan Giaimo and Stuart White 2001
Chapters 2–15 © Palgrave Publishers Ltd 2001

All rights reserved. No reproduction, copy or transmission of
this publication may be made without written permission.

No paragraph of this publication may be reproduced, copied or
transmitted save with written permission or in accordance with
the provisions of the Copyright, Designs and Patents Act 1988,
or under the terms of any licence permitting limited copying
issued by the Copyright Licensing Agency, 90 Tottenham Court
Road, London W1P 0LP.

Any person who does any unauthorised act in relation to this
publication may be liable to criminal prosecution and civil
claims for damages.

The authors have asserted their rights to be identified
as the authors of this work in accordance with the
Copyright, Designs and Patents Act 1988.

First published 2001 by
PALGRAVE
Houndmills, Basingstoke, Hampshire RG21 6XS and
175 Fifth Avenue, New York, N. Y. 10010
Companies and representatives throughout the world

PALGRAVE is the new global academic imprint of
St. Martin's Press LLC Scholarly and Reference Division and
Palgrave Publishers Ltd (formerly Macmillan Press Ltd).

ISBN 0–333–91564–X hardback
ISBN 0–333–91565–8 paperback

This book is printed on paper suitable for recycling and
made from fully managed and sustained forest sources.

A catalogue record for this book is available
from the British Library.

Library of Congress Cataloging-in-Publication Data
New labour : the progressive future? / edited by Stuart White.
    p. cm.
    "Many of the papers in this book have their origin in a conference
    'Labour in government : the 'Third Way' and the future of social
    democracy' which took place at the Munda de Ginzberg Center for
    European Studies, Harvard University, November 13–15, 1998"–
    –Acknowledgments p.
    Includes bibliographical references and index.
    ISBN 0–333–91564–X
    1. Labour party (Great Britain) 2. Great Britain—Politics and
    government—1997– 3. Comparative government. 4. Socialism.
    5. Liberalism. I. White, Stuart, 1966–

    JN1129.L32 N495 2000
    324.24107—dc21
                                                        00–062598

10   9   8   7   6   5   4   3   2   1
10   09   08   07   06   05   04   03   02   01

Printed in Great Britain by Antony Rowe Ltd, Chippenham, Wiltshire

Contents

Notes on Contributors

Samuel H. Beer is Eaton Professor of of the Science of Government, Emeritus, Harvard University. He is the author of a number of classic works on British politics, including *British Politics in the Collectivist Age* (1969) and *Britain Against Itself: the Political Contradictions of Collectivism* (1982).

Laurent Bouvet is Lecturer in Political Science, University of Lille and Institute for Political Studies, Paris. He is editor-in-chief of *La Revue Socialiste*, the quarterly review of the French Socialist Party.

Andreas Busch teaches in the Department of Politics and International Relations, Oxford University. He is co-editor, with Dietmar Braun, of *Public Policy and Political Ideas* (1999).

Anna Coote is Programme Director at the King's Fund, London. She has written widely on gender politics and is the editor most recently of *The New Gender Agenda: Why Women Still Want More* (2000).

Colin Crouch is Professor of Sociology at the European University Institute, Florence. His recent publications include *Social Change in Western Europe* (1999) and *Are Skills the Answer? The Political Economy of Skill Creation in Advanced Industrial Countries* (1999), co-edited with David Finegold and Mari Saho.

Susan Giaimo is an Assistant Professor in the Department of Political Science, Massachusetts Institute of Technology. She is the author of a forth-coming book on the politics of healthcare, *Markets and Medicine: Health Care Governance in Britain, Germany, and the United States*.

Anton Hemerijck is a political scientist at the Max Planck Institute for the Study of Societies, Cologne. He is co-author, with Jelle Visser, of *'A Dutch Miracle': Job Growth, Welfare Reform and Corporatism in the Netherlands* (1997).

Paul Johnson is an economist in the Department of Education and Employment and formerly a director of research at the Institute for Fiscal Studies, London. He is the author of numerous articles and monographs on income distribution, personal taxation and social security, including *Two Nations? The Inheritance of Poverty and Affluence* (1996).

Marc Landy is a Professor in the Department of Political Science, Boston College. He is co-editor, with Martin A. Levin, of *The New Politics of Public Policy* (1995).

Philip Manow is a political scientist at the Max Planck Institute for the Study of Societies, Cologne.

Frédéric Michel is Director of the Policy Network, London (www.policy-network.org) and a correspondent for *La Revue Socialiste*.

Pippa Norris is a Professor at the John F. Kennedy School of Government, Harvard University. She is co-author, with Geoff Evans, of *Critical Elections: British Parties and Votes in Long-Term Perspective* (1998) and editor of *Critical Citizens: Global Support for Democratic Government* (1999).

Carey Oppenheim works in the Prime Minister's Policy Unit and was formerly a director of research at the Institute for Public Policy Research, London. Her publications include *An Inclusive Society: Strategies for Tackling Poverty* (1998). She writes here in a personal capacity.

Michele Salvati is a member of the Commissione Lavoro Gruppo Democratici, Rome.

Steven M. Teles is an Assistant Professor in the Department of Politics, Brandeis University. He is the author of *Whose Welfare?: AFDC and Elite Politics* (1996).

Frank Vandenbroucke is Minister for Social Affairs in the Belgian government. He is the author of *Globalization, Inequality and Social Democracy* (1998) and *Social Justice and Individual Ethics in an Open Society* (forthcoming).

Jelle Visser is affiliated with the Amsterdam School for Social Research, Amsterdam, and the Max Planck Institute for the Study of Societies, Cologne. He is co-author, with Anton Hemerijck, of *'A Dutch Miracle': Job Growth, Welfare Reform and Corporatism in the Netherlands* (1997).

Margaret Weir is a Professor in the Department of Sociology at the University of California, Berkeley. Her publications include *Politics and Jobs* (1992) and *The Social Divide: Political Parties and the Future of Activist Government* (1998).

Stuart White is Tutorial Fellow in Politics at Jesus College, Oxford.

Stewart Wood is Fellow in Politics at Magdalen College, Oxford.

Acknowledgements

Many of the papers in this book have their origin in a conference, 'Labour in Government: the "Third Way" and the Future of Social Democracy', which took place at the Munda de Ginzberg Center for European Studies, Harvard University, 13–15 November 1998. I would like to thank the Center for European Studies at Harvard, the Dean's Fund at the Massachusetts Institute of Technology and the Social Market Foundation in London for their financial assistance with the conference. I would also like to offer more personal thanks to Suzanne Berger, Joshua Cohen, Philip Khoury and Richard Locke at MIT; to Abby Collins, Peter Hall, Charles Maier, Paul Pierson and George Ross at Harvard; to Robert Skidelsky of the SMF; and to Lloyd Gruber of the University of Chicago, for their advice, input and encouragement in putting the conference together. My special thanks to Lisa Eschenbach for her advice and for her efficient organization and running of the conference; and to Susan Giaimo, who has patiently listened to and greatly assisted my efforts to comprehend European and US politics over the past few years. I would like to thank those who participated in the conference who, even if they have not contributed a paper to this volume, will have nevertheless contributed to its substance through their interventions and presentations. I am immensely grateful to those who have contributed chapters to the volume for their good grace and commitment to the project. Finally, I would like to thank Diana Gardner for her support and for patiently enduring more conversations about third way politics than I had a right to expect.

Introduction: New Labour and the Future of Progressive Politics

Stuart White

1. The uncertain revival of progressive politics

For many advanced capitalist nations, certainly for Britain and the USA, the 1980s was a decade dominated by the forces of political and economic conservatism. In the 1990s, gradually at first, and gathering pace towards the end of the decade, progressive political parties have climbed their way back into office. In Britain the change has perhaps been most acutely felt in the form of Labour's emphatic victory in the 1997 general election, ending almost twenty years of uninterrupted Conservative government. But Labour's victory was preceded (and to some extent guided) by earlier Democratic victories in the US presidential elections of 1992 and 1996. It was also preceded by the victory of the centre-left 'Olive Tree Coalition' in the Italian legislative elections of 1996, and was followed by victories for the French Socialists in the legislative elections of June 1997 and for the coalition of Social Democrats and Greens in the German legislative elections of September 1998. In the Netherlands, the 'Purple Coalition' of liberal and socialist parties that took office in 1994 was returned with an increased majority following the elections of 1998. In 1999, social democratic parties held office in the vast majority of the European Union's 15 member states.

This apparent revival in the fortunes of progressive political parties has generated much excitement. But it has also generated much confusion and debate. In essence, the debate is about the extent to which the electoral success of these notionally progressive political parties really will, or can, translate into a reassertion of progressive values at the societal level. Are we witnessing a political realignment in the advanced capitalist world that will further progressive commitments to social justice (understood in reasonably egalitarian terms), effective freedom, and the extension and deepening of democratic self-government? Or are these new governments of the 'centre-left' destined merely to tinker with the terms of established conservative political settlements or to act as reluctant agents of pro-market economic reform?

Ironically, the world changed considerably during the years in which conservatism was the dominant force in the politics of the advanced capitalist world. There were, of course, dramatic and far-reaching economic changes: the further internationalization of trade and industrial operations; the voluminous expansion and internationalization of capital markets; the rise of new information technologies and the 'knowledge-based economy'; the continued shift from a manufacturing-based to a service-based, or 'post-industrial', economy. A notable continuity with the 1970s, however, is that for much of this period productivity growth remained rather sluggish across the advanced capitalist world, depressing growth in living standards and perhaps increasing citizens' aversion to a politics of 'tax and spend' (Glyn 1998). These economic developments have in part driven and have certainly interacted with important social changes: increased social and economic differentiation within the class-based communities from which the left has historically drawn support; changes in the position of women, reflected in their growing labour-force participation; demographic changes such as population aging and, in some countries, rapid growth in single-parent families; an erosion, in some countries, of citizens' 'trust in government' (Nye et al. 1997).

In the face of these developments – 'globalization', population aging, fundamental changes in family structures, less trust in state capacity – is it possible for governments to reaffirm progressive values? The question only increases in urgency when one adds to the foregoing list certain other developments of the last two decades: substantial growth in earnings and income inequality (at least in the nations of 'Anglo-Saxon capitalism'); attendant growth in poverty; persistently high levels of unemployment or economic inactivity (a severe problem in some continental European states); and the emergence of deprived subcommunities that are effectively cut off and alienated from mainstream society. On the one hand, economic and social changes have generated a new demand for progressive government; on the other, these same, or related, changes have generated widespread anxiety about the capacity for governments to reaffirm progressive values.

In Britain, the hopes and anxieties surrounding the future of progressive government are particularly acute, not least because of the length and intensity of the preceding period of Conservative government. 'New Labour' – the Labour Party as led by Tony Blair since his election as party leader in 1994 – embodies and evokes these hopes and anxieties. New Labour claims to offer a fresh approach to progressive politics, one that is uniquely fitted to the demands and constraints imposed by contemporary economic and social developments. New Labour politicians and intellectuals argue, moreover, that this approach is relevant not only to Britain, but to other advanced capitalist countries. In this vein, New Labour portrays itself as being in the vanguard of a new politics of the 'third way' or 'radical centre' that is winning power and reshaping public policy throughout Europe, in North America, and which has potential relevance to the wider world.

Do these claims stand up to critical scrutiny? Is New Labour's political project, in the British context, one that can be expected to reaffirm progressive values, in particular that of social justice? Moving to the comparative context, how is New Labour's project related to that of notionally progressive parties and governments in other countries? To what extent does it represent a project with wider international relevance and potential applicability, and to what extent is it of specifically British (or perhaps Anglo-American) relevance?

Of course, New Labour tends to be seen, not least by its strongest supporters, as a long-term political project with the same scope and ambition as 'Thatcherism'. But Thatcherism *evolved* as a political project, to a great extent defining itself only once in government and over a number of years. If the electorate grants it the opportunity, New Labour will also evolve in the course of time, and it is hard to anticipate at this stage exactly how it will evolve. It is, then, as yet too soon to offer a definitive assessment of New Labour. But it is still possible to offer a provisional assessment of New Labour's progressive credentials and of the relationship between New Labour and rhetorically cognate political movements elsewhere in Europe and in the USA. And that is what this book attempts: a report on political work-in-progress, mixing analysis, evaluation and a modest degree of prescription.

2.   Three approaches to the puzzle of New Labour

We shall examine New Labour's claims to be in the vanguard of a new form of progressive politics from three complementary angles: from the standpoint of ideology; from the standpoint of major policy initiatives; and by looking at what progressive parties and governments elsewhere are doing with a view to casting a comparative eye on New Labour.

2.1   The ideological angle: what does New Labour stand for?

How far has New Labour succeeded in fleshing out a distinctive, coherent and progressive public philosophy? How does New Labour stand in relation to pre-existing ideological traditions that have shaped British political debate? Is it plausible to see New Labour as a purely populist political movement which, for all its talk about the 'third way', actually eschews ideology in the interest of tracking the preferences of the median voter?

These questions are the focus of the papers in Part I of the book. In Chapter 1, I examine the concept of the 'third way' which has thus far guided New Labour's more explicit efforts to articulate a distinctive, coherent and progressive public philosophy. I argue that the third way is best understood, in Steven Luke's phrase, as a particular 'rhetorically defined space'. The space in question is quite capacious. It can be 'decontested' in both progressive and relatively conservative ways. It contains, in other words, a number of fundamental ambiguities, ambiguities that may (and perhaps already do) serve to obscure latent and potentially deep divisions over what New Labour stands for. In Chapter 2, Samuel Beer offers a historical perspective on New Labour's public philosophy. Beer finds much affinity between New Labour and various currents within the British Liberal tradition, particularly with the 'positive liberalism' of David Lloyd George and Jo Grimond. These two theoretical essays are then complemented by Chapter 3 on New Labour and public opinion. Pippa Norris looks at how far New Labour policy-positioning tracked the preferences of voters at the 1997 general election. This gives us some indication of the electoral pressures that may drive or constrain New Labour's efforts to articulate and act from a progressive public philosophy.

2.2 The policy angle: what is New Labour doing?

What is New Labour actually doing in government, and do its actions support its claims to represent a new form of progressive politics? More specifically, how far are New Labour policies distinctive from the policies pursued by the preceding Conservative administrations? And how far is government policy true to New Labour's stated (broadly progressive) ambitions, for instance, to create a society of 'lifelong learning', to reverse 'social exclusion', to create a more 'pluralistic' politics? Could government policy feasibly be modified so as to be more distinctive and/or true to these stated ambitions? If so, how?

These questions are the focus of Part II of the book. First, in Chapter 4, Stewart Wood examines and evaluates New Labour policy in the flagship area of education and training. Education and training lie at the heart of New Labour's strategy for both improved economic performance and social justice. Can existing policy commitments carry the heavy weight thus assigned to them? What assumptions implicitly underpin these policy commitments, and do these assumptions need to be challenged? In Chapter 5, Paul Johnson offers a critical survey of New Labour's approach to social security and the welfare state, exploring the points of continuity and change with the previous Conservative government, and the possibility of finding savings in the existing welfare bill so as to release funds for other areas (such as education or healthcare). Probably no policy initiative will have more immediate effect on social justice than

New Labour's welfare-to-work policies. In Chapter 6, Carey Oppenheim takes an in-depth look at some of New Labour's strategies for helping those who are typically disadvantaged in the labour market such as the young unemployed, single parents, and the disabled. She outlines another possible direction for active welfare policy based on participation income and discusses its strengths and weaknesses relative to the government's present tax-credit based approach.

The concerns of Chapters 4–6 are closely intertwined, relating as they do to the central progressive objectives of economic empowerment and security as requirements of social justice. Chapters 7–9 range more widely, albeit very selectively, over the field of government policy. In Chapter 7, Colin Crouch analyses New Labour's early initiatives in the field of industrial relations. Does New Labour have an original third way conception of industrial relations or can its initiatives be readily understood in terms of existing neo-liberal and social democratic models of industrial relations? In Chapter 8, Steven Teles and Marc Landy take a critical look at New Labour's commitment to constitutional reform and, in particular, at its policies to devolve political power to the nations and regions of the United Kingdom. In Chapter 9, Anna Coote concludes our discussion of New Labour in government with a consideration of the position and likely impact of New Labour on one of the prime objectives of modern progressive politics: gender equity.

Clearly, we do not cover the full range of government policy in Part II of the book. Important policy areas such as macroeconomic policy, environmental policy, policy towards Europe (to name but three) are not discussed as such. And it is important to emphasize that each chapter offers a snap-shot of policy at what could prove to be a relatively early stage of New Labour's development. Nevertheless, we do examine policy across quite a wide range of areas, and, most importantly for our purposes, in areas where the progressive values of social justice, effective liberty and democratic self-government are deeply implicated.

2.3 The comparative angle: New Labour and progressive politics abroad

'Third ways', 'Neue Mittes', 'active centres', 'radical centres', and so forth, have proliferated of late in the politics of the advanced capitalist world. Beyond commonality of rhetoric, what substantive points of commonality are there between the various national projects? To what extent is New Labour the British expression of an international sea-change amongst these parties? Does New Labour offer lessons in progressive politics from which parties abroad can learn? Does the experience of other nations offer lessons from which New Labour can and should learn?

Part III of the book focuses on these questions. Comparisons with Bill Clinton and the 'New Democrats' in the US emerged quite early in Tony Blair's leadership. In Chapter 10, Margaret Weir considers the record of the

Clinton administrations, explains why Clinton failed to translate the rhetoric of a progressive 'third-way' politics into real policy achievement, and considers how the left in the US might seek in future to promote a more progressive agenda. Our attention then turns to the relationship between New Labour and continental social democracy. To begin the discussion, Chapters 11–12 offer overviews of the current and ongoing debate within European social democracy (though also to some extent implicating the US Democrats) on the future direction of progressive politics. In Chapter 11, Michele Salvati, a member of the Italian parliament for the Party of the Democratic Left, argues that social democracy has in fact *long been* a third way (a principled compromise between the two historic lefts of liberalism and socialism), and that while there may be a need for adjustment within the terms of this compromise we are not in a period of epochal transformation on the left akin to the rise of socialism or the split between communism and social democracy. In Chapter 12, Frank Vandenbroucke, a social democratic minister in the Belgian government, identifies a number of broad public-policy positions on which European social democrats, including British Labour, seem recently to have converged. But he also identifies some important points of difference between mainstream continental social democracy and the philosophy of New Labour's 'third way' and a common challenge at the level of values: the challenge of clarifying what form of equality social democracy aspires to enact.

Chapters 13–15 then look at the current situation in three continental European states. The New Labour project is often said to have much in common with, if not to have inspired, the 'Neue Mitte' politics of Gerhard Schroeder, leader of the German Social Democratic–Green coalition government. Blair and Schroeder have themselves reinforced the impression of being engaged in essentially the same reformist project by issuing a joint declaration on the future of social democracy prior to the 1999 EU elections. In Chapter 13, Andreas Busch and Philip Manow examine prospects for Germany's 'Neue Mitte' and how far the comparisons with Blair and New Labour really hold up. In Chapter 14, Anton Hemerijck and Jelle Visser offer an account of the much-discussed Dutch third way and consider what lesions (if any) the Dutch experience may have for progressive governments in other advanced capitalist countries. In Chapter 15, Frédéric Michel and Laurent Bouvet discuss the developing theory and practice of the French socialists. The French socialists are often presented in the British press as the conservatives of continental social democracy, resistant to the innovative third way politics of Blair, Schroeder or the Dutch 'Purple Coalition'. How accurate is this image? Finally, in Chapter 16, Susan Giaimo and I try to draw together some lessons from the foregoing chapters and offer some provisional conclusions as to the progressive credentials of New Labour and the relationship between New Labour politics and contemporary progressive politics elsewhere.

References

Glyn, Andrew, 'The Assessment: Economic Policy and Social Democracy', *Oxford Review of Economic Policy*, 14(1), 1998, pp. 1–18.
Nye, Joseph, Zelikov, Phillip and King, David, *Why People Don't Trust Government* (Cambridge: Harvard University Press, 1997).

Part I
The Ideology of New Labour

1
The Ambiguities of the Third Way

Stuart White[1]

'...the worst thing one can do with words is to surrender to them.'
George Orwell, 'Politics and the English Language'

1. Introduction: a problem of self-definition

What does New Labour stand for? What is its ambition for British society? What is the public philosophy in terms of which it seeks to mobilize activists and citizens and how does this public philosophy differ from that of the right? These questions are posed by many political commentators, both in Britain and abroad. The puzzle to which they point, however, is one that is not confined to external commentators, but is to a great extent shared by many supporters and perhaps even members of the government. New Labour is clear about what it is not. It is not old-fashioned 'statist social democracy' and it is not free-market neo-liberalism. But how to state in more positive terms what it stands for?

This question, the question of New Labour's public philosophy, has become a major theme of the first years of the Blair government. Intriguingly, the government has to some extent purposefully raised the profile of the issue. And it has itself tried to frame the terms of the discussion by introducing the concept of the 'third way'. The questions with which we began have been translated and collapsed into one simple question: 'What is the third way?' Intellectuals close to Tony Blair have given their answer (Giddens 1998; Halpern and Mikosz eds 1998), and so too has Blair himself (Blair 1998).

Nevertheless, it seems fair to say that the third way has thus far failed to capture the public's imagination. One reason for this, I believe, is that despite recent efforts to clarify the concept, the nature of the third way remains fundamentally vague and elusive. It is not really a concept or an ideology, but, to use Steven Lukes's phrase, a rhetorically defined space (Lukes 1999: 3–4).[2] This space is defined in terms both of values and of receptivity to certain kinds of policy instruments. But the space involved is an expansive one, large enough to spread over a number of important intellectual divisions which correspond to potentially very different political projects. Some of these projects are clearly continuous with the Labour Party's tradition of egalitarian social democracy. Others are much less so.

Thus, what progressives ultimately have to decide is not simply whether they support 'the' third way, but what kind of third way project they favour; and whether, given its apparently inherent ambiguities, the discourse of the third way is in fact one that they wish to employ at all. A distinction might be made between the substance of the third-way debate, which has raised some interesting questions and stimulated some interesting contributions as regards possible futures for progressive politics; and the form of this debate, the insistence on framing questions under the rubric of a search for a third way. Form has almost certainly damaged substance. Those interested in the future of progressive politics should, I believe, renounce the form, focus more clearly on the substantive issues at stake, and state more precisely in their own terms where they stand – accepting that when they do this, they may well find themselves standing in somewhat different positions.

2.   The value framework: opportunity, responsibility and community

One way in which people have attempted to answer the question 'What is the third way?' is by reference to values. It is often said that the third way is about finding ways to promote 'traditional values in a changed [or modern] world' (Blair 1998: 1). What values, then, supposedly animate the putative third-way approach to economic and social governance?

When one looks over recent attempts to articulate a left or 'centre-left' philosophy of government (e.g., Commission on Social Justice 1994, Brown 1994, Blair 1996), as well as more recent explicit efforts to define the third way (Giddens 1998, Blair 1998), three concepts occupy the centre-stage: opportunity, responsibility and community. Interestingly, all three concepts also feature in statements of 'New Democrat' belief in the USA, including many of President Clinton's speeches.[3] At least in the Anglo-American context, then, the putative third way may be defined at the normative level by commitment to these three values, regarded, moreover, as mutually implicated and reinforcing.

1) *Real opportunity*: The value of 'opportunity' can obviously be interpreted in various ways. Within the framework of recent left (or 'centre-left') thinking it refers primarily to substantive or real opportunity to enjoy and deploy strategic goods such as education, jobs, income and wealth. The ideal of a society in which all citizens enjoy adequate levels of real opportunity, in something like this sense, is often described in contemporary left (or 'centre-left') literature as a 'stakeholder society' (see Layard 1997: 5–6,

for an example of such usage). And the evil of 'social exclusion' can be understood in terms of patterns of distribution that deny people access to minimally decent shares of these goods, i.e., which deprive them of their rightful 'stake'. The commitment to real opportunity is typically linked to notions of 'equality' or 'equal worth' (Blair 1998: 3, Giddens 1998: 102). In essence, the commitment to real opportunity embodies a principle of equal concern and respect and may require certain kinds of substantive equality for its satisfaction.

2) *Civic responsibility*: Within the value framework of putative third-way thinking the commitment to real opportunity is conjoined with an emphasis on civic responsibility. Once again, the concept of 'civic responsibility' can obviously be elaborated in various ways. Concretely, individuals should not try to free-ride on the productive efforts of their fellow citizens; they should take primary responsibility for nurturing and providing for their children; they should bear a fair share of the taxes necessary to ensure adequate opportunities and public goods for all; and they should recognize and act on their responsibilities to the natural environment. Those who ignore these civic responsibilities offload certain costs of a civilized, common life onto others and thereby live at the latter's expense. As a matter of justice, the state should clearly define and, where necessary, enforce the obligations which derive from these basic responsibilities. As Giddens puts it (1998: 65): 'One might suggest as a prime motto for the new politics, *no rights without responsibilities*.'

3) *Community*: A third key value in putative third-way thinking is 'community' (Blair 1994, 1996, 1998; Brown 1994). Perhaps even more contestable than the preceding two values, this concept is employed in two distinct ways, in what one might call 'macro' and 'micro' senses. In the first, macro sense, it can be said to refer to the quality social relations have when the preceding two values are satisfied: a society exhibits the good of community when, and only when, it secures real opportunity for all on the basis of shared, equitably enforced, civic responsibilities. There is no genuine community without real 'opportunity for all', for without this some will suffer exclusion and second-class membership. But there is also no genuine community without a general acceptance of civic responsibilities, for without this some will live 'aristocratically', at the expense of others. In the second, micro sense community refers to local attachment and attendant solidarities, a localized public good that contributes in itself to real opportunity and which may also help to undergird a sense of civic responsibility (see Teles and Landy in this volume, Chapter 8, and the brief discussion of social capital in section 3 below).

Another putative third-way value, given particular emphasis by Giddens (1998: 70–8), is 'democracy'. For Giddens, the putative third way must be centrally about 'deepening democracy', about making sure that there is 'no authority without accountability'. This implies not merely the conventional British reform agenda of devolution, and perhaps electoral reform, but a willingness to establish new democratic fora to connect citizen and state and to build legitimacy thereby for controversial public decisions in areas like science and technology. In some versions of the third way, therefore, the value of democracy rests alongside the 'core' values of opportunity, responsibility and community described above.

If this is the value framework of the putative third way, then it is by no means vacuous or empty of implication. It is clear, for example, that the commitment to real opportunity rules out libertarianism or a conservative form of meritocracy of the kind defended by Friedrich Hayek in *The Constitution of Liberty*. The commitment to civic responsibility – and to its enforcement – also distinguishes the putative third way from certain other ideological positions. It arguably marks a difference, for example, with what David Piachaud has termed 'mid-century Fabianism', perhaps the dominant ideology of social-democratic reformists in Britain for much of the late twentieth century (Piachaud 1993). Mid-century Fabianism saw the state as having all sorts of enforceable responsibilities towards its individual citizens, but, as Piachaud argues, tended to downplay the idea that the individual citizen also has enforceable responsibilities towards the wider community. In this respect, the putative third way has more in common with earlier currents of progressive thinking, such as 'New Liberalism' (and perhaps turn-of-the-century Fabianism). As articulated in the work of Leonard Hobhouse, for example, New Liberalism affirmed the state's role in defining and enforcing responsible behaviour on the part of the individual citizen even as, at the very same time, the state seeks to secure real opportunity for all (see especially Hobhouse 1994: chs 7, 8).

The third-way conception of civic responsibility should probably also be distinguished, however, from the New Right's ethic of 'self-reliance'. If people discharge responsibilities of the kind described above – to work, to nurture and provide for their children, and so on – many of them will thereby attain a state of economic self-reliance. By the same token, a failure of self-reliance will sometimes be symptomatic of a failure to carry out these basic responsibilities. But it does not follow that this ethic of civic responsibility is coterminous with universal self-reliance. For people can obviously suffer great misfortunes – unemployment, ill-health, etc. – through no fault of their own, and they will then have a legitimate claim to assistance that in no way impugns their status as responsible citizens. To deny this and to insist that people always 'stand on their own two feet' would be to renege on the commitment to guarantee real opportunity for all.

However, while the value framework of the putative third way is by no means vacuous and without some substantive implications, it cannot be said that the framework amounts, in itself, to anything like a complete political philosophy. It is a *framework*, and a relatively general one at that, which can be rendered more determinate and concrete in a number of ways. As I shall show in section 4, different elaborations of the core values of real opportunity and civic responsibility can issue in very different political philosophies and projects.

3. The broad policy framework: rethinking collective action

An alternative way of trying to define the putative third way is by reference to distinctive policy stances and instruments – the 'means' of collective action rather than the 'ends' with which we were concerned in the previous section. In recent years there has been a wave of new thinking about how governments can and should act to promote progressive values, and the resulting ideas have acquired considerable saliency in the course of efforts to define the putative third way. Here I shall simply list and describe, in no particular order, what I take to be the most important ideas or sets of ideas:

1) The state should be seen as the guarantor, but not necessarily as the direct provider, of opportunity goods.
2) A receptivity to forms of 'mutualism' as a way of achieving progressive ends.
3) New thinking about public finance in connection with the state's role as guarantor of opportunity goods.
4) Employment-centered social policy.
5) 'Asset-based egalitarianism'.

1) *The state as guarantor, not necessarily provider.* According to one tradition in social-democratic thinking, the state is obliged to guarantee citizens access to certain opportunity goods (healthcare, education, etc.) and in general it ought itself to provide these goods. An alternative view insists that the state has the responsibility of guaranteeing access to such goods but denies that the state must directly provide these goods itself in order to discharge this responsibility.

First the state might continue to finance provision of certain opportunity goods while at the same time leaving actual production of the goods to other agencies. For example, the state might grant each citizen funds to acquire some high minimum of education and training (through such things as 'Individual Learning Accounts'), but it does not necessarily have to provide that education and training itself. Another means of separating finance and production roles is through the use of 'quasi-markets' in organizing the provision of goods such as healthcare and personal social services (Le Grand 1989, 1997, Bartlett et al. 1998).

Secondly, the state need not necessarily even be the primary financer of provision, but may confine itself to erecting a regulatory framework within which citizens are guaranteed access to opportunity goods. A pertinent example here would be recent proposals for a system of universal compulsory second pensions (Field 1996, Layard 1997). Citizens would be required to save some proportion of their income in funded pensions schemes, with subsidies for low earners, so as to ensure an adequate second pension for all. This is a potential example of what Julian Le Grand terms 'legal welfarism' in contrast with conventional 'fiscal welfarism' (Le Grand 1997). Under legal welfarism, the state requires the citizen, or more usually third parties, to undertake actions which ensure that he/she subsequently has access to important goods. Other examples of legal welfarism include: minimum wage legislation (requiring employers to pay their workers at least some prescribed amount); child support legislation (requiring absent parents to contribute to the upkeep of their children); and school–parent contracts (which might, for example, require parents to prevent their children playing truant). Legal welfarism clearly coheres with the emphasis on civic responsibility in the value framework of the putative third way.

2) *Receptivity to forms of mutualism.* Intersecting with this concern to rethink how the state might secure access to opportunity goods, on equitable terms, without necessarily providing them itself, is a renewal of interest in various forms of 'mutualism'.

One set of proposals, for example, is that the state should help and encourage Friendly Societies and other secondary associations to play a greater role in the organization and administration of welfare provision (Hirst 1994, 1997, Field 1996, Hargreaves 1998). Similarly, it has been argued that the state should help and encourage the formation of local Credit Unions to provide financial services to vulnerable, low income families (Toynbee 1998: 6).[4] There is related interest in 'time currencies' and Local Exchange and Trading Schemes as ways of reviving economic activity in disadvantaged communities (Boyle 1999). Tim Bentley and Geoff Mulgan have argued for a new form of association, the 'employee mutual', to provide protection for individuals in the labour market. Owned by their members, employee mutuals would organize training for their members and would negotiate the sale of their members' services to employers (Bentley and Mulgan 1996). They could also take on other welfare functions. Peter Kenway and Guy Palmer, along with Gerald Holtham, have argued that public utilities and other service industries should be reorganized as customer mutuals as an alternative both to conventional nationalization and privatized industry (Kenway and Palmer 1997, Holtham 1998).

An emphasis on the good of mutuality can also be discerned in recent thinking about business strategy and organization. Enterprises should not be seen as necessarily hierarchical entities which exist solely for the good of shareholders, but as sites of long-term, mutually advantageous cooperation between capital-holders and employees. Institutionally, such enterprises will be characterized by the use of various forms of revenue/profit-sharing and employee involvement in decision-making. It is argued that such 'mutual gains' enterprises are likely to be more efficient, especially in pursuing quality-centered product market strategies (Fernie and Metcalf 1995, Levine 1995, Layard 1997). There are important disagreements, however, as to the appropriate extent and form of state intervention in developing such enterprises. For some, exhortation is sufficient. Others countenance tax incentives to encourage employee share ownership (Mulgan and Murray 1994). Others favour legally mandated works councils, and legislating to discourage hostile takeovers (Hutton 1995, 1997, Kay 1996).

The growing interest in mutualism is also related to a growing interest amongst social scientists in the effects and construction of so-called 'social capital' (see Putnam 1993) – roughly speaking, stable interactive relationships that help bind people to cooperative norms and which thereby help to promote desirable social outcomes (economic, social and political). Mutualist initiatives, such as the establishment of new Credit Unions in low-income communities, may provide a way of rebuilding social capital where it is currently lacking, with, it is argued, a wide range of positive knock-on effects for these communities and the wider society (Commission on Social Justice 1994, King 1997).

3) *New thinking about public finance.* While many have argued in recent years that the state should recast its role in securing citizen access to opportunity goods, few have denied that the state will continue to have a significant role in providing and financing the provision of these goods. Given the perceived tax aversion of electorates in advanced capitalist societies, progressive policy thinkers have been under pressure to come up with new ideas as to how the state can raise the necessary revenues. I list just a few of the more notable ideas here.

a) Environmental taxes and charges: These would seem to cohere with the commitment to civic responsibility described above (they seem to follow from the obligation to make responsible use of the environment, paying the community for the extra costs one inflicts upon it). But some also argue that increased use of such taxes will allow for a reduction in taxes on earnings so boosting employment (Robertson 1996, Holtham and Tindale 1996). Thus there may be a link between this policy proposal and the idea of an employment-centred social policy which I shall describe below.

b) Hypothecation at the margin: Some argue that voter resistance to new taxes can be reduced if the link between new taxes and benefits is made clearer. Hypothecation of new taxes to specific goods, e.g. education, healthcare, or long-term care in old age, is thought to offer one way of doing this (Mulgan and Murray 1994, Hills 1997).

c) New consultative procedures on tax: Governments should connect with citizens on tax issues more directly through new consultative procedures akin to 'deliberative opinion polls' (Halpern 1997).

d) Community Fund ('Topsy Turvy Nationalization'): Under this proposal (Holtham 1995, Meade 1991, 1994), the state gradually acquires a share of the nation's productive assets and places these assets in a special fund (private-sector institutions may be contracted to manage the fund). The returns on the assets can then be used to finance provision of goods like education and healthcare. Initial capital for the fund could come from a revitalized inheritance tax or a wealth tax. While this idea is not on the immediate policy agenda in Britain, similar ideas have been floated in the US, not least by President Clinton, as a way of securing the long-term viability of the public pensions system (Blackburn 1999).

4) *Employment-centred social policy.* A fourth theme of recent policy discussions on the left is employment-centred social policy (a term I borrow from Haveman 1997): the central aim of social policy must be to enable citizens to achieve a decent standard of living through employment, and, since employment is becoming increasingly knowledge-based, this must be based on encouraging the ongoing acquisition of skills (Rogers and Streeck 1994, Commission on Social Justice 1994, Brown 1994, Layard 1997). Consequent policy proposals focus on enhancing the capabilities of disadvantaged workers (through increased access to education and training and childcare); and increasing the work incentives of disadvantaged workers (through some combination of a minimum wage and new or reformed 'in-work benefits' (see Ellwood 1988)). Since it will take a long time for new educational initiatives to feed through, it is sometimes argued that other complementary measures are necessary in the meantime to increase the demand for unskilled workers and/or to prevent entry into long-term unemployment (Phelps 1997, Haveman 1997, Layard 1997).

5) *Asset-based egalitarianism.* Closely linked with the idea of employment-centred social policy is the idea of 'asset-based egalitarianism' (Freeman and Rogers 1997). The basic idea is that the left's traditional distributive objectives should not only be pursued through income redistribution, or solidaristic wage policy, but by more concerted action to change the initial distribution of assets and productive endowments, such as skills, which people bring to the market in the first place (Rogers and Streeck 1994, Commission on Social Justice 1994, Freeman and Rogers 1997, Bowles and Gintis 1998). Employment-centred social policy can be seen as one application of this general idea. Another area of application is *asset-building policies*, such as the aforementioned proposals for universal second pensions (Field 1996) or tax incentives to encourage saving amongst the asset poor. More radical still are policies of explicit *asset-based redistribution*, such as the proposal to provide every citizen on maturity with a basic capital grant that he/she would then be free to use for approved activities such as education and training or setting up a new business (Haveman 1988, Le Grand 1989, White 1991, Ackerman and Alstott 1999). In this vein, for example, Ackerman and Alstott advocate endowing each US citizen on maturity with

a grant of some $80,000 to be paid for out of a tax on wealth and inheritances.

4.   Not one third way, but many

We have now reviewed the value and broad policy frameworks of the putative third way. I want now to suggest, however, that there can be (and currently are) important differences of opinion concerning the interpretation of the core values and how the state should seek to advance them. And these differences ultimately suggest very different, to some extent opposing, political philosophies and projects.

There are at least two important lines of division within the rhetorical space of the putative third way. There is, firstly, an important and potentially fractious division between 'leftists' and 'centrists' over the commitment to real opportunity: a philosophical division over exactly what this is a commitment to and, derivatively, a division over exactly what policies are needed to satisfy it.

Secondly, there is a no less important and potentially fractious division between 'liberals' and 'communitarians' over the commitment to civic responsibility – more specifically, over the precise range of behaviours for which individuals are appropriately seen as responsible to the community and which the state may therefore legitimately seek to regulate.

1) *Leftists vs. centrists: the ambiguity of real opportunity.* The people whom I am here terming centrists understand the commitment to real opportunity primarily in meritocratic terms. The people I am terming leftists, on the other hand, interpret the commitment to real opportunity in more egalitarian terms. Perhaps influenced by contemporary egalitarian political philosophy (see especially Rawls 1972, Dworkin 1981, and Cohen 1989), the leftists argue that meritocracy allows for unjust inequalities in real opportunity grounded in morally arbitrary ('brute luck') differences in natural ability. They believe that, in principle, policy ought to seek to mitigate for these undeserved brute luck inequalities.

From this philosophical difference, certain policy differences can of course follow. In particular, while accepting the need for a general reorientation towards 'asset-based egalitarianism', leftists will accord a larger continuing role to income redistribution in promoting genuine equality of real opportunity than centrists. Centrists will downplay the importance of income redistribution. Indeed, as qualified meritocrats, they will think it *unjust* to tax away the returns to superior ability beyond a moderate point. Blair (1998: 3) is perhaps endorsing the centrist position when he writes of how the left has in the past 'stifled opportunity in the name of an abstract equality'. While not strictly inconsistent with the leftist position as here defined, this is probably intended as a rejection of the level of income redistribution that leftism calls for. On the other hand, as we saw above,

Blair does state that 'equal worth' is a defining value of the third way, and it is precisely this foundational value to which leftists appeal when they critique meritocratic arrangements for arbitrarily penalizing the less talented (Rawls 1972, Dworkin 1985) and/or for creating a society riven by inequalities of status and respect (Tawney 1964). It would, moreover, be quite wrong to suppose that all social-democratic modernizers, either in Britain or elsewhere in the advanced capitalist world, embrace the centrist position (see especially Vandenbroucke in this volume, Chapter 12). There is no reason why those who are committed to a form of equal opportunity that goes beyond meritocracy cannot try to rethink their 'strategy of equality' by reference to the broad policy framework described in section 3. It is perfectly possible to be an egalitarian of a Rawlsian or near-Rawlsian variety at the philosophical level, and at the same time an open-minded modernizer at the level of policy.

2) *Liberals vs. communitarians: the ambiguity of civic responsibility.* Those sympathetic to the value framework of the putative third way claim that individuals have important civic responsibilities and that the state may and often should act to enforce the obligations which derive from these responsibilities. There is, moreover, a plausible range of consensus on what these responsibilities include: the responsibility to work (in return for a share of the social product) and to make an effort to acquire relevant skills for work; the responsibility to be a good parent (if one chooses to be a parent); the responsibility to pay a fair share of taxes; the responsibility to respect the environment. Nevertheless, there can be (and currently are) important disagreements about the precise range of behaviours for which people can reasonably be held responsible to the community and which the state may therefore legitimately regulate. The people I am here calling communitarians interpret this range of behaviours quite broadly, while those I am calling liberals interpret it more narrowly.

Take the case of family policy. The typical communitarian, as I am here using the term, will argue that the state has a legitimate interest in encouraging married two-parent families and that public policy ought to reflect this interest, for example by favourable tax treatment, tougher divorce laws, etc. Through such policies, the state encourages or requires individuals to act on their responsibilities as spouses and parents with positive repercussions for the community as a whole. The typical liberal, on the other hand, will see such policies as unfairly restricting or infringing personal freedom. Or take the case of drugs policy. The typical communitarian will see drug use as paradigmatically irresponsible behaviour which ought to be prohibited and punished. The typical liberal, on the other hand, will make the basic Millian distinction (Mill, 1985) between punishing someone for harmful behaviour which results from use of a given substance (which punishment is legitimate), and punishing someone for mere use of the substance regardless of how the person then behaves (which punishment is illegitimate). Relatedly, the liberal will in general be more hesitant about recourse to 'legal welfarism' (Le Grand 1997).

In short, the liberal will want to identify a limited number of very specific civic obligations and will acknowledge the legitimate role of the state in enforcing these specific obligations (witness, for example, John Stuart Mill's trenchant defence of the state's right to force parents to support and educate their children). But what the liberal will reject is the idea that the state may and should enforce 'good behaviour' in any very general sense. The liberal will see this as dangerously moralistic, i.e., as providing an alarming opportunity for elites or majorities to attack non-conformity for its own sake. On the other side, the communitarian, following such thinkers as Etzioni (1993) and Galston (1991), might argue that the liberal has an impoverished view of the rich social capital which undergirds civilized life, and of what is necessary to protect such capital from erosion.

There are thus at least two lines of division – leftist vs. centrist, liberal vs. communitarian – that cut across the rhetorical space of the putative third way. This space contains significant differences of opinion on values and public policy and these differences in turn define distinct, potentially opposing, political projects. On the one hand, for example, it is possible to speak of a 'leftist liberal' conception of the third way. This would combine a relatively strong emphasis on the continuing importance of income redistribution in pursuing the goal of real opportunity with a relatively narrow conception of the types of behaviour which the state may seek to regulate in the name of civic responsibility. On the other hand, it is also possible to discern a possible 'centrist communitarian' third way which would reverse these directions of emphasis. The former political project, I would argue, is genuinely social democratic (as well as liberal), whereas the latter project could conceivably end up having as much or more in common with a leftish one-nation Toryism of the Macmillan variety or leftish variant of continental Christian Democracy. Nor do these two positions exhaust the possibilities. It is perfectly possible to conceive of a 'centrist liberal' conception of the third way or, indeed, a 'leftist communitarian' conception of the third way.

There may also be further dimensions of disagreement pertaining to other values that I have not considered in depth here. In particular, Steven Lukes (1999: 3) has suggested that the value of democracy is the focus of another fundamental division within the camp of the putative third way between 'those inclined to concentrate power in the hands of the specially qualified, whether politically or managerially or technically, and those who favour its wide dispersion into the hands of the governed, enabling them to participate maximally in public deliberation and decision-making.'

5.   Conclusion: moving the 'third-way debate' beyond the 'third way'

Contrary to some critics, it is possible to identify distinctive value and policy frameworks that define a putative third-way approach to economic and social policy. But this does not mean that the third way amounts to a distinctive, coherent and progressive public philosophy. For its defining frameworks are broad enough to accommodate some quite basic disagreements on values and policy – disagreements that cut across opposing public philosophies in the true sense of the word.[5]

This capaciousness and ambiguity reflects the coalitional character and ambition of New Labour. It is also, relatedly, a reflection of the 'newness' of New Labour: of the fact that this political current contains many possible futures, not all of which can ultimately be squared with each other. But this capaciousness and structural ambiguity do mean that the putative third way cannot perform the function that its proponents claim for it. It cannot serve as a public philosophy, simply because it skirts over the hard choices across values and policy orientations that define genuine public philosophies.

George Orwell recognized that to engage in serious and truly free political thinking we have to get our ideas clear first and *in the process* choose the words that are most appropriate to express them: freedom of thought *is* autonomy in the use of language (Orwell 1983). But this is exactly the reverse of the way in which the third-way discussion has proceeded in Britain. Contrary to Orwell's advice, those who have tried to answer the question, 'What is the third way?', have 'surrendered' to a phrase and have then cast frantically about for its meaning. This does not mean that the 'third-way debate' has been useless. It has provoked people into a real discussion, not only within Britain, but across Europe and (probably to a lesser extent) in the USA, about the future of progressive governance – though some have also probably been discouraged from entering into this debate by what they perceive as the shallowness of the third-way concept. But in the spirit of Orwell, with his acute sense of how language can control and distort thought, progressives should now put the ambiguous language of the third way aside and focus directly on the questions at stake in this debate: What values ought progressives to affirm (in particular, what kinds of equality)? What institutional arrangements can significantly advance these values in contemporary circumstances?

Notes

1   This chapter is taken, with some revisions, from an earlier article, 'The "Third Way": Not One Road, But Many', *Renewal*, 6, 1998: 17–30. I am particularly indebted to Steven Lukes for comment on the earlier paper, and am grateful to the editors of *Renewal* for permission to draw upon it.

2 Lukes sharpens and extends a line of argument towards which I was groping in 'Not One Road, But Many'.
3 See the website of the Democratic Leadership Council (DLC) at <www.dlcppi.org> which contains an archive of speeches and policy statements by New Democrat thinkers and politicians including Al Gore and Bill Clinton.
4 At time of writing, the Labour government has already announced plans to reform the laws governing Friendly Societies and Credit Unions so as to facilitate their growth.
5 For other analyses which reach similar conclusions, see Freeden (1998) and Klein and Rafferty (1999).

References

Ackerman, Bruce and Alstott, Anne, *The Stakeholder Society* (New Haven: Yale University Press, 1999).

Bartlett, Will, Roberts, Jennifer and Le Grand, Julian, *A Revolution in Social Policy: Quasi-Market Reforms in the 1990s* (Bristol: The Policy Press, 1998).

Bentley, Tim and Mulgan, Geoff, *Employee Mutuals: The 21st Century Trade Union?* (London, Demos, 1996).

Blackburn, Robin, 'The New Collectivism: Pension Reform, Grey Capitalism and Complex Socialism', *New Left Review*, 233, Jan./Feb. 1999: 3–65.

Blair, Tony, *Social-ism* (London: Fabian Society, 1994).

——, *New Britain: My Vision of a Young Country* (London: Fourth Estate, 1996).

——, *The Third Way: New Politics for a New Century* (London: Fabian Society, 1998).

Bowles, Samuel and Gintis, Herbert, *Recasting Egalitarianism* (London: Verso, 1998).

Boyle, David, *Alternative Currencies, Alternative Identities* (London: Centre for Reform, 1999).

Brown, Gordon, 'The Politics of Potential: a New Agenda for Labour', in David Miliband, ed., *Reinventing the Left* (Cambridge: Polity, 1994), pp. 113–22.

——, *Fair is Efficient* (London: Fabian Society, 1995).

Cohen, G. A., 'On the Currency of Egalitarian Justice', *Ethics*, 99, 1989: 912–44.

Commission on Social Justice, *Social Justice: Strategies for National Renewal* (London: Vintage, 1994).

Dworkin, Ronald, 'What is Equality? Part 2: Equality of Resources', *Philosophy and Public Affairs*, 10, 1981: 283–345.

——, 'Why Liberals Should Care About Equality', in Dworkin, *A Matter of Principle* (Cambridge, Mass.: Harvard University Press, 1985), pp. 205–213.

Ellwood, David, *Poor Support: Poverty in the American Family* (New York: Basic Books, 1988).

Etzioni, Amitai, *The Spirit of Community: the Reinvention of American Society* (New York: Touchstone, 1993).

Fernie, Sue and Metcalf, David, 'Participation, Contingent Pay, Representation and Workplace Performance: Some Evidence from Great Britain', *British Journal of Industrial Relations*, 33, 1995: 379–415.

Field, Frank, *How to Pay for the Future: Building a Stakeholders' Welfare* (London: Institute of Community Studies, 1996).

Freeden, Michael, 'The Ideology of New Labour', *The Political Quarterly*, 69, 1998.

Freeman, Richard and Rogers, Joel, 'The New Inequality and What to Do About It', *The Boston Review*, Dec. 1996/Jan. 1997.

Galston, William, *Liberal Purposes* (Cambridge: Cambridge University Press, 1991).

Giddens, Anthony, *The Third Way: the Renewal of Social Democracy* (Cambridge: Polity, 1998).

Halpern, David, 'A New Consultative Procedure for Taxation' (London: Nexus, 1997).

Halpern, David and Mikosz, David, eds, *The Third Way: Summary of the NEXUS Online Discussion* (London: Nexus, 1998).

Hargreaves, Ian, 'A Step Beyond Morris Dancing: the Third Sector Revival', in Ian Hargreaves and Ian Christie, eds, *Tomorrow's Politics: the Third Way and Beyond* (London: Demos, 1998), pp. 65–79.

Haveman, Robert, *Starting Even: an Equal Opportunity Program to Combat the Nation's New Poverty* (New York: Simon and Schuster, 1988).

——, 'Employment with Equity', *The Boston Review*, Summer 1997.

Hayek, Friedrich, *The Constitution of Liberty* (London: Routledge, 1993 [1960]).

Hills, John, 'How Will the Scissors Close? Options for UK Social Spending', in Alan Walker and Carol Walker, eds, *Britain Divided: the Growth of Social Exclusion in the 1980s and 1990s* (London: Child Poverty Action Group, 1997), pp. 231–48.

Hirst, Paul, *Associative Democracy: New Forms of Economic and Social Governance* (Cambridge: Polity, 1994).

——, *From Statism to Pluralism* (London: University College London Press, 1997).

Hobhouse, Leonard T., *Liberalism* (Cambridge: Cambridge University Press, 1994 [1911]).

Holtham, Gerald, 'A Community Fund Could Save Social Democracy', *The Independent*, 18 April 1995.

——, 'Ownership and Privatized Utilities', *The Political Quarterly*, 69, 1998: 386–93.

Holtham, Gerald and Tindale, Stephen, *Green Tax Reform: Pollution Payments and Labour Tax Cuts* (London: Institute for Public Policy Research, 1996).

Hutton, Will, *The State We're In* (London: Jonathan Cape, 1995).

——, *The State to Come* (London: Vintage, 1997).

Kay, John, *The Economics of Business* (Oxford: Oxford University Press, 1996).

Kenway, Peter and Palmer, Guy, 'Stakeholding in Service Industries: Public Action to Change Institutional Behaviour?', *The Political Quarterly*, 68, 1997: 406–11.

King, Loren, 'Constructing Democratic Solidarity in US Cities: Two Paths to Local Empowerment', paper presented to the Annual Conference of the American Political Science Association, Washington DC, Sept. 1997.

Klein, Rudolf and Rafferty, Anne Marie, 'Rorschach Politics: Tony Blair and the Third Way', *The American Prospect*, July/Aug. 1999.

Layard, Richard, *What Labour Can Do* (London: Warner, 1997).

Leadbeater, Charles and Mulgan, Geoff, *Mistakeholding: Whatever Happened to Labour's Big Idea?* (London: Demos, 1996).

Le Grand, Julian, 'Markets, Welfare, and Equality', in Julian Le Grand and Saul Estrin, eds., *Market Socialism* (Oxford: Oxford University Press, 1989), pp. 193–211.

——, 'Knights, Knaves or Pawns? Human Behaviour and Social Policy', *Journal of Social Policy*, 26, 1997: 149–69.

Levine, David, *Reinventing the Workplace: How Business and Employees Can Both Win* (Washington DC: The Brookings Institution, 1995).

Lukes, Steven, 'The Last Word on the Third Way', *The Review*, London, Social Market Foundation, March 1999, pp. 3–4.

Meade, James, *Agathatopia: The Economics of Partnership* (Aberdeen: University of Aberdeen Press, 1991).

——, *Full Employment Regained* (Cambridge: Cambridge University Press, 1994).

Mill, John Stuart, *On Liberty* (Harmondsworth: Penguin, 1985 [1859]).

Mulgan, Geoff and Murray, Robert, *Reconnecting Taxation* (London: Demos, 1994).

Orwell, George, 'Politics and the English Language', in *Inside the Whale and Other Essays* (Harmondsworth: Penguin, 1983 [1946]).

Phelps, Edmund, *Rewarding Work: How to Restore Participation and Self-support to Free Enterprise* (Cambridge, Mass.: Harvard University Press, 1997).

Piachaud, David, *What's Wrong With Fabianism?* (London: Fabian Society, 1993).

Putnam, Robert, *Making Democracy Work: Civic Traditions in Modern Italy* (Princeton: Princeton University Press, 1993).

Rawls, John, *A Theory of Justice* (Oxford: Oxford University Press, 1972).

Robertson, James, 'Towards a New Social Compact: Citizen's Income and Radical Tax Reform', *The Political Quarterly*, 67, 1996: 54–8.

Rogers, Joel and Streeck, Wolfgang, 'Productive Solidarities: Economic Strategies and Left Politics', in David Miliband, ed., *Reinventing the Left* (Cambridge: Polity, 1994), pp. 128–45.

Tawney, R. H., *Equality* (London: Allen and Unwin, 1964 [1931]).

Toynbee, Polly, 'Not Quite a Wonderful Life, But a Whole Lot Better', *The Independent*, 19 Jan. 1998.

White, Michael, *Against Unemployment* (London: Policy Studies Institute, 1991).

2
New Labour: Old Liberalism

Samuel H. Beer

'Division among radicals almost one hundred years ago,' Tony Blair informed the Labour Party conference in 1997 'resulted in a 20th century dominated by Conservatives. I want the 21st century to be the century of the radicals.'

It takes time for that statement to sink in.

What happened in 1899 was that the TUC, which had been acting as a pressure group in 'the interests of labour,' voted to set up a separate political party. At first called the Labour Representation Committee, the new organization in 1906 took the name Labour Party.

Yet here, in 1997, is the Leader of the Labour Party telling us that the founding of the Labour Party was a great mistake and that he looks forward to reversing that fatal deviation.

Nor does it misrepresent his views to say that this reversal is made even more urgent by the further damaging division in the forces of radicalism dating from 1918. Until then the infant Labour party had been the junior partner to the Liberals, helping them to win their landslide victory in 1906 and to enact a sweeping program of social and constitutional reform in great part inspired and led by Lloyd George. The decisive break did not come until 1918 when Labour committed itself to socialism.

Tony Blair's history is sound. Division on the Left has done much to keep the Right in power. That view of history also clarifies and magnifies Blair's current achievement in reducing the trade unions once again to little more than a powerful pressure group and in returning Labour to its roots in a radical liberalism. His achievement owes a good deal to the defeats suffered by Old Labour at the hands of a Conservative Party, which at the same time was also undergoing a profound ideological purge under Margaret Thatcher. Does the resulting bipartisan embrace of the free market make Blair a clone of Thatcher? Or does his adaptation of the liberal tradition offer the nation the clear, firm choice which his towering electoral victory in 1997 would seem to give him the power to execute?

18

Socialism as blind alley

To appreciate what Blair has brought forth one must make the effort necessary to recall Labour's age of faith. That term with its religious overtones is no exaggeration. The ideology of the party was at once a damning analysis of capitalist society as a whole and a utopian vision of the Socialist Commonwealth. It called for revolutionary change: the substitution of common ownership for private property, public administration for the free, competitive market, and, above all, fellowship for self-interest as the governing value. Common ownership, which in practice came to mean nationalization, was the key concept, since, as spokesmen for the cause had long preached, this change in economic structure would bring about the cultural transformation of capitalistic self-interest into socialist fellowship.

In 1918 the party, breaking with the Lib-Lab alliance, had declared its independence and its commitment to that ideology. In 1931, it showed that it meant what it said on both counts. Not a single constituency party or trade union, and only a tiny handful of MPs and leaders followed MacDonald into the National government. In this campaign, although the Labour government of 1929–31 had shown its total incapacity to deal with the economic crisis, the party proclaimed that no reform of capitalism would help and only its policy of 'public ownership' could provide a solution.

That ideology continued to flourish in the party right through the first years of the Labour government of 1945. It was sincerely believed, for instance, that once the coal mines had been transferred from private to public ownership under the flag of the National Coal Board, the ancient strife between managers and miners would cease. As late as 1946, as sensible a man as Clement Attlee, then prime minister, could declare before the party conference that 'the distinctive side of Labour's programme' is 'our Socialist policy, the policy of nationalization.'

In the next few years, as nationalization and planning failed as instruments of economic control, administrators turned more and more to the mechanisms of the market. This collapse of the old ideological premises created problems not only for managers trying to increase production, but also for party leaders trying to write a manifesto and for socialist intellectuals trying to restate their beliefs so that they would fit the facts and give coherent direction to party and government. A leading example of that intellectual crisis and the effort to cope with it was the volume *New Fabian Essays* published in 1952 under the editorship of R. H. S. Crossman, with a foreword by Attlee.

I vividly recall its reception by the Harvard liberals. Much as we sympathized with the programs of economic management and social services being pioneered in Britain, we were disappointed by the confusion and sense of drift in the *Essays* and expressed our opinions in some highly critical reviews as well as in our private conversations with the socialist dons and journalists with whom we exchanged visits. The sticking point was common ownership as the central principle of industrial policy, in contrast with what we regarded as the superior New Deal approach of regulation, trust-busting and other forms of countervailing power. One Sunday afternoon in the American Cambridge, after the rural walk obligatory when our visitors were British, we got into a long wrangle with them on this question. Finally, Arthur Schlesinger Jr. exploded: 'Do you really think that everything should be nationalized, even newspapers, magazines, book publishing? How could you maintain freedom of the press under these conditions?' Needless to say, that was a clinching argument among a bunch of aspiring authors.

Revisionism triumphed – and in a remarkably short time. The essence was to drop control, exemplified by common ownership, as the means for achieving economic equality. Instead, this traditional objective would be achieved by the redistributive spending of the expanding social programs of the welfare state, which would now depend on a managed economy admittedly capitalistic and embracing private property and self-interest.

In the fortunes of the new doctrine, the unions played a decisive role, first by assuring its acceptance within the party and then by destroying any chance of its success as economic policy.

I recall how at the party conference of 1953 trade union power crushed the effort to commit the party to further nationalization. The key figure was Arthur Deakin, a roly-poly sort of person, plump, genial, and autocratic, who as general secretary of the transport workers, faithfully administered from a tiny office for a minuscule salary the affairs of his gigantic organization. When the critical vote loomed at the conference, he took the floor, denounced the resolution as 'meaningless mumbo-jumbo,' or, to be more exact, 'the worst abortion ever conceived by the mind of man,' and cast against it as a block the 835,000 votes of his union, a figure not too far short of the total cast by all the individual members of the constituency parties.

In the late 1960s the Wilson government, desperately trying to control the effect of wage increases on the rising inflation, to which the new policy of spending had contributed, sought to win the unions' acceptance of pay restraint. The unions were unwilling and/or unable to cooperate, the TUC exercising a veto which was accepted by the cabinet. The subsequent 'self-defeating bonanzas' of the wage scramble finally produced the winter of discontent of 1978–9, which brought Thatcher to power.

The pursuit of socialist equality by spending had proved as fruitless as by common ownership. Understandably, moreover, the experience of what Tony Blair has repeatedly denounced as 'the tax and benefit regime' powerfully supports New Labour's stubborn insistence on fiscal prudence.

The demise of Tory paternalism

'I think of myself,' Margaret Thatcher has said, 'as a Liberal in the 19th century sense – like Gladstone.' Her fiscal prudence, which she shares with

Tony Blair, would surely have won the approval of Mr Gladstone, who liked to see 'money fructify in the pockets of the taxpayers.' Historically speaking, her repudiation of the Tory element in the Conservative heritage is even more far-reaching than Blair's repudiation of socialism. Her ideological ancestry excludes Harold Macmillan, Rab Butler, Neville Chamberlain, Stanley Baldwin, Disraeli, and Bolingbroke.

What the Conservatives did with their landslide victory of 1931 exemplifies that strain of Tory statism. The National government, which in all but name was a Conservative administration, was the agent of a reassertion of state power which not only broke with the free-trade policy of the previous hundred years, but also laid the foundations of the managed economy with its corporatistic structure which the bipartisan consensus established after the Second World War. When one looks at the instruments of economic control utilized in that system, one continually comes across the contributions of pre-war Conservatism, such as a managed currency, import quotas, subsidies, controls on the location of industry, and those first initiatives in nationalisation, the BBC, London Passenger Transport Board, and Central Electricity Generating Board.

While Tory statism was mainly directed toward control of the economy, it also embraced a concern for 'the condition of the people.' Making and keeping the party electable was one cause of the occasional appearance of this concern, but it was not the only cause. Mr Attlee, who was not unduly disposed to give Tories the credit for good intentions, admitted as much. When I once asked him about 'Disraelian conservatism,' he agreed that this belief in a 'patriarchal nation' was real and after mentioning several leaders from Shaftsbury to Salisbury, he conceded that 'the Tories have a better record of social reform in some respects than the Liberals.' In the early 1960s, very much an exemplar of this tradition, Harold Macmillan, who had once said that 'Toryism has always been a form of paternal socialism,' eagerly plunged into the rapid expansion of social benefits in competition with Labour.

As in Blair's case, a historical background helps one see what Margaret Thatcher attempted and achieved. As prime minister she conducted a fierce, persistent, and highly ideological attack not only on the interventions of Labour governments but also upon Tory statism and paternalism, reversing, so far as she was able, just about every such innovation of interwar and postwar Conservatism.

We are all liberals now

Margaret Thatcher has proclaimed and practiced Gladstonian liberalism. Tony Blair is returning his party to the liberalism of Lloyd George. And there is another party, until recently led by Paddy Ashdown, which actually puts the term Liberal in its title. It would be no surprise if British voters were to conclude, 'We are all liberals now.' Tony Benn has said as much when he refers contemptuously to the present party alignment as 'a coalition.' British politics has lost something important. With Blair's purge of socialism supplementing Thatcher's demotion of Tory paternalism, two distinctive elements have disappeared from the political culture. Both Toryism and socialism brought sentiments and values from a distant past into contemporary politics. The Tory tradition still managed to show recognizable traces of the deference and *noblesse oblige* of premodern hierarchy. Likewise the sense of solidarity among socialists drew on the values of an older organic society. It makes sense, therefore, to use the term 'modernization,' much fancied by Tony Blair, to identify the disappearance of these vestiges of traditionalism.

Britain, however, has not wholly taken leave of the collectivist age which it entered while these premodern sentiments still had force. Tony Blair confronts a huge public sector. Thatcher's assaults on nationalization and the privileged position of organized labour were immensely successful in preparing the way for New Labour. From a financial point of view, however, the welfare state has survived more than a decade of Conservative hostility virtually intact – as William Hague recognizes. Moreover, while Thatcher could convert the corporatist structures of the managed economy into quangos, she could not reduce, but indeed increased their number.

In Britain no more than in America has the era of Big Government come to an end, although Tony Blair said it has at the party conference of 1995 and Bill Clinton in almost the same words so informed Congress a few months later. Not only are their speech-writers in touch. The two chief executives face a similar predicament. The management of these huge public sectors cannot be left to the *ad hoc* responses of pressure politics. There must be some clear defining purpose, some concept of the common good, which will impose coherent direction and control on the unruly pluralism of these modern, democratic, capitalistic welfare states. Is the liberalism that Tony Blair brings to the new party alignment up to that formidable task?

Two conceptions of liberty

When I look for the ideological foundations of the present party alignment in Britain my thoughts turn back to a dinner on 16 March 1954 with virtually the whole of the Parliamentary Liberal Party. Reduced to a mere six MPs and supported by only 2.6 per cent of the voters, the Liberals and their cause were, according to all expert opinion, destined for extinction. Yet the senior at the table, Sir Rhys Hopkin-Morris, QC, born in 1888, an MP from Wales since 1923 and Deputy Speaker for the Standing Committees, stated his libertarian creed with clarity and conviction. 'No one,' he said, setting out his premise, 'is to tell anyone else what is good for him.' He rejected the claim to such authority, whether asserted on the 'aristocratic principle' or on behalf of 'the community.' In the economy, as in matters of opinion, individual freedom must also prevail. When some farmers in his constituency had recently asked him if he supported 'guaranteed prices,' he replied that the very concept was a contradiction in terms. 'You can have a guarantee, or a price, but not both.' When my host, Jo Grimond, reminded him that Adam Smith himself had thought that government should provide roads, bridges, docks and the like, Sir Rhys conceded that in some respects the father of laisser-faire was a bit too interventionist.

So nourished on what I called in my notes at the time, 'the pure milk of Gladstonian liberalism,' Sir Rhys cogently identified 1906 as the moment when the Liberal party had deserted the old faith. He could bear no mention of Lloyd George and his social reforms. What was on his mind is made vividly clear when one reviews how radically the direction of policy had been changed by the communitarian liberalism brought to power by the famous landslide of 1906: protection of trade union funds, eight-hour days for miners, wage tribunals, labor exchanges, old age pensions and health and unemployment insurance, heavy taxation of the well-to-do, all rudely capped by the emasculation of the aristocratic veto in 1911. Then and there Lloyd George laid the foundations of the welfare state on which Labour later built a larger structure, according to the architecture of those two Liberals, Beveridge and Keynes.

Informing the conflict between the two branches of liberalism, as recalled by Sir Rhys, are two concepts of liberty which in modern times have received a good deal of attention from philosophers and have had considerable influence on government and politics. One side, the libertarian, puts great stress on the rights of the individual, holding in the language of a recent editorial in *The Economist*, that 'men and women are entitled to live their lives as they choose, according to their own idea of what is good, provided their choices do not harm others.' Support for this principle can be found among great thinkers – Locke, Kant, Mill. It can be used to identify the general drift of policies, such as Margaret Thatcher's effort to restrict government interference with the free market. The idea has had exhilarating effects in breaking down archaic taboos; it also has the weakness of fostering a moral relativism, which loosens social bonds and undermines the capacity for self-government.

The other concept of liberty, the communitarian, is also individualist, but holds that the individual person needs and seeks closer ties with others, as he or she takes part in deciding on and enjoying a common life with them. A better description of the powerful bonds of mutual identification, which we actually find among people, this approach has the weakness of tending toward an oppressive moral absolutism.

Compassion with a hard edge

Moral relativism is not a weakness of Tony Blair. 'I tell you,' he said to the 1997 party conference, 'a decent society is not based on rights. It is based on duty. Our duty to each other.' Blair stated the defining purpose of that society in a vivid oxymoron, 'compassion with a hard edge.' What he meant was sharply expressed in his warning to young people not to lapse into dependency, but to work, to improve their skills, to avoid crime, sloth, and disorderly conduct. Both the compassion and the hard edge appeared in his pledge to end not only the Britain where children go hungry, but also the Britain where 'gangs of teen-agers hang around street corners, nothing to do, but spit and abuse passersby.'

Blair does not hold out the socialist promise of equality of condition, but the liberal promise of equality of opportunity. To offer opportunity is to require a responsible use of that opportunity. And in Blair's view that means not just for any purpose one may choose, but for the purpose of making Britain, if no longer 'the mightiest,' now and in the future 'the best place to lead a fulfilled life.' Neither of the two leading British philosophers of communitarian liberalism, T. H. Green and L. T. Hobhouse, has stated more earnestly the ideal of a society in which individuals find fulfillment in a common good.

Populism and nationalism

Some critics call this hard edge of Blair's message social conservatism. That doesn't fit. Blair is not speaking as the voice of privilege talking down to lesser folk. He claims to speak for The People. That claim has a basis in present fact and draws on an old and honored usage. It is emphatically meant to be inclusive and certainly not confined to 'the working class,' not even under the elastic Webbian definition of 'workers by hand and brain.' Blair's doctrine of responsibility gets a warm response from all classes, not least the working class. Among the four social strata identified in opinion surveys, Labour, needless to say, enjoys more support from the lower than from the upper brackets. But Blair has demonstrated a remarkably strong trans-class appeal. According to a MORI survey, the shift of opinion to Labour between the elections of 1992 and 1997 was by almost exactly the same percentage in each of the social strata surveyed.

Blair's populism, as rhetoric and philosophy, descends from England's failed democratic revolution of the seventeenth century. As in the famed *Agreement of the People* of 1647, it is an appeal to an authority beyond king and parliament to a body of individuals perceived as sufficiently responsible and united to be the sovereign. These sentiments, while never dead, were revived in the late nineteenth century, as radical democrats moved up in the Liberal party. Lloyd George became their acclaimed champion, fighting his fiercest battles for 'the People's Budget' and against the Peers by appealing beyond parliament to 'the great assize of the People.'

And which people? The British people, the British nation. In Blair's lexicon the terms are synonymous. Strongly as he supports Scottish devolution, Blair's British nationalism is as fundamental as his populism. In his 1997 conference address this year, references to 'Britain' abound, the four concluding sentences including the term no less than five times. In Tony Blair's view of the world, the British nation-state is alive and well and on its way to becoming 'a beacon of good to the world,' which includes a leading role in the European Community. If the term were not so unpopular, I would call his doctrine a New Nationalism.

From Jo Grimond to Tony Blair

To this anticollectivist, communitarian doctrine, the Liberal party remained remarkably faithful even during its long years of decline and defeat. How the party framed its purpose and program under the leadership of Jo Grimond (1956–67) strikingly illustrates this continuity, looking back to Lloyd George and forward to Tony Blair. In the 1950s the political fortunes of the party had reached their lowest point, while the centralized, bureaucratic welfare state had won almost universal acceptance. Only a few months after Grimond became leader of his party, Harold Macmillan took office as prime minister. Soon known as Super Mac, he led the Conservatives to their third victory in a row, completing the convergence of policy between the two big parties under the auspices of his pronounced Tory paternalism.

In these circumstances, partisan and ideological, to suggest that liberalism might rise again as an effective public philosophy was unconventional to the point of eccentricity. Grimond nonetheless launched an intellectual renewal of liberal doctrine which, reflecting in essence the old faith in free enterprise and social reform championed by Lloyd George, fiercely rejected the consensus. Accordingly, about this time in a letter to an American friend, I found Grimond's effort 'charming, but archaic.' No less remarkable, moreover, as one can see now, what Grimond proposed fits not at all badly with Blair's Third Way. The comparisons are interesting as history, but what makes them particularly useful today is that they testify to Blair's incontestable liberalism, despite the fact that he still calls himself a socialist or social democrat. They also radically distinguish what he stands for from Thatcherism.

The Liberal Future, published in 1959, lays out Grimond's beliefs. It is not a mere collection of speeches such as political leaders sometimes offer as a political testament. Although the work of an author who claims to eschew philosophy, it invokes some fairly high-order theory. Not strange really, since after all Grimond read PPE at Balliol. Serious and systematic, this little book ranges from a brief statement of principles to a detailed examination of issues and programs. Reminding one of the primacy Blair gives not to rights, but to duty, Grimond at the very start states that the 'first principle' of his liberalism is 'responsibility.' This is a clue to much that follows in this demanding, as well as liberating credo. Its premise is the rationality of the individual. That capacity enables and obliges a person to make choices. These are personal, when directed at making one 'better off materially or morally,' and social, when exercised in democratic deliberations on the conditions of 'a liberal society.'

Again as with Blair, these conditions include not only preventing people from harming one another, but also 'positive government,' specifically that system of welfare state services which, as Grimond boasts, originated with Lloyd George and was elaborated by latter-day Liberals, such as Keynes and Beveridge. Grimond is no advocate of 'endless welfare benefits.' As in Blair's thinking, the purpose and limit of the system is 'equality of opportunity,' which means that in the competitive race some will fall behind, while others forge ahead. There is the hint of a hard edge here. While discussing eligibility, Grimond uses exactly the same phrase Lloyd George employed when he specified that benefits were intended for persons suffering disadvantage 'through no fault of their own.' Some years later Grimond expressed the same statement even more sharply when he criticized the view he found to be fashionable among some supporters of the Beveridge system that 'the individual has not the responsibility to do the best he or she can and should be encouraged to rely entirely on public charity.'

The rationale of Grimond's view on economic and social policy was in a profound sense political. In his later years he once summarized it thus: 'Value on earth it seems to me must appertain to individual consciousness and the voluntary use of individual faculties.' The paradox of his stout defense of the free market and his advocacy of wide government intervention is reconciled and rationalized by that premise. In this view, the free economy, in contrast with the planned economy, is an arena of opportunity for the exercise of individual rational choice. That arena, however, is not a mere fact of nature, but an artifact of human creation. The capitalist economy, he emphasized, depends on a complicated system of law and policy. In this sense it is a political product, a grand example of what Grimond liked to call approvingly 'social engineering.' For government to intervene in order to modify and supplement some aspect of this system did not violate its purpose, but was an expression of the values which informed its creation. It was only logical and moral for the liberalism, which in the course of history had created and supported this system of free enterprise, to take further action by economic and social reforms to enlarge its field of human choice.

Unless justified on such ultimately liberal grounds, government intervention was 'bureaucracy,' one of Grimond's prime targets of attack. The same background of thought led him to detest even more fiercely any form of class politics, whether socialist or Tory, which indeed he viewed as the source of 'bureaucracy.' What particularly excited his hostility, it seemed to me, was the suggestion that there is some great economic or social machine, which stamps out individuals into solidary groups, determined in their behavior not by reflection and choice but by a given identity. In this deterministic way, for instance, the individual manual worker did not by taking thought decide that he preferred the doctrine and program of the Labour party; he simply looked around and discovered that he belonged to the working class and therefore automatically supported the party by which that class acted in politics. For the true blue Tory, on the other hand, the class division was vertical with upper and lower levels joined by the submission of the great majority to 'a hereditary officer-class conservative elite,' in Grimond's phrase.

While Grimond recognized that the two big parties often won votes by their appeals to feelings about class, he refused to compete with a similar rhetoric. And in fact, although the Liberal activists came mainly from the middle class, the Liberal voters were much more evenly distributed among the various social strata than were the Conservative and the Labour voters. Today Blair's leadership is in the same mold, trans-class in the rhetoric of the leader and in the support of the public.

The primacy of individual choice in Grimond's political thinking appears in the prominence he gave to constitutional reform. Believing that 'liberal rationalism' was the way individuals should and, he hoped, often did take part in self-government, he strongly favored electoral reform. This meant some form of PR, although he thought this reform might best be realized in the vote for an elected second chamber, since he valued the close connection of MP and constituents fostered by the existing plurality system. In other fields of constitutional reform, Grimond also anticipated the proposals Tony Blair has championed. Echoing the old Liberal commitment to Home Rule, he favored devolution for Scotland, Wales, Northern Ireland, and possibly the English regions. Decentralization, which as 'community politics' became increasingly a field of activity and achievement for the Liberal party, occupied more and more of Grimond's attention. In the way of procedural reform he wished to enhance the role of specialist committees and enlarge the opportunities for individual MPs to take part in framing bills even before the government draft had been introduced. From the early days of the Iron and Steel Community, Grimond was pro-European, ready to see Britain surrender bits of sovereignty for specific purposes.

'Liberal rationalism' informed not only his views of the institutions of self-government, but also his approach to economic and social issues, including that central problem, industrial relations. He was acutely concerned with the way the conflict of organized labor and organized capital heightened the inflationary pressures which increasingly plagued the British economy in the 1960s and 1970s. He persistently and decisively rejected, however, the solution widely advocated by economists and politicians that a national wages policy be negotiated under government auspices by the two sides. This smacked of 'class politics' and 'bureaucracy.'

Instead Grimond proposed that the democratic idea be applied to industry, in some such form as 'co-ownership.' By giving workers the same interest as managers in productive and profitable enterprise this arrangement in his opinion would make it easier for the two combatants to reach agreement on wages. Proposals of this sort, however, although attempted in a few, notable instances, have never caught on in the private sector. Nor, apart from the Liberal party, have they been widely taken up by political leaders. Still, this element of Grimond's liberalism has survived and achieved some notoriety as the 'stakeholder' concept promised in Tony Blair's public pronouncements and to some extent realized practically in his attempts to encourage 'partnerships at work.'

The Thatcher contribution

If we want to know where New Labour belongs among the operative ideals of modern British politics, this backward glance gives an emphatic answer. New Labour can be classified neither with the socialism of Attlee nor with the social democracy of Gaitskell, but rather with the liberalism of Jo Grimond. Blair's incontestable liberalism also separates him radically from Thatcher, yet her so-called revolution in theory and practice made essential contributions to his purpose. The essence of this contribution was her three great negatives: her radical reduction of trade union privileges; her demolition of the 'bureaucracy' of the nationalized industries; her persistent attempts to curb spending. Blair has made no effort to reverse any of these departures from postwar collectivism. Indeed, New Labour has so fully embodied these reforms that at one point I characterized the victory of 1997 as 'that psephological monster, a landslide for the status quo.' What that characterization misses is that these reactionary negatives were a body of affirmative reforms dictated by a powerful and coherent version of libertarian ideology, radically at odds with the communitarian ethic of New Labour. Thatcher emphasized this significance in her claim of kinship with the Liberalism of Gladstone. My anecdotal recollection of the opinions of Sir Rhys Hopkin-Morris shows that even the party of Lloyd George harbored support for this brand of liberalism. Academic authorities like Hayek and Friedman maintained the tradition. If we look for a political figure who led this charge against collectivism, in the manner of Jo Grimond, but form the opposite, libertarian angle, Enoch Powell fills the bill. Powell made his appearance in this role about the same time Jo Grimond rose to prominence. In 1958 with two other ministers he resigned from Macmillan's government in protest against excessive spending and in the name of sound money. After the Conservative defeat of 1964, he broadened his attack to embrace the whole Butlerite consensus and its acceptance of the mixed economy, grounding his criticism in a brilliant exposition of the merits of the free market. During the troubled 1970s, his influence spread in the party and his ideas were taken up by Sir Keith Joseph, who became Thatcher's mentor.

From public goods to the common good

So what is that radical difference between the two branches of liberalism? Sir Rhys Hopkin-Morris went to the heart of the matter in his bold assertion of the libertarian premise that no one, the democratic community no more than the aristocracy, has the authority to dictate to anyone what is good for them. The individual separately and by free association with others has the right to do as he/she chooses, so long as they do no harm to others. By such freely formed associations of mutually interdependent persons, great things can be accomplished, especially by the free market. To be sure, some forms of social cooperation which answer to the wants of the public cannot be mounted solely by voluntary effort, but require that the coercive power of government intervene to assure each of the cooperation of all. Such 'public goods,' however, do not violate the libertarian premise, since the benefit they confer on each individual is enjoyed as a separate good.

Jo Grimond's liberalism firmly committed him to the free market, as displayed in his rejection of 'planning' and 'bureaucracy.' Grimond also recognized the necessity for 'public goods,' such as defense, to make up for the deficiencies of the market. At this point in his thought, Grimond breaks from the libertarian view and greatly broadens and deepens the role of nation and state. As set forth particularly in his 1978 volume, *The Common Welfare*, he argues that the liberal state should intervene not only to provide 'public goods,' but also to care for 'the common good,' which in relation to the market is not merely perfecting, but rather 'overriding.'

This common good, he continues, involves 'certain states of human consciousness.' By sharing in a common consciousness and the common life it entails, the many think and act as one, each seeking and finding in certain respects the fulfillment of his/her promise in the achievements of the social whole. This is the essence of a 'community.' In size a community may be great or small. It is exemplified in the common life of Grimond's Orkney neighbors, as affectionately portrayed in his *Memoirs*. Tony Blair also finds it in the British nation, which he hopes to make 'the best place to live a fulfilled life.' In a classic summary, the idea has been set forth by T. H. Green, the intellectual forefather of communitarian liberalism in Britain. 'The final good,' he wrote, 'can be realized only in a society of persons who, while retaining their individuality, find their perfection attainable only when their separate qualities are integrated as part of the social whole.'

The national community is not a separate system in conflict with the free, competitive economy in which individuals seek to maximize their personal gain. On the contrary, it is that community, the nation, which, acting through the democratic state, has created and continues to maintain, regulate, and reform the system of free enterprise. As Grimond repeatedly emphasized, the free market is not a fact of nature, but a human artifact, depending for its existence and operation upon a complicated system of law and policy, supplemented by the norms of modern culture legitimating self-interested endeavor. This economy, if properly designed in law and morals, will enhance the efficiency of its constituents and the productivity of the nation. These functions of the economy, however, are not the ultimate purpose of the community which created it. In the communitarian view, the greater wealth of the nation will enlarge its power by private and public action to provide for the material and cultural needs of its citizens, not least those who falter in the competitive race 'through no fault of their own.' The overriding obligations of the common good, moreover, require that the economy be regulated with regard not only to the uses of its product, but also to the processes of its production. A greater GDP makes possible the more abundant life of better schools, more hospitals, longer holidays, more satisfying recreation, and the like. But the conditions under which that increment of national product is produced also bear upon the quality of the common life, for better or for worse. Measures to perfect the economy also serve ultimately to make the community more of a community.

The dangers, constitutional and political

Blair's communitarian purpose entails his populism. The programs of the common good may have a hard edge. Wider participation in their formulation will serve to make these imperatives not only more acceptable, but also more justifiable. More acceptable simply by broadening and deepening the base of consent. More justifiable also by reconciling a variety of interests and opinions through a process of deliberation which enriches and elevates the policy outcomes. For the sake of such beneficent results, liberalism of the communitarian persuasion has typically displayed a concern for constitutional reform. Blair is very much in this tradition. His populism embraces a massive program of constitutional reforms, most of which would increase popular participation. I heartily agree with his pledge to reform what he has called 'THE most centralized government of any large state in the western world.' But when, in the light of American experience, I review the program of constitutional reform which is widely advocated in Britain today – a written constitution, bill of rights, judicial review, elected second chamber, decentralization and devolution, freedom of information, proportional representation, and a fixed term for parliament – I shudder. The USA has tried them all, and as a result enjoys a confusion of voices in its political discourse, which often threatens to deprive the ship of state of any sense of direction.

A truism makes the point: representative government must not only represent, it must also govern. Constitutional reform should be fitted to the need not only for participation, but also for coherence and effectiveness in the enactment and administration of programs of government action. Blair we may hope will not carry these constitutional reforms so far as to destroy that concentration of constitutional and political power, which enable him to reshape the welfare state. And which, surely, must be the envy of his fellow executive, Bill Clinton, locked in the embrace of a system so responsive to pressures that sometimes it is hardly able to move. The prime minister should bear in mind that Lloyd George launched his reform of the Lords in order to clear the way for his revolutionary financial and social measures. I cannot imagine that Tony Blair, who has done so much to coordinate power within the party in the leadership, indeed in the Leader, will as prime minister turn around and dissipate that ancient and formidable monopoly of power in the state which has made possible the great achievements of Britain's liberal past.

Tony Blair's New Labour offers the nation a choice. His communitarian liberalism, exemplified in British history and honored in the classics of political thought, distinguishes his views sharply enough from the libertarian brand of liberalism to sustain a lively and significant democratic dialogue. His emphasis upon the responsibilities entailed by the opportunities to be opened up by New Labour promises to give a defining purpose to the remodeled welfare state.

Some critics doubt that he can deliver on the promise. His immense personal popularity is a source of weakness as well as strength. While differences of economic class will remain in the New Britain as in any society where there is considerable equality of opportunity, the old class system with its premodern solidarities, Tory and socialist, is fading. This loss deprives the political parties of that unwavering support which surveys of the electorate used regularly to report in the 1950s and 1960s. As in the 1997 general election, today's more volatile electorate will be more likely to vote for the Leader than the party. Thus far, Tony Blair has been a formidable vote getter. But, again to reflect on American experience, can a chief executive dependent on such a volatile constituency turn aside the pressures against the hard edges of his policies? Judging by what Tony Blair has said and done, I am betting that he has what it takes.

The author and editor are grateful to *The Economist* for permission to use extracts from 'The Roots of New Labour' © *The Economist*, London, Feb. 7, 1998.

3
New Labour and Public Opinion: the Third Way as Centrism?

Pippa Norris

1. Introduction

The strategic shifts in Labour's attempt to dominate the center ground of British politics started under the leadership of Neil Kinnock, strengthened with John Smith, but only received an apotheosis under Tony Blair. Like Thatcherism in the early 1980s, the project has continued to evolve and take concrete shape in the early years of the Labour government. In a series of subsequent speeches Blair has sought to develop and flesh out the core components of a so-called 'third way' approach to governance. In the words of his 1998 Fabian Pamphlet: 'The Third Way stands for a modernized social democracy, passionate in its commitment to social justice and the goals of the centre-left, but flexible, innovative and forward-looking in the means to achieve them. It is founded on the values that have guided progressive politics for more than a century – democracy, liberty, justice, mutual obligation and internationalism. But it is a third way because it moves decisively beyond an Old Left preoccupied by state control, high taxation and producer interests; and a New Right treating public investment, and often the very notions of "society" and collective endeavour, as evils to be undone' (Blair 1998: 1).

Yet despite successive attempts to nail down the core ideas, the meaning of the so-called third way remains elusive. Understood as an ideological project the intellectual origins of the so-called third way are open to different interpretations: as the adoption of 'soft' Thatcherism; as a return to the early roots of social liberalism; or as a genuinely new reworking of social-democratic values (see, for example, Sopel 1995; Rentoul 1995; Mandelson and Liddle 1996; Giddens 1998; White, Chapter 1 in this volume). In addition, it remains unclear how far the third way is a product of marketing and spin, a framing device symbolizing the abandonment of past left-wing shibboleths but lacking substance, or whether it represents a more deep-rooted phenomenon, a genuinely new public philosophy. If 'Blairism' is interpreted in terms of concrete policy initiatives, then, like the first term of Thatcherism, it remains a work in progress, and at this stage it is probably too early to identify its defining features.

One way to explore the nature and scope of the third way is to examine ideological shifts within the parliamentary Labour Party and to consider how these relate to patterns of party competition in the British electorate. This chapter examines how Labour has positioned itself between the traditional left and right positions on the political spectrum, and how far this development has permeated different levels of the party. Previous work has demonstrated that from 1992–7 the Labour Party moved sharply center-right in its manifesto policies (Budge 1999), and towards the center in its membership (Webb and Farrell 1999). Other work has also demonstrated the emergence of a new cleavage in parliament revolving around issues of constitutional issues, where all the parties except the Conservatives are strongly in favor of the reform agenda (Norris 1999). Building upon this foundation, we can map the ideological profile of each parliamentary party on some of the classic cleavages in British party politics, offer a plausible electoral explanation for the shift towards the center within the Labour ranks, and consider the implications for future patterns of British party competition.

2.   Measuring left–right ideology

How far did Labour move closer towards the ideological position of the median British voter from 1992 to 1997? And were the Conservatives out of touch with their own supporters? To consider these issues we can compare the ideological position of politicians with that of voters in the 1 May 1997 British general election. For the elite level we draw on evidence from more than 1,000 MPs and prospective parliamentary candidates surveyed in the British Representation Study (BRS) prior to the election (for technical details see the Appendix at the end of this chapter). For the electorate we utilize the 1997 British Election Study (BES) post-election cross-sectional survey (for details see the technical appendix in Evans and Norris 1999). This study examines ideological scales that asked people to identify their own position on six key issues traditionally dividing the parties. The 11-point scales measured the trade-off between inflation versus unemployment; taxation versus public spending; nationalization versus privatization; integration within the European Union; gender equality; and general left–right self-placement. These represent some of the classic 'old politics' cleavages about the economy that have long divided British parties, along with the key issue of Britain's role within Europe and women's rights, which reflect 'new politics' concerns. In western Europe the left–right self-placement scale has also been widely used as one of the most valuable ways to identify voters.

If the parliamentary Labour Party had adopted a third-way strategy in the 1997 election we would probably expect to find that they had abandoned traditional socialist concerns with state ownership of industry and Keynesian public-spending programs, as well as high taxation. Instead the party should have moved into the center ground on the economy, as well as taking a more pro-European stance, in line with Blair's emphasis on internationalism, while also adopting a progressive position on women's rights and gender equality.

The scales were designed to tap the actual and the perceived position of voters and elites across the left–right ideological spectrum. The BRS asked politicians to use the scales to identify their own position, and also to estimate the position of their own party's voters. Using the same issue scales, the BES asked voters to identify their own actual position and also to estimate the position of the major parties. Combining these data-sets allows us to compare the actual position of voters (how they rated themselves) with the actual position of politicians. For the first time they also allow us to compare the actual with the perceived position of different actors across the British political spectrum.

3.   Mapping party competition: Labour tracking the median voter?

If we map the (self-assigned) actual position of voters and politicians across the left–right ideological scale, the results in Figure 3.1 show that voters were fairly tightly clustered in the center of the spectrum while politicians were more dispersed to left and right. This was not unexpected since a similar pattern was found in 1992, where the elite also proved more polarized than voters (Norris 1994).

Perhaps more interestingly for our purposes, however, Figure 3.1 also reveals that in the 1997 election on the overall left–right ideological scale Labour politicians were slightly closer than Conservatives to the median British voter. This provides important evidence for the adoption of a 'third way' in terms of a Labour shift towards the political center ground. And it indicates that this shift was not confined to the top ranks of the Labour leadership but was also evident in the attitudes of the party's MPs and parliamentary candidates. If the Labour party was radically out of touch with mainstream public opinion in the early 1980s, as many commentators assume (Shaw 1994, 1996), then by the time of the 1997 election their politicians more closely reflected the prevailing ethos. Of course this, by itself, is not enough to win elections, as otherwise the Liberal Democrats, as the closest party to the median voter, would have been in power for decades. Nevertheless Labour's position on the ideological spectrum placed them in a more advantageous position than the Conservatives to maximize potential support.

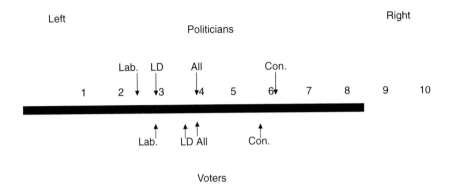

Figure 3.1   Left–right ideological position of politicians and voters, 1997

Note: 'In politics people sometimes talk of left and right. Using the following scale, where 1 means left and 10 means right, where would you place yourself?' The figures represent the mean position of different groups based on their actual self-placement (where they placed themselves) on the scale.

Sources: British Representation Study 1997 including all MPs and parliamentary candidates (N = 999); British Election Study 1997.

This pattern is shown in even starker relief when we turn to the position of the parties on the key economic issues that have so long divided British party politics. Figure 3.2 shows a consistent and revealing pattern: across all the economic issues Labour and Liberal Democrat politicians were closer to the median voter, and also closer to the average Conservative voter, than Conservative politicians. Conservative politicians proved to be furthest away from their own supporters. This gap becomes a veritable chasm when one turns to the issues of unemployment versus inflation, taxation versus spending, and privatization versus nationalization. Across all three scales Conservative politicians took a distinctive stance that was far more right-wing than that of their own supporters. In contrast, on these economic issues Labour and Liberal Democrat politicians placed themselves fairly close to each other and close to the position of the median British voter (see Figure 3.2 and Table 3.1). Indeed, *on the issue of taxation versus public spending Labour actually leap-frogged into the center ground*, leaving them flanked to the left by the Liberal Democrats (who promised raising taxes to subsidize education) and to the far right by the Conservatives. Only the contentious issue of Europe provides some exception to this picture, with Conservative politicians more closely in touch with their own supporters than either of the other major parties. The Liberal Democrats proved the most pro-European, some distance away from their own voters.

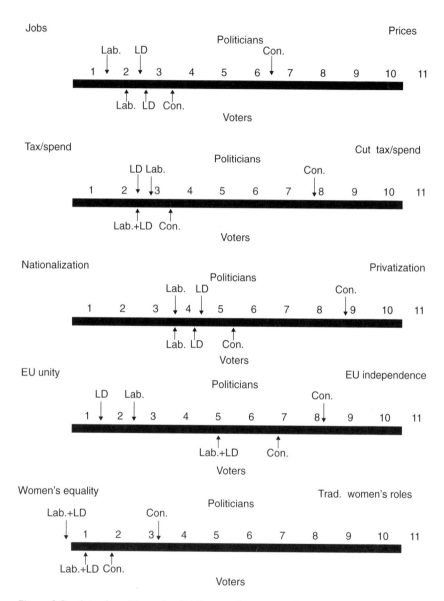

Figure 3.2   Actual position of politicians and voters on the major issues

Finally, on the issue of gender equality, all parties and voters clustered fairly closely on the egalitarian end of the spectrum. If we compare the relative position of all politicians against each other in the last election on the five issue scales, Labour proved the most left-wing on only two (unemploy-

Table 3.1 Actual position of politicians and voters on the issue scales, 1997

	Actual position of voters (i)				Actual position of politicians (ii)				Difference (i – ii)			
	Con	LDem	Lab	All	Con	LDem	Lab	All	Con	LDem	Lab	All
Left–right	6.8	4.9	4.0	5.0	7.3	4.0	3.4	4.7	0.5	–0.9	–0.6	–0.3
Jobs *v.* prices	4.4	3.6	3.1	3.6	7.4	3.4	2.4	4.0	3.0	–0.2	–0.7	0.9
Tax *v.* spend	4.4	3.3	3.3	3.7	8.9	3.4	3.7	5.0	4.5	0.1	0.4	1.3
Privatization	6.3	5.2	4.7	5.3	9.9	5.4	4.7	6.4	3.6	0.2	0.0	1.1
EU	7.8	6.0	6.0	6.6	9.2	2.5	3.5	5.0	1.4	–3.5	–2.5	–1.6
Women's role	2.6	2.0	2.0	2.3	4.1	1.5	1.3	2.2	1.5	–0.5	–0.7	–0.1

Notes: The scales run from left (low) to right (high). All the scales are 11-point except for the left–right scale which is 10 points. The figures represent the mean position on the scales. The '*actual*' position is the self-placement on the scales by voters and by politicians.
Source: British Representation Study 1997, including all MPs and parliamentary candidates (N. 999); British Election Study 1997.

ment and nationalization). Labour took much the same position as the Liberal Democrats on gender equality, and they were the most centrist party on two issues (taxation/spending and Europe). Labour did therefore leapfrog over their nearest rivals to take the center ground on these last two issues, a development which challenges the familiar postwar party order. And the Conservative politicians took the most clear-cut and distinctive relative position with clear blue water between themselves and the other major parties, but also, unfortunately for them, clear blue water between their stance on the economic issues and the position of their own voters.

What explains this phenomenon? Why should Labour have moved towards the center and why should the Conservative parliamentary party have remained so far from their supporters on the economy? If all politicians shift positions strategically along the ideological spectrum to maximize their vote, as Downsian theory suggests (Downs 1955), then the failure of Conservatives to capture the center ground poses an interesting puzzle.

One important clue to this phenomenon lies in the perceptual error of how politicians saw voters. We can compare the actual position of voters (where they rated themselves) with how politicians perceived them (in Table 3.2). In turn, we can also compare the actual position of politicians (how they rated themselves) with how voters perceived them (in Table 3.3). The difference between the actual and the perceived represents the 'perceptual error'.

The results show a strikingly consistent pattern that provides important insights into party competition. Table 3.3 demonstrates that across all the scales except Europe at the time of the 1997 general election *politicians generally believed that the electorate was more right-wing than was actually the case*. This misplacement was found in all parties but the perceptual error was far

Table 3.2   How politicians saw voters, 1997

	Actual position of voters (i)				How politicians saw their own voters (ii)				Perceptual error (i − ii)			
	Con	LDem	Lab	All	Con	LDem	Lab	All	Con	LDem	Lab	All
Left–right	6.8	4.9	4.0	5.0	7.2	5.0	4.6	5.4	0.4	0.1	0.6	0.4
Jobs v. prices	4.4	3.6	3.1	3.6	6.9	4.5	3.5	4.7	2.5	0.9	0.4	1.1
Tax v. spend	4.4	3.3	3.3	3.7	8.1	4.5	4.9	5.6	3.7	1.2	1.6	1.9
Privatization	6.3	5.2	4.7	5.3	8.4	5.5	5.3	6.2	2.1	0.3	0.6	0.9
EU	7.8	6.0	6.0	6.6	9.3	4.9	5.7	6.4	1.5	−1.1	−0.3	−0.2
Women's role	2.6	2.0	2.0	2.3	5.3	3.0	3.0	3.8	2.7	1.0	1.4	1.5

Notes: The scales run from left (low) to right (high). All the scales are 11-point except for the left–right scale which is 10 points. The figures represent the mean position on the scales. The *'actual'* position is the self-placement by voters. The *'perceived'* position is the estimated position of their own party voters by politicians. The *'perceptual error'* is the difference between 'actual' and 'perceived'.

Source: British Representation Study 1997, including all MPs and parliamentary candidates (N. 999); British Election Study 1997.

Table 3.3   How voters saw politicians, 1997

	Actual position of politician			How voters saw parties			Perceptual error (i − ii)		
	Con	LDem	Lab	Con	LDem	Lab	Con	LDem	Lab
Left-Right	7.3	4.0	3.4	7.4	5.0	4.5	0.1	1.0	1.1
Jobs v. Prices	7.4	3.4	2.4	5.4	3.8	3.0	−2.0	0.4	−0.6
Tax v. spend	8.9	3.4	3.7	6.0	3.2	3.4	−2.9	−0.2	−0.3
Privatization	9.9	5.4	4.7	7.4	5.2	4.6	−2.5	−0.2	−0.1
EU	9.2	2.5	3.5	6.8	4.7	4.8	−2.4	2.2	1.3
Women's Role	4.1	1.5	1.3	3.5	2.7	2.4	−0.6	1.2	1.1

Note: See Table 3.2.

Source: British Representation Study 1997, including all MPs and parliamentary candidates (N. 999); British Election Study 1997.

stronger among Conservative politicians, who believed that their own voters were far more right-wing than was the case. In contrast, Labour and Liberal Democrat politicians estimated the position of their own voters remarkably accurately. Conservative politicians proved out of touch with the attitudes of their core supporters on the core economic issues including the pursuit of further privatization programs and the priority of tax cuts over public spending.

This raises the question of why the Conservatives were not damaged even more badly by their economic policies. One answer to this is shown if we examine how politicians rated their own position, compared with how voters perceived them. Again the actual position of Labour and Liberal Democrat politicians corresponded remarkably well with how most voters perceived them, the sizes of the perceptual errors are extremely low on all issues except the EU. But once more the perceptual errors concerning the Conservatives were larger than for other parties, which may have prevented the party from losing even more support than they actually did. Conservative voters believed that Conservative politicians were more moderate than was in fact the case. What this pattern suggests is a self-reinforcing projection that was particularly marked in the Conservative party, as voters and politicians tended to perceive each other as closer to their own attitudes and values than was the case. Therefore the misperception of Conservative voters and politicians to some extent canceled itself out.

4. Why did the Conservatives not shift back to the center?

If Labour was able to occupy the center ground so effectively this was not only because of its own willingness to shift policy and attitude, but also, as we have seen, because of the apparent unwillingness and/or inability of the Conservatives to offer serious competition for the center ground. What explains the failure of the Conservatives to adopt the rational vote-maximizing strategy that would move them back to the center? Answering this question is important not only for analyzing the result of the 1997 British general election, but also for understanding the real limits on how far any party, in Britain or elsewhere, can shift ground ideologically in the face of electoral pressures. How difficult will it be for the Conservatives to move back to the center and offer a credible centrist alternative to New Labour's self-styled third-way approach to government? Four possible interrelated reasons may plausibly limit any party's ideological movement.

First, spatial theories of electoral competition emphasize that party leaders can only move their party along the left–right spectrum to a limited extent, at least in the short term (Budge, Robertson, and Hearl 1987). One of the most important reasons for this 'stickiness' concerns party images, since politicians gradually come to be associated in the public mind with 'ownership' of certain issues. Hence social-democratic parties are usually positively associated with welfare policies concerning health, pensions, and education, while parties of the right are conventionally seen as stronger on the issues of defense and crime. Images can be carefully crafted by political communications, and the last election saw growing use of the techniques of strategic news management and political marketing (Norris et al. 1999). Nevertheless, in the short term, given the pattern of issue ownership, if parties try to change their historic policy commitments too fast then the danger is the loss of credibility and trust, as parties are suspected of becoming 'all things to all voters' just to court support. John Major carried the legacy of 18 years of Conservative government, whereas opposition parties travel light without such ideological baggage. Clearly, this obstacle to the emergence of a new Conservative centrism should diminish over time.

Another possible reason for party stickiness in shifting to the center rests in the limited control that leaders can exercise over their party machine. Modern mass-branch parties are complex organizations rather than unitary actors. Short-term radical ideological change incurs potential problems of internal party fragmentation and factionalism, since the leader needs to carry the parliamentary party and grassroots membership with him or her. As shown by the deep divisions over Europe, John Major proved powerless to heal the Conservative rifts. A recent attempt to abandon some Thatcherite icons by Peter Lilley was regarded as outrageous heresy by many backbenchers. Any attempt by Hague to move the party back towards the center on the economy, thereby perhaps appearing to the right wing to undermine the legacy of Thatcherism, might prove equally fraught. After all, the evolution of Labour's ideological move towards the center ground had taken four successive election defeats. Perhaps the Conservative government required the shock of hard opposition benches to adjust their electoral strategy. We cannot conclude, however, that one such electoral shock will be enough to convince them of the need for a centrist realignment.

In addition, perhaps the demonstrable electoral success of Thatcherism encouraged all politicians to assume that public opinion was more right-wing than was actually the case. Certainly this seems the most plausible explanation for why *all* parties exaggerated the extent to which the public favored tax cuts rather than public spending.

Finally, the most plausible explanation for why the Conservatives failed to move back to the center is that, quite simply, they did not realize quite how far their party platform had become out of touch, particularly on the economy, with their grassroots supporters and with public opinion more widely. Downsian analysis of electoral competition assumes that electoralist parties attempt to gain popularity by moving to the centre of the ideological spectrum. But any effective party strategy to maximize support requires politicians to pinpoint public opinion fairly accurately. The results of this analysis suggest that the Conservatives were more mistaken in their perception of their supporters than politicians in other parties.

We can only speculate at this stage about the causes of this intriguing phenomenon. This perceptual error may have been due to the Conservative government having been in power for 18 years, which may have made them increasingly ideologically dogmatic and out of touch with their grassroots supporters and public opinion. In opposition Labour had employed all the black arts of political marketing to get in touch with the electorate. After 1992 Labour realized that elections are not usually won or lost in the official campaign, and they subsequently designed their strategy for the long haul. Opinion polling was carried out regularly from late 1993. Philip Gould and Deborah Mattinson conducted a program of focus group research to monitor reaction to Labour's policies, including daily groups during the 1997 campaign. Strategy meetings were conducted almost daily from late 1994, tackling Labour's weaknesses on taxation, trade unions, and crime well before the official campaign came close. Labour renewed their interest in constituency campaigns with strategic targeting of key voters under the guidance of Millbank Tower. For two years before polling day, a Labour task force was designed to switch 5,000 voters in each of 90 target marginals. Those identified as potential Labour converts in these seats were contacted by teams of volunteers on the doorstep, and by a canvassing operation run from 20 telephone banks around the country, co-ordinated from Millbank during the campaign. Information from the canvassing operation, especially issues of concern raised by voters, was also fed back to Philip Gould, to help shape Labour's presentations. Labour's long climb back to power, which involved such exercises as the 'Labour Listens' campaign, may have made their electoral antennae more sensitive to the nuances of public opinion.

Certainly William Hague's attempt to emulate the 'Labour Listens' exercise suggests that he recognizes its value in principle. But all the 'town-hall' meetings and 'meet-the-people' sessions are useless unless the Conservatives learn from the feedback by revising their policy platform and thereby recapturing the middle ground. The evidence so far is that under William Hague the party has been more preoccupied by reorganizing central office, and changing some aspects of party presentation and communication, than tackling the thorny issue of new policies. Indeed, in terms of the divisions over Europe, Hague has opted to adopt a more hard-line stance, rather than moving towards a softer compromise over Britain's future adoption of the euro. The Conservative Party's continuing overdraft and financial restrictions mean that they are also unable to afford extensive public opinion polling and the services of professional political consultants to road-test new themes and issues. To some extent public meetings, dispatching shadow ministers on an Away-Day out to the provinces, are a cheap and easy alternative to systematic polling and market research. At the mid-term of the Labour government, the evidence from monthly opinion polls, from the June 1999 European elections, and from by-elections like Eddisbury, indicated only faint stirrings of a revival in Conservative fortunes. These stirrings may be sufficient to encourage the Conservatives to believe that, because they lost so much support in the 1997 election, by the usual law of swings and round-abouts they will almost inevitably recover some of Middle England in the next general election, *if* they batten down the hatches on sleaze, if they polish up their presentation, and, above all, if Blair stumbles. This is a not unreasonable expectation. But Conservatives should look over their shoulder and recall that in 1979 Callaghan was slaughtered by the swing to the Conservatives, but Labour even fell further into the abyss in 1983, before clawing back a slow, painful recovery. By all the usual expectations, Labour's massive majority should be reduced in the next general election, but there is nothing inevitable about this.

5.   Conclusions

This analysis carries some important implications for understanding the results of the 1997 general election, for patterns of British party competition, as well as for Downsian theories of party competition. On the basis of this analysis we can conclude that the traditional pattern of party competition was transformed on the economy by Labour's move towards the center ground of the British political landscape. Spatial theories of electoral competition assume that 'catch-all' parties have the capacity to gain popularity by moving strategically to the center of the ideological spectrum (see, for example, the discussion in Kitschelt 1994). The most plausible explanation of why Labour moved center-right is that, in accordance with this spatial theory, it rationally adopted an electoralist strategy to gain the votes of 'Middle England' after 18 years in the opposition wilderness. It remains to be seen how far the Conservatives learn these lessons and start to return home to their supporters.

Appendix A: The 1997 British Representation Study

The 1997 British Representation Study (BRS) is the second in a series of national surveys of parliamentary candidates and MPs from all major parties standing in British general elections. In mid-summer 1996 a mail survey was sent to 1,628 candidates selected by the main British parties (Conservative, Labour, Liberal Democrat, SNP, Plaid Cymru, and Green). In total 999 politicians replied, representing a response rate of 61.4 per cent. The survey includes 272 MPs elected into the May 1997 parliament (or 43 per cent of all British MPs), distributed as a representative cross-section by party (for details see the Technical Appendix and www.ksg.harvard.edu/people/pnorris). The results can be compared with a similar survey, the 1992 British Candidate Study, involving 1,658 politicians in the previous election (Norris and Lovenduski 1995). Attitudes among the politicians can be compared with the electorate using the 1997 British Election Study.

Issue scales

The following items were includes in the 1997 BRS and the 1997 BES:
   Q24: Some people feel that getting people back to work should be the government's top priority. These people would put themselves in Box 1. Other people feel that keeping prices down should be the government's top

priority. These people would put themselves in Box 11. Other people have views in-between. Using the following scales ... where would you place your view?

Q25: Some people feel that government should put up taxes a lot and spend much more on health and social services. These people would put themselves in Box 1. Other people feel that government should cut taxes a lot and spend much less on health and social services. These people would put themselves in Box 11. Other people have views in-between. Using the following scale ... Where would you place your view?

Q26: Some people feel that government should nationalize many more private companies. These people would put themselves in Box 1. Other people feel that government should sell off many more nationalized industries. These people would put themselves in Box 11. Other people have views somewhere in-between. Using the following scale ... Where would you place your view?

Q27: Some people feel Britain should do all it can to unite fully with the European Union. These people would put themselves in Box 1. Other people feel that Britain should do all it can to protect its independence from the European Union. These people would put themselves in Box 11. Other people have views somewhere in-between. Using the following scale ... Where would you place your view?

Q28: Recently there has been discussion about women's rights. Some people feel that women should have an equal role with men in running business, industry, and government. These people would put themselves in Box 1. Other people feel that a woman's role is in the home. These people would put themselves in Box 11. Other people have views somewhere in-between. Using the following scale ... Where would you place your view?

Q23: In politics people sometimes talk of left and right. Using the following scale, where 1 means left and 10 means right, where would you place yourself?

Identical items are also carried in the 1997 BES.

References

Note: The directors of the 1997 British Election Study were Anthony Heath, Roger Jewell, John Curtice, and Pippa Norris and the research was funded by the ESRC. The 1997 British Representation Study was directed by Pippa Norris in conjunction with the CREST team, with fieldwork conducted at the University of East Anglia, funded by the Nuffield Foundation. I am most grateful to all my colleagues at CREST and East Anglia for collaborating on this data-set.

Blair, Tony. 1998. *The Third Way: New Politics for the New Century*. Fabian Pamphlet 588. London: Fabian Society.
Budge, Ian. 1999. 'Party Policy and Ideology: Reversing the Fifties?' In Geoffrey Evans and Pippa Norris, *Critical Elections: British Parties and Voters in Long-term Perspective*. London: Sage Publications.

Budge, Ian, David Robertson, and Derek Hearl, eds. 1987. *Ideology, Strategy and Party Change: Spatial Analysis of Post-War Party Programmes in 19 Democracies.* Cambridge: Cambridge University Press.

Downs, Anthony. 1955. *An Economic Theory of Democracy.* New York.

Evans, Geoffrey and Pippa Norris. 1999. *Critical Elections: British Parties and Voters in Long-term Perspective.* London: Sage.

Giddens, Anthony. 1998. *The Third Way.* Cambridge: Polity Press.

Kitschelt, Herbert. 1994. *The Transformation of European Social Democracy.* New York: Cambridge University Press.

Mandelson, Peter and Roger Liddle. 1996. *The Blair Revolution: Can New Labour Deliver?* London: Faber & Faber.

Norris, Pippa. 1994. 'Labour party Factionalism and Extremism'. In Anthony Heath, Roger Jewell, and John Curtice, eds., *Labour's Last Chance?* Aldershot: Dartmouth.

Norris, Pippa. 1999. 'New Politicians? Changes in Party Competition at Westminster'. Geoffrey Evans and Pippa Norris, eds., *Critical Elections: British Parties and Voters in Long-term Perspective.* London: Sage.

Norris, Pippa, John Curtice, David Sanders, Margaret Scammell, and Holli A. Semetko. 1999. *On Message: Communicating the Campaign.* London: Sage.

Norris, Pippa and Joni Lovenduski. 1995. *Political Recruitment: Gender, Race and Class in the British Parliament.* Cambridge: Cambridge University Press.

Rentoul, John. 1995. *Tony Blair.* London: Little Brown.

Shaw, Eric. 1994. *The Labour Party Since 1979.* London: Routledge.

Shaw, Eric. 1996. *The Labour Party Since 1945.* Oxford: Blackwell.

Sopel, Jon. 1995. *Tony Blair: The Moderniser.* London: Bantam.

Webb, Paul and David M. Farrell. 1999. 'Party Members and Ideological Change'. In Geoffrey Evans and Pippa Norris, eds., *Critical Elections: British Parties and Voters in Long-term Perspective.* London: Sage.

Part II
New Labour in Government

4
Education and Training: Tensions at the Heart of the British Third Way

Stewart Wood

Introduction

Education is central to the New Labour world-view. In an age of globalization, the mantra goes, it is only through education that individuals can find stable sources of income and employment security. Only through education can we break the cycle of dependency that threatens the British welfare state. And only through education can we hope to overcome the British disease of low productivity, chronic long-term unemployment and supply-side constraints to growth. Education and training policy under the Blair government has therefore come to assume a new weight of responsibility, performing a pivotal role in a whole range of economic and social policy areas.

This fundamental position of education and training in the New Labour world-view and policy toolkit is a defining feature of its self-proclaimed 'third way'. Critics from left and right charge that the third way is at best an intellectual fig-leaf for sheer pragmatism, and at worst a justification for abandoning the commitment to improving the welfare of the disadvantaged. The early years in the philosophical life of the third way have seen it attacked from many sides. It may still be too early to pass judgement on many of the new government's policies. But it is not too early to look at the principles underlying these policies, to point to emerging strengths and weaknesses, and to formulate some initial responses to the criticisms launched against them.

This paper presents an overview of the main education and training initiatives launched by the Blair government, and examines the extent to which they reflect putative third way principles. Secondly, it assesses the initiatives themselves, how successful they are likely to be, and tensions between education policy and other notionally third way policies. Thirdly, it points to specific features of British economic and political life that pose significant problems in implementing New Labour's conception of the third way in the area of education policy. Predictably, perhaps, the verdict is mixed. There is considerable ambition and coherence in the educational strategy of the Blair administration that deserves encouragement. But the obstacles facing the government, stemming from familiar structural problems of the British economy, and from incompatibility between its own policies, are sizeable.

1. Education and training at the heart of the third way

The goals and toolkit of the third way

New Labour's third way seeks the extension of real opportunities to all within a framework that fosters civic responsibility (see White, this volume). According to this view, every citizen should have meaningful access to a minimal range of 'basic goods' necessary for a freely-chosen, fulfilling life. When these conditions are met, citizens must be expected to bear the costs of the free choices they make. Where access to basic goods is denied by poverty, lack of education, or other 'brute luck' factors beyond individual control, i.e. where citizens are 'socially excluded', the state has a duty to step in to clear the way. In the philosophy of the third way, therefore, inclusion rather than equality is the primary goal. And when the state assists, it must be with the aim of restoring self-reliance rather than replacing it. Furthermore, as White argues (see Chapter 1), the third way is arguably distinguished by a broader conception of the policy toolkit available to centre-left governments than that of post-war British social democracy. The third way is agnostic about the appropriate balance between public and private funding, or state versus market methods of public provision. These are questions whose answers should be determined by technical rather ideological considerations.

Two features of this package of ends and means are of particular relevance to the domain of education and training policy. First, state intervention in the name of empowering individuals should be concerned with a broad range of assets rather than simply income levels. The central emphasis here is clearly on opportunity goods that secure future income streams, in particular (though not only) education and skills. Second, the third way emphasizes the centrality of employment to the welfare and opportunities of its citizens. The success of social and economic policy is largely measured by the extent to which it returns individuals from welfare to work, and helps to equip them with the skills required for security and self-sufficiency. These emphases have the effect of concentrating much of the transformative ambition behind the third way into the realm of education policy, particularly in light of the government's self-imposed restrictions on expansive monetary and fiscal policy.[1]

A third way world-view?

Ideologies are underpinned by certain characteristic world-views from which their defining principles spring. The third-way view of the world has at least four distinctive elements.

Globalization: The third way sees globalization as irresistible and inescapable. Individuals must therefore learn to adapt to new types of work, new technologies, the need for increased occupational and geographical mobility, and heightened employment insecurity. Governments, for their part, must realize that the traditional solutions of the post-war world are no longer relevant in an age of mobile capital and new global competition (Blair 1995). Rather than ignore or fight the tide of globalization, the third way recommends that governments and citizens alike must combine forces to exploit the opportunities it presents. Of paramount importance here is the need for education and training to enable individuals to participate in the new 'knowledge-driven economy'.

Harmony of interests: The third way also subscribes to a benign view of social organization. Where social democracy sees class conflict and neo-liberalism sees atomistic individuals, the third way sees individuals laden with both rights and responsibilities to communities. It rejects the individualism of the New Right, but it also refuses to believe that society is stratified by classes, with fundamentally antagonistic interests engaged in zero-sum conflicts over the distribution of resources. If we view society instead as communities of mutual dependence, it argues, the interests of all can be pursued simultaneously, through consensual rather than adversarial politics.

Partnership with business: Following on from this, the third way rejects what it sees as the traditional antipathy of the left towards business. In the new world economy, one of the central tasks of government is to work with rather than against business to create favourable conditions for economic growth. This requires governments (especially Labour governments) to assure business that it will restrain its interventions in the economy, both by reducing the fiscal burden of state expenditure, and by committing itself to a stable macroeconomic policy regime. More indirectly, the interests of business and of improving competitiveness should be guiding principles in the formulation of economic and social welfare policy.

Electoral constraints: Technological and global economic changes provide technical reasons for thinking that traditional social-democratic policy programmes are no longer feasible. But the electoral constraints on such solutions are equally important. New Labour is clearly wedded to the view that the British electorate will not tolerate redistribution to the extent it once did. As a result, governments are forced to face up to electoral limits on what they can achieve through tax-and-spend policies.

The implications for education

Clearly education looms large in the philosophy of the third way. It is central to the vision of a civic community in which individuals have access to basic economic and social goods, and are in a position to take responsibility for their own choices. In a world of global competition among knowledge-based industries, we have no choice but to acquire new and better skills. And the task of developing these skills is one which should be accomplished in partnership by business, government and individuals.

In some respects, of course, this picture is not as far removed from the traditional social-democratic emphasis on supply-side investment as many proponents of the third way would like to think. There is a tendency to caricature social democracy as essentially an ideology resting on income redistribution and generous welfare entitlements. In many north European countries, however, supply-side investment in human- and physical-capital assets (both by the state and by employers) has always been an integral part of social democracy. Even within the somewhat different ideological tradition of British 'Labourism', social democrats such as Anthony Crosland argued in the 1960s for a reorientation of ideology and policy away from emphasizing income redistribution towards the equalization of initial wealth endowments and of educational opportunities (Crosland 1962). The newness and distinctiveness of the third way must therefore not be exaggerated. Rather, the invocation of the term by third wayers is designed to draw a distinction between themselves and a stylized notion of crude state intervention that, rightly or wrongly, has come to be associated with the Labour Party during the 1970s and 1980s.

A comparison of 'New' and 'Old' Labour views on education brings out the extent of their differences. On the surface, both see education policy as an instrument of egalitarianism. For 'Old Labour', education was also about extending opportunities, but with the ultimate goal of bringing about greater equality of outcome. There was a far stronger emphasis on the redistribution of opportunities than in Blair's Labour Party. This in turn implied a focus on the structures within which education was delivered. Equality of educational opportunity implied equality of educational formats and in the distribution of resources – hence Labour's hostility towards private education (which remained largely rhetorical), and its initiative after 1965 towards single-format comprehensive state schooling. In the sphere of vocational training, Labour laid the blame for Britain's poor skills record on the reluctance of business to invest in workers. Employers therefore required statutory intervention in order to force them to invest in human capital, initially in the form of a training levy, and subsequently through the direct intervention of the centralized Manpower Services Commission. Indeed Labour remained wedded to the idea of a training tax on companies until the early 1990s (King and Wickham-Jones 1998).

The third way of New Labour differs from these analyses and prescriptions in a number of ways:

Tolerating inequality: Certainly there is an egalitarianism implicit in the emphasis on universalizing access to opportunities. But there is less of a concern for achieving equality in outcomes. New Labour sees inequalities of income and wealth as perfectly consistent with widespread real opportunities. In some respects inequality is not just begrudgingly accepted, but considered natural and even desirable.

Standards not structures: New Labour's education policy is not oriented towards redistribution of educational opportunities, because there is no reason to think that improving access for the disadvantaged implies reducing opportunities for the advantaged. This in turn implies an agnosticism towards the structures within which education is delivered, a sharp departure from Labour's traditional concern to develop common educational formats. New Labour is now prepared to accommodate private schools alongside state schools, and both selection and nonselection within the state system.

The economics of education: Labour's primary interest in education is in its contribution to improving individuals' labour-market prospects. In other words, education is regarded ultimately from an economic point of view. The government's Green Paper, *The Learning Age*, begins with the sentence: 'Learning is the key to prosperity' (DfEE 1998). One major implication of this emphasis is that business should be invited into 'delivery structures' of education and training in a larger way than before. The intended effect is both to inject private-sector principles into the management of education, but also to encourage an orientation of learning towards skills. While the Labour governments of the 1960s and 1970s resorted to state power to force companies to invest in training, the Blair administration sees harmony between the economic interests of companies, the employment interests of students and trainees, and the national interest.

2. New Labour's policies on education and training

Within a year of the 1997 election David Blunkett, Education and Employment Secretary, announced plans for an increase in education spending of 5 per cent in real terms from 1999 to 2002. The main (though not only) aim of this spending boost was to expand the number of places for 3- to 5-year-olds, and to reduce class sizes to under 30 for all 5- to 7-year-olds by 2001. Expanding opportunities by concentrating resources at the early years of education is a clear priority of the new government.

At the other end of the age range, Labour's main initiative is to spread the gospel of 'lifelong learning'. The government's aim is to break the exclusive association of learning with schooling by emphasizing the variety of formats in which learning can take place, and by stressing that education continues throughout working lives rather than exclusively prior to them. Though this campaign has so far been largely a rhetorical one, there have been some innovations. In 1998 the University for Industry (UfI) scheme was launched – in essence, an internet-based brokering service which will offer information on a range of education and training courses in different regions. The UfI was accompanied by 'Learning Direct', a new freephone national advice and information service about learning and career options (Milner et al. 1999). In June 1999 the government announced a new Learning and Skills Council to assume responsibility for the administration of the myriad forms of post-16 education in Britain.

Labour's main financial instrument for boosting lifelong learning remains in the planning stage. Individual Learning Accounts (ILAs) are intended to enable all individuals to invest in upskilling and reskilling throughout their careers. Although ILAs are one of the centrepieces of Labour's pre-election consultation document, *Lifelong Learning*, worries about the programme's coherence, implementation and spending implications led to delay in its introduction. The Chancellor announced in his March 1999 Budget that a million ILAs were to be created in the following year. Any individual wishing to open such an account will receive a government contribution of £150, and both employers and employees will be able to contribute supplementary amounts tax-free. In addition, any adult with an ILA will be able to claim a discount of 20 per cent, or an additional grant of up to £100, on the cost of the training they choose. Adults signing up to improve their basic education – including computer literacy – will receive a discount of 80 per cent on course fees.

Reform of student funding arrangements in higher education has been one of the most controversial changes introduced by New Labour. While the Blair administration is completing the transition from state-financed maintenance grants to a loan-repayment system, it has also broken the principle of 'free tuition' with the introduction of a £1,000 (now £1,050) flat-rate tuition fee on all students entering higher education. This seems to mark the beginning of a transition towards a system of mixed funding, in which individuals, the state and companies will be expected to share the costs of paying for higher education.

Policy towards the education of 5- to 16-year-olds has been particularly active. New Labour sees itself as the guarantor of improving standards in schools (of whatever status), and to this end it has continued the preceding Conservative government's reliance upon targets. National literacy targets (supported by the establishment of 50 summer literacy schools) and numeracy targets have now been joined by the publication of homework guidelines for parents. Most notably the government has demonstrated its willingness to intervene directly in a variety of ways to improve the quality of schools and of teaching. The teacher-training curriculum has been beefed up and modernized, as has the teacher appraisal system. Legislation has been introduced to allow the government to send 'SMART' teams to turn around failing schools (named, publicly, by the independent regulatory body, OFSTED).

The flagship policy for correcting under-performance of schools in deprived areas has been the creation of 25 regional 'Education Action

Zones'. Within each zone, local partnerships between schools, business and community organizations will be given up to £750,000 to develop innovative strategies for raising standards. Further attempts to open the door of the state education system to market mechanisms notably include the involvement of private-sector companies to help run a local education authority in east London, as well as a state school in Surrey. Education authorities will also be encouraged to introduce Advanced Skills Teachers, or 'superteachers', on higher salary scales than their colleagues in more advantaged areas. Superteachers will be paid up to £40,000 a year in return for taking on additional tasks such as visiting schools to absorb and disseminate successful teaching techniques. Meanwhile Blair is determined to press ahead with the introduction of performance-related pay for teachers despite intense opposition from teachers' unions. According to the Green Paper published in March 1999 teachers will be subject to annual appraisals which could result in bonuses of up to 10 per cent as a reward for teaching excellence.

Finally, Labour's welfare-to-work strategy has attempted to introduce new educational options for the non- and un-employed. 'New Deals' for the unemployed, for lone parents and for the disabled attempt to move people off benefits and into employment or education. The New Deal for the 18- to 24-year-old long-term unemployed (i.e., out of work for over 6 months) presents individuals with the choice of work placement, education or training, voluntary work or a place on a new Environmental Task Force (though there is no option to refuse all the options and continue drawing benefit). To encourage take-up employers are offered tax incentives to take on programme participants either in employment or in training. In other respects New Labour's approach to learning in the workplace is a mixture of exhortations to train more, calls for partnership between government and business, and a continuation of structures and schemes developed under the previous government. Despite the marginalization of the Training and Enterprise Councils (TECs) created by the previous Conservative government, the Learning and Skills Council that is assuming its roles has the same commitment to forging 'a strengthened strategic role for business in education and training'. New Labour's view of education and training, like that of its Conservative predecessor, stresses 'the tripartite responsibility of employers, learners and government' (DfEE 1999), but conspicuously sees no role for trade unions (King and Wood 1999).

3. How much third way is there in New Labour's education policy?

Although Labour's education strategy is still in its infancy, it clearly bears the imprint of third-way ideas. Both the language and the structures of new policies exemplify the third-way view of harmonious interests between workers, employers and the state. In particular, employers are being encouraged to develop new, innovative roles in the delivery of education and training. Furthermore the policy instruments used to deliver these initiatives have lived up to the third way's emphasis on public–private partnerships and public–private finance – Education Action Zones and Individual Learning Accounts are perhaps the clearest examples.

Many of these policies are also consistent with the principle that individuals should be expected to bear the costs of lifestyle choices that are genuinely freely made (see Halpern and White 1998). For example, requiring students to contribute to their tuition in higher education is justified in part by the fact that the minority of individuals who undertake degree courses not only choose to do so, but will also thereby add significantly to their future earnings. In contrast, education in the crucial early years of schooling should be financed collectively, because to deny this would be to make access to opportunities that are fundamental to individual and social welfare a matter of brute luck. Taken together this implies a principled justification for shifting public resources down the educational age-ladder.

If the argument from principle supports a shift of public expenditure, spending trends in Britain over the past two decades or so illustrate the need even more vividly. Attendance of British pre-schoolers in publicly funded education remains comparatively low, despite a catalogue of evidence that high-quality pre-school provision generates persisting gains in educational development. In the mid-1990s Britain spent far more on each student in tertiary education than any other OECD country, but conspicuously underspent on primary education; only Ireland and Turkey enjoyed higher pupil to staff ratios (Hillman 1996). In the post-16 age band past policy has concentrated disproportionately on the most able students, who stay in schooling and then move on to university education, rather than those of lesser ability who either leave formal schooling altogether and/or undertake vocational training courses. Charging tuition fees to university entrants can thus be seen as enabling redistribution of public resources within the post-16 age group to those with greater need of collective support (Layard 1997).

Inconsistencies in the application of third way principles to policy are also clear, however, even at this early stage:

Central control versus local initiative: There is, first, a striking conflict between New Labour's principled repudiation of old-style state intervention and policies that have increased intervention in schools and teaching. The new self-restraint of the state in economic policy is clearly not being matched by a similar restraint in educational policy. There are surely good reasons to think that central government should not be involved in the management of schools at the local level (often circumventing local governance structures), let alone prescribing homework guidelines. Accusations of excessive interference by Whitehall are beginning to surface in the 13 new Education Action Zones that were recently launched. Although business is supposed to play the leading role in EAZs, there have been grumblings that central government is reluctant to cede control over one of its dearest policy experiments.

Does content match ambition?: A further worry is the apparent gap between the ambition and the content of policies. While the Labour government has displayed a strong concern with tackling social exclusion, it is unclear how much substance has so far accompanied the rhetoric. New Labour's commitment to Lifelong Learning, for example, is largely still in the stage of being a campaign, rather than a genuine policy with schemes, organizations and money to match. Indeed there is a widespread suspicion that the downgrading of the Lifelong Learning strategy from the status of a legislative proposal to that of a consultative document was motivated by concerns about finance. If this reflects a general reluctance to support the commitment to extending opportunities with significant resources, many of these policy initiatives (such as the Individual Learning Accounts) may prove ineffectual.

Whatever the doubts about the coherence of Labour's education policies in terms of the ideology that lies behind them, however, the more pertinent question is whether or not these policies will work. A closer examination reveals three broad problems that face New Labour in implementing its most cherished set of policies.

4. Obstacles to a British third way in education

The absence of appropriate economic institutions

Britain's record in cultivating vocational skills is poor by international standards. In 1990 63 per cent of British workers had no vocational qualifications at all, compared to 26 per cent of the German workforce. In the same year intermediate vocational qualifications had been earned by 56 per cent of German workers, but by only 20 per cent of British workers (Prais and Beadle 1991). A number of studies have demonstrated a persistent and sizeable gap in the skill levels of British workers compared to their occupational equivalents in other west European countries. Equally worrying is the evidence of a parallel gap in employers' demand for skills between British and European firms (Finegold 1993). As a result, about a third of British workers have never received training from their employers (Keep and Mayhew 1998).

The failure of British firms and schools to deliver a workforce equipped with flexible skills has been at the forefront of the public-policy agenda for about 40 years. Despite a barrage of policy initiatives since the Carr Report of 1957, the problem has remained severe. Finegold and Soskice have persuasively argued that this record of policy failure can be explained by the concept of a 'low-skill equilibrium' (Finegold and Soskice 1988). Low levels of industrial training, they argue, are the result of a network of institutions that give companies incentives to adopt production and competitive strategies that do not rely on transferable skills, and thus depress the demand for them. The problem of training cannot, therefore, be addressed in isolation from other institutional features of the British economy (Soskice 1993).

Soskice argues that the key organizational requirement for a flourishing vocational training system is that business be collectively organized. Where employer organizations are strong and cooperation between companies is close, employers are both more willing and able to invest in the skills of their workers. Coordination between employers helps to prevent poaching of skilled workers; strong, inclusive employers' organizations can offer advice and expertise in developing company training systems; and powerful employers' organizations counter the collective market power of skilled workers.

In the absence of coordination between employers, Britain's capacity for developing a successful system of vocational training is weak. Efforts to increase the supply of or demand for skilled labour run up against the barriers of opposing incentives and constraints that confront employers (Wood 1997). Managers dependent upon short-term capital, for example, face short-term planning horizons that militate against investment in human capital. Without coordination between employers the danger of trained workers being poached by other companies acts as a disincentive to train at all.

The result of this cocktail of incentives is a low capacity for organizing training collectively, coupled with a low demand for skilled labour in general (Wood 1999). The second of these features follows on logically from the first. Where collective action to solve the problem of providing skilled labour is either absent or ineffective, surviving firms will become progressively less reliant on product market strategies that rely on such skills. Those firms that do conduct in-firm training emphasize firm-specific training (i.e., skills that are not transferable, and skilled workers who are less 'poachable') rather than training which produces marketable skills.

This analysis does not bode well for some of the core policies of the British third way. New Labour's education policy is fundamentally about partnerships between government, business and individuals to develop marketable skills. But exhortation, partnerships and other policy initiatives cannot overcome the obstacles of inadequate institutions and weak incentive structures. It seems likely therefore that many of Labour's attempts to turn around Britain's dismal record on training will go the same way as the long list of its failed predecessors, stretching from the Industrial Training Board experiment of the 1960s to the Youth Training programmes of the 1980s.

However, there is an alternative to this bleak scenario of repeated policy failure. Rather than concentrating on the development of vocational training systems in the private economy, governments may serve a valuable role by investing in an education system that develops general skills (Finegold and Soskice 1988). General skills include basic capabilities in numeracy and literacy; interpersonal or 'social' skills; autonomy skills such as competence in time management; and the ability to use automated equipment and new technologies. These are skills that are particularly crucial to the service sector in which Britain's employment growth over the past ten years has been concentrated. Gallie and White present data suggesting that there has been a 'widespread increase in industry [in Britain] in the demand for higher social skills, for instance with respect to communication and handling people' between the mid-1980s and early 1990s (Gallie and White 1993). These general skills can be acquired in formal public education through the school and university system, providing that more people can be induced to remain within the education system rather than exiting at age 16. In particular an expanded and more flexible higher education system, with a wider range of programmes of different content and duration, may well be a profitable way of increasing the general skill level of new entrants to the workforce.

There have been encouraging leaks from Downing Street indicating their willingness to pursue such an expansion, with the aim of ensuring at least 50 per cent of under-30s pass through the HE system, and of promoting shorter and more flexible 'career-friendly modular courses' (*The Guardian* 1999). The establishment of the Learning and Skills Council as an umbrella body to coordinate the fragmented educational options available to those over 16 who do not go to university is an important initial step. A pilot project has also been launched which offers means-tested educational maintenance allowances to 16-year-olds as an incentive to stay in school. These are policies that accept the limits imposed by Britain's economic institutions rather than seeking to overcome them. Nevertheless they are ultimately likely to prove more successful than more ambitious but less realistic alternatives.

Conflicting incentives of employment and education policies

Both Sweden and Germany have been successful in generating high levels of educational achievement and vocational skills in the post-war period. Crucial to both regimes have been the presence of the sorts of coordinated institutions between employers and companies discussed above. But equally important is the way in which labour-market policies have been used to impose 'benign constraints' on employers to support high-skill outcomes. In the German case, for example, employers' commitment towards their workforce's human capital is reinforced by employment protection legislation that makes downsizing difficult and costly (Streeck 1992). Restrictions on the availability of short-term contracts have a similar effect. Employer participation in genuine education and training activity in the workplace has thus been secured by labour-market regulations that force companies to rely upon high-skill strategies.

The danger in Britain is that the quest to raise the supply of intermediate skills within the framework of deregulated labour markets will be self-defeating. If employment protection is weak, contractual flexibility high, and a ready supply of low-wage labour available, employers face few incentives to depart from strategies based upon minimizing labour costs rather than maximizing the long-term productivity of their workers. One result of this is that so-called 'training programmes' in the context of deregulated labour markets become temporary employment programmes, mechanisms for providing companies with cheap, unskilled labour to meet their short-term manpower needs. For example, the training programmes brought in by the Conservative government in the 1980s, and administered by the employer-run Training and Enterprise Councils, clearly confirmed rather than challenged Britain's low-skills equilibrium.

The criticism that training schemes in Britain are little more than subsidized low-skill employment schemes may soon be turned in the direction of Labour's 'New Deal'. One part of the New Deal explicitly offers employers subsidies for taking on long-term unemployed workers for a period of only six months. The possibility that a scheme such as this will open new avenues of opportunity for the unemployed seems remote. Of course the New Deal for the long-term unemployed also offers places on education and training courses. But the quality of these courses, and their limited duration, again suggest that their supply-side impact can only be marginal. Other options – participation in voluntary work and on an Environmental Taskforce – have the flavour of old-style public-works schemes rather than components of a comprehensive 'skills agenda'.

To put the criticism at its strongest, there seem to be contradictory impulses at the heart of the New Deal. One impulse is to push the unemployed back into employment (and off benefits), for which flexibility at the low end of the labour market is considered essential. The other impulse is to use the New Deal to raise the skill levels of the unemployed. But if employers use the scheme to fulfil their short-term manpower needs, as the structure of the programme seems to encourage them to do, it is difficult to see how the two impulses can coexist. Forcing the unemployed into subsidized work or 'training' seems to be a more effective means of managing unemployment than of nurturing real opportunity. And as long as the terms of being out of work remain relatively onerous, the balance of carrots and sticks facing the low-skilled unemployed favours re-entering low-skill, low-wage employment rather than investing in skills with distant pay-offs.

Addressing the needs of the excluded

Many of the education and training schemes introduced so far by New Labour presume a minimal amount of general or social skills. But there is little substantive policy so far for the children, workers and unemployed from the most disadvantaged backgrounds. The government has set up a Social Exclusion Unit within the Cabinet Office, but its effect so far has been limited to a handful of reports on isolated subjects. The welfare-to-work initiative, on the other hand, may well prove to be a revolving door for the socially excluded, moving them in and out of low-wage employment and public employment schemes without seriously improving their long-term prospects. Meanwhile the devolution of most social policy levers to the newly launched Scottish Assembly makes a coordinated country-wide attack on social exclusion even more difficult. Given the importance of overcoming social exclusion to New Labour's third way, this is an area that is still desperately in need of new ideas.

If the government is to respond to this challenge it will require radical policy innovation. Instead of thinking in terms of programmes and schemes, it must address the more fundamental question of reforming the incentive structures that maintain disadvantage over time. A comprehensive approach to this problem will need a combination of policies that attack the multiple social and economic causes of social exclusion. But in the area of education policy, there are clear problems with existing incentive structures that need, somehow, to be remedied.

Let me identify three of the major problems:

Weak incentives of disadvantaged children: First, children from disadvantaged backgrounds have weak incentives to put in great effort at school. Children (and parents) take hard work seriously when there is a perceived link between effort and good job prospects. For many in the 'bottom 30 per cent', the only types of jobs that they see themselves as likely to get are low-skill jobs with poor mobility prospects. These children know they face a relative disadvantage because they come from low literacy and numeracy backgrounds; learning is difficult in schools which are usually dominated by students from a similar background; and the lack of family links to employment networks in underprivileged areas lowers the prospects of finding work anyway.

Weakened incentives to cater to disadvantaged children: Second, schools face strong financial incentives to cater to children from advantaged rather than disadvantaged backgrounds. Funding for schools has become increasingly a function of good performance, while the promotion of parent choice (which New Labour has further encouraged) increases the incentive to attract affluent, high-performing families.

Limited options beyond 16: Third, genuine educational options for the post-16 age group in Britain are limited to an elite group of students who take the academically specialized A-level route (which in turn leads on to university education). If students think or know that they will not be good enough to pursue the university route to employment, they have good reason to exit the education system altogether at the age of 16.

Addressing these problems will require radical reforms that will demand high levels of collective resources. Breaking the calculus that leads students to put in low effort in school is a particularly complex task. Government and business could play a role in extending employment networks into underprivileged areas. A more radical step would be to reverse the process of self-selection that leads to concentrations of affluent and disadvantaged students in separate schools. This would require government-assisted integration, and (less attractively for New Labour) limits on the autonomy of schools and of parents. Children from poorer backgrounds should be offered financial incentives to stay on at school after the age of 16, subject to the condition of meeting lower-level academic requirements (Soskice 1998). As noted earlier, the Labour government seems to be endorsing this proposal, but in order for the incentive to be attractive there will need to be massive investment in relevant and accessible higher and further education courses – perhaps in the form of one- and two-year degree courses, or modulized courses with mixtures of vocational and academic elements.

All of these solutions require money that has to come from the pockets of the better-off. However, this brings out perhaps the most deep-seated tension within the third way. A community of civic responsibility and real opportunity is not built cheaply. Redistribution of resources is an inescapable part of achieving these goals. But if the perception persists that significant redistribution is both politically intolerable (because it will lead to voter flight) and economically intolerable (because it will lead to capital flight), it is difficult to see how these lofty ambitions can really be met. Social inclusion is not an alternative to redistribution but requires redistribution in order to be more than an electoral sound-byte.

The greatest threats to the viability of a consistent British third way lie in the tensions between its component parts. The Labour government wants to 'stabilize' state spending, taxation and intervention, but also to attack inequalities of opportunity. It aims to make labour markets more flexible and convert benefit claimants into employees, but also to encourage long-term investments in human capital as a means of escaping welfare dependency. And it wants to empower employers to lead the skills agenda, without addressing the institutions and incentive structures responsible for British employers' depressing record on industrial training. These are tensions that require tough choices between different elements of the package of nostrums, goals and policy instruments that have been bundled together under the banner of 'the third way'.

Notes

1 Prior to the 1997 general election the Labour government assured the electorate of its fiscal prudence by announcing specific self-binding constraints in monetary and fiscal policy – no increases in the basic rate or top rate of income tax for five years; a long-term objective of introducing a 10p starting rate (introduced in

1999); and a commitment to the incumbent Conservative government's tight public expenditure targets for the following two years. Once in office, Labour not only observed these constraints but added to them by introducing operational autonomy for the Bank of England over the setting of interest rates within two days of winning the election. For details see Glyn & Wood (2000).

Bibliography

Blair, Tony, 1995, article in *The New Statesman*, 29 Sept.

Crosland, Anthony, 1962, *The Conservative Enemy: a Programme of Radical Reform for the 1960s*, London: Cape.

Department for Education and Employment (DfEE), 1998, *The Learning Age: a Renaissance for a New Britain*, Feb.

Department for Education and Employment (DfEE), 1999, 'Blunkett to Transform Post-Sixteen Learning', 30 June, located at http://www.dfee.gov.uk/news.cfm?PR_ID=302.

Finegold, David, 1993, 'The Changing International Economy and its Impact in Education and Training', in D. Finegold, L. McFarland and W, Richardson, eds, *Something Borrowed, Something Learned? the Transatlantic Market in Education and Training Reform*, Washington, DC: Brookings Institute.

Finegold, David and David Soskice, 1988, 'The Failure of Training in Britain: Analysis and Prescription', *Oxford Review of Economic Policy*, 4, no. 3.

Gallie, Duncan and M. White, 1993, *Employee Commitment and the Skills Revolution: First Findings from the Employment in Britain Survey*, Policy Studies Institute, London.

Glyn, A. and Stewart Wood, 2000, 'New Labour's Economic Policy', in Glyn, ed., *Social Democracy and Economic Policy*, Oxford: Oxford University Press.

The Guardian, 1999, 'Blair's Revolution for Learning', 8 March, p. 1.

Halpern, David and Stuart White, 1998, 'The Principle of Partitioned Responsibility', mimeo (available at Nexus Library at www.netnexus.org).

Hillman, Josh, 1996, 'Education and Training', in D. Halpern, Stewart Wood, Stuart White and Gavin Cameron, eds, *Options for Britain: a Strategic Policy Review*, Dartmouth.

Keep, Ewart and Ken Mayhew, 1998, 'Vocational Education and Training and Economic Performance', mimeo, Oxford University.

King, Desmond and Mark Wickham-Jones, 1998, 'Training Without the State? New Labour and Labour Markets', *Policy and Politics*, 26, no. 4.

King, Desmond and Stewart Wood, 1999, 'The Politics of Neoliberalism: Britain and the United States in the 1980s', in H. Kitschelt, P. Lange, G. Marks and J. Stephens, eds, *Continuity and Change in Contemporary Capitalism*, New York: Cambridge University Press.

Layard, Richard, 1997, *What Labour Can Do*, London: Warner.

Milner, Helen, Josh Hillman, Nick Pearce and Michael Thorne, 1999, *Piloting the University for Industry: Report of the North East Project*, Institute of Public Policy Research, London.

Prais, S. and E. Beadle, 1991, *Pre-Vocational Schooling in Europe Today*, London: National Institute for Economic and Social Research.

Soskice, David, 1993, 'Social Skills from Mass Higher Education: Rethinking the Company-Based Initial Training Paradigm', *Oxford Review of Economic Policy*, 9, no. 3.

Soskice, David, 1998, 'The Bottom 30 per cent', mimeo, Wissenschaftszentrum, Berlin.

Streeck, Wolfgang, 1992, *Social Institutions and Economic Performance*, London: Sage.

White, Stuart, 1998, 'Interpreting the Third Way: Not One Road, But Many', *Renewal*, 6, no. 2 (spring).

Wood, Stewart, 1997, *Capitalist Constitutions: Supply-Side Reform in Britain and West Germany 1960–1990*, unpublished dissertation, Government Dept, Harvard University.

Wood, Stewart, 1999, 'Creating a Governance Structure for Training: the TECs Experiment in Britain', in Pepper Culpepper and David Finegold, eds, *The German Skills Machine*, Berghahn.

5

New Labour: a Distinctive Vision of Welfare Policy?

Paul Johnson

1. Introduction: then, and now

Imagine this world. A third of the population lives in publicly owned housing paying hugely subsidized rents; the state promises to pay a generous earnings-related pension at retirement, leaving little need for private top-ups for most; unemployment benefits are earnings related; higher education is free and student grants are publicly provided at levels generous enough to live on; lose your job and the whole of your monthly mortgage interest is paid by the state; long-term care of the elderly is free and universal.

That was Britain in 1979. But things have changed. A series of reforms has increased the degree of targeting in the welfare system and, especially with regard to housing and pensions, there has been substantial privatization. Nobody can now expect a decent pension without a private supplement; at least a third of the publicly owned housing has been sold off; help for those without adequate incomes to pay for their housing or to survive in retirement is much more closely related to income; student grants have been replaced by loans; free higher education is only for the poor; home owners expect to insure themselves against loss of earnings; provision of long-term care is subject to a severe income and asset test.

The other really big difference between the late 1970s and the late 1990s lies in the sheer scope of the social security system. Cut back in its generosity it most certainly has been. But in terms of spending and the numbers dependent on it the reverse is very much the case. So where does that leave us at the end of the 1990s? Is there anything distinctive about the actual or prospective policies of the new Labour government by comparison with what went before?

To provide some preliminary answers to these questions we start with a brief description of what the Conservatives did and where they left the welfare system. Labour's attitude to welfare reform can only be seen in this historical context. We then divide the analysis of the policies followed between those for working-age individuals and policy on pensions, to which a large part of the chapter is devoted. Inevitably in a chapter of this length a great deal of interest and importance is simply ignored. We say nothing about welfare outside of the social security area even though health policy has been very important to this government. We say little or nothing about housing despite its central role in the reform of the welfare system over the past two decades and the fact that it is crying out for further change. What is covered, however, should be adequate to gain some sort of useful view of Labour's welfare vision.

2.   Welfare under the Conservatives

To understand Labour's stance one needs to realize that historically the system of social security provision in the UK, and the one that Beveridge had foreseen, was never a generous one. The state pension was not intended to be more than a minimum on which to build. From the start, and unlike most European countries, means-tested benefits formed an integral part of the system.[1] Unemployment benefits were never meant to do more than tide people over a short period between jobs. It was not until the 1960s and 1970s that the first serious steps were taken towards introducing earnings-related benefits on the continental model. First there were earnings-related supplements to Unemployment Benefit and then, after 1978, the state earnings-related pension scheme (SERPS) and earnings-related additions to Invalidity Benefit.

Projected future costs of this system were large. Without reforms an earnings-indexed basic pension and SERPS would have swallowed up more than 10 per cent of GDP by the middle years of the twenty-first century – as much as the entire social security system costs now. So a very major part of the reforms enacted by the Conservatives during the 1980s was just a rowing back from big new promises from the relatively recent past. The UK had stood on the brink of following the continental European model of social insurance and the Conservative governments of the 1980s pulled it back away from the brink. Earnings-related supplements to UB were abolished in 1980, the future value of SERPS was cut in half in 1986 legislation and reduced again in the early 1990s. Earnings-related additions to Invalidity Benefit were abolished for future claims in 1990. From 1980 the basic state pension was indexed only in line with price increases, not by the greater of price and earnings growth – another generous policy only implemented on a statutory basis in the 1970s. So Labour's predecessor government had already steered the course of reform back to the UK's historical norm.

This movement away from earnings-related provision and earnings indexation of benefits was accompanied by a series of more fundamental reforms to the basis of the welfare state and social security system in the

UK. Private provision of pensions was encouraged, with substantial incentives provided for taking out *Personal Pensions*. Privatization was also a central element of housing policy. First there was widespread privatization of the housing stock through 'right-to-buy' legislation which allowed incumbent tenants to purchase their property from the local council at well below market value. Second, there was an almost complete end to new public-sector house building. In combination these policies led to a swift fall in the importance of public housing. Third, a policy of removing 'bricks and mortar' subsidies led to rents in the social sector moving up much closer to private-sector rents. As a result, reliance on means-tested Housing Benefit rose very swiftly.[2] So housing policy combined state withdrawal from provision through privatization alongside a move away from universal rent subsidies to means-tested benefits.

The move towards means-testing was also evident in the long series of reductions in entitlement to the non-means-tested Unemployment Benefit.[3] These changes culminated in the transformation of this benefit in 1994 into Job Seekers' Allowance (JSA). JSA took the principle of means-testing benefits to the unemployed much further by restricting non-means-tested assistance to the first six months of unemployment. Perhaps more importantly, however, it made much more explicit and formal the link between job search and receipt of benefit. It incorporated a whole series of schemes to help with the job search process with names like 'job search plus', 'jobplan', 'workwise' and 'restart'. In this way the Conservatives made the link between the right to benefit and the responsibility to look for work very explicit.

Accompanying these changes to unemployment benefits and the whole list of welfare-into-work programmes that went with them was the in-work benefit *Family Credit*. Introduced in 1988,[4] this benefit was designed both to directly increase the incomes of low earning families with children and also specifically to make it worthwhile for them to take work by providing a means-tested benefit once a certain number of hours were worked.[5] Spending on Family Credit has risen rapidly, reaching £2 billion a year by 1997. This rise has come largely as a result of continuing increases in the generosity of the benefit. Just as in the US it has been politically relatively easy to raise the in-work *Earned Income Tax Credit* (EITC), so increasing the generosity of Family Credit has occurred at a time when increases in most benefits for those out of work have been seen as politically unpalatable.

As an interesting aside it is worth noting that the emphasis put on the purpose of Family Credit changed over time. By the mid-1990s it was seen in policy terms largely as a means of giving people a financial incentive to work.[6] But in 1988 it was introduced at the time of a great controversy over the future of the universal Child Benefit, and was largely seen as a more generous but affordable means-tested alternative to Child Benefit. (Never generous, Child Benefit is worth less than 3 per cent of average earnings but is paid in respect of each child, irrespective of parental income.) For three years at the end of the 1980s it was frozen in value, but one of the first actions of John Major's government in 1991 was to restore a large part of its value and then to index it to prices each year. There were clear tensions within the government over the extent and role of universal as against means-tested benefits.

This brief history of welfare policy under the Conservatives is necessary introduction to understanding where Labour started from. Two more points need to be made by way of background, however. The first just relates to the cost of the system and the number of people dependent on benefits. Despite all the privatization, cuts and increased targeting set out above, the cost of the social security system rose throughout the period of Conservative government.[7] And it rose largely as a result of vast increases in the number of people of working age receiving benefits. The greater part of this increase was not in the registered unemployed but in other non-workers, particularly lone parents and the sick and disabled. There has been a quadrupling, to one million, in the number of lone parents dependent on Income Support, the UK's minimum means-tested benefit. Over the same period the numbers on Sickness and Invalidity Benefits have trebled so that there are now 1.2 million recipients of (the less generous and harder to qualify for) Incapacity Benefit.

The impact of this on progress towards reform and saving money is clear enough. It makes it very hard. It is one thing to means test the registered unemployed or to insist on them doing work; quite another to do the same for lone parents and those on disability benefits.

The second important background point to recall relates to the distribution of income. It became very dramatically more unequal during the 1980s.[8] And the most important feature of that increased inequality is that it was pervasive. It was pervasive in the sense that it wasn't just, indeed it wasn't particularly, that workers became more different from non-workers and the working age more different from those of pension age, rather inequality grew within each group. Workers got more different from one another. Inequality among pensioners grew enormously.[9]

This increase in inequality has a number of important consequences. Perhaps most important from our point of view is that it makes a return to universality in the social security system both more difficult and less efficient as a means of relieving poverty. Take pension policy for instance. In a world in which the great majority of pensioners are poor, the most efficient way of delivering them benefits is likely to be through a universal system paid at a rate adequate to live on. Little is gained by means-testing, the costs of which in terms of administration, less than full take-up and reduced savings incentives, outweigh the financial benefits derived from spending less. As the proportion with substantial income from private sources rises, so a universal benefit becomes more 'wasteful' and the balance of advantage between universal and means-tested benefits shifts towards means-testing.

So Labour came to power in 1997 facing a very different world to the one it had left in 1979. It was a world of vastly greater inequality and with a much reformed welfare state. It came to power with a set of policies unrecognizable by comparison with those which it had set before the electorate just five years previously in the general election of 1992. Back then the main planks, not just of its welfare policy but of its whole manifesto, had been substantial increases in the universal basic pension and in child benefit. By 1997 its main platform was much more vague, but certainly didn't involve any plans to raise universal benefits. The central plank was probably its 'welfare-to-work' policies with the 'New Deal' for the young unemployed at its heart.

There was without question a (perhaps naive) belief that *something could be done* about welfare dependency and welfare spending, that money could be unlocked from the £100 billion welfare bill to spend elsewhere, that work incentives could be improved, and that all this could be done without hurting people. It took a good year, a green paper[10] with little in the way of specific proposals, disputes over a rather hasty cut to benefits for lone parents, politically unwise (in the absence of any actual proposals) speculation *from the government* about the genuineness of the disabilities of many of those receiving disability benefits, and the eventual sacking of the cabinet minister and her deputy at the DSS, before a clearer understanding of some of the difficulties and fundamental trade-offs involved in designing social security systems became apparent to the government.

By the middle of 1999, though, a number of changes have been made or proposed, or the general thrust of policy has become clear. In a paper of this length there is only room to explore one of those areas in any detail, and here we choose to look at pensions, at least in part because it is in this area that some of the most detailed proposals for change have been set out.[11] Pension policy, though, is also an area in which a number of the more general issues raised by social security reform are particularly explicit. The relative roles of means-testing and universality, the role of the private sector and the importance of incentives (to save rather than to work) are all at the heart of the new pension policy.

There is of course a great deal more to Labour's welfare plans than pension policy. Plans to change the whole focus of the system for working-age individuals to promote work are central. They are dealt with in some detail elsewhere in this volume by Carey Oppenheim (see Chapter 6). Other changes have been made or proposed with regard to benefits affecting the family, to targeting in other contexts and to disability and widows' benefits. A brief summary of some of these policy changes within the overall context of Labour's welfare strategy forms the next part of this chapter, before we move on to look in more detail at pension policy.

3.   The strategy for those of working age

For working-age people the government's clear priority is to encourage work, to 'make work pay' and in particular to increase the skills and employability of the young unemployed. Details are provided by Oppenheim (Chapter 6). But right from the start a serious problem with which the government is having to grapple is what the New Deal and the welfare-to-work rhetoric means with regard to those who are of working age and not employed but not registered as unemployed – largely lone parents and those on sickness and disability benefits. It is among these groups that the number dependent on welfare has really exploded in the past two decades, and it is among these groups that really long-term dependency on welfare is most evident. With regard to the sick and disabled in particular there is only a limited amount that one can draw from welfare-to-work rhetoric or talk of an 'active not passive' welfare state. What does 'a hand up, not a hand out' mean when it refers to this group?

In part some of the strategies that are part of the New Deal for the young unemployed are being used, and a New Deal for the disabled has been launched. Individual help and advice about how to look for work, what work is available and so on is being tried and might prove to be productive. But the government will have to tread a very careful path here. Any suggestion that eligibility criteria will be tightened will result in (and indeed already has resulted in) considerable hostility from the press and fear among benefit recipients. Protests from clearly vulnerable groups will always be difficult to deal with.

Even so, a package of benefit changes for the long-term sick and disabled has been agreed. The changes announced are not hugely radical but, like many of the policy changes of the last Conservative social security secretary, Peter Lilley, they chip away at the generosity of the system and will, over the longer run, have a growing impact on social security bills. One major part of the changes, which may well be built upon by future governments, is the effective means-testing of Incapacity Benefit (IB) against receipt of private pension income. IB is the major social security benefit for the those long-term sick or disabled and unable to work, and it is a long-standing contributory benefit receipt of which has not previously depended on income in any way.

The actual proposals are not hugely draconian as they stand – the benefit will be withdrawn at a rate of 50 pence in the pound for every pound of pension income in excess of £50 a week. But this increased targeting of benefits seems likely to be a continuing theme of Labour policy. It is also evident in proposals made to limit the availability of widows' benefits, another long-standing contributory benefit though one that has become of increasingly limited importance as increased male longevity has reduced the number of widows of working age.

This move in the direction of targeting benefits represents an important step for Labour. In the first place it marks yet another break with the past in which the party was traditionally hostile to means-testing. It also marks a decisive break with those in the party – including Frank Field, a social security minister until mid-1998 – who see means-testing as a major source of perverse incentives not to earn, not to save or just to defraud the system. These are serious issues for a party which appears to be basing its ethos on rewarding rather than penalizing 'civic virtue'. But of course, in the end the arguments pro and contra means-testing are essentially the same as they have always been. We now have some evidence of the direction in which this government is jumping, but there are clear limits to its ability, and probably its desire, to go a great deal further down this path.

Further targeting has not been a policy response available to tackle the issue of benefit dependency among lone parents. There is rather little scope for squeezing their benefits, for these are already paid on an almost entirely means-tested basis at a level that could never be construed as generous. A relatively minor cut in these benefits announced in November 1997 brought down such a heap of opprobrium on the heads of ministers that the Chancellor effectively more than reversed the cut in his budget four months later. The government is also evidently nervous about making looking for work a condition of benefit receipt for lone parents.[12] Instead we have rather more of a carrot than a stick for lone parents, and other low-paid families with children, in the shape of the *Working Families Tax Credit*. Sold as a major new policy innovation, this is effectively a more generous version of the Family Credit benefit introduced and expanded by the Conservatives.[13] This is probably no place to go into the largely theological arguments about the alleged benefits of delivering income through something called a tax credit as opposed to something called a social security benefit; but a belief in the importance of the packaging as well as the product clearly does extend to welfare policy.

The stress being put on the WFTC, and the significant amount of money being spent on it, are further evidence of the profound belief in the ability of supply-side changes to alter the performance of the labour market and of the wider economy. The WFTC increases work incentives somewhat by raising the benefit that low earners with children receive once they work 16 hours or more; and by lowering the withdrawal taper, the incentive to work more than the minimum 16 hours is also increased. The down side, of course, is that many more people will be drawn into the net and will face the full new 55 per cent withdrawal rate.

The really big innovation within the WFTC, though, is to do with the introduction of a 'childcare credit' which, within relatively generous limits, will pay childcare costs for low earners, especially single parents. The future cost of this is unclear, but is potentially large.

This policy does give people more incentive to move into work, and the childcare credit especially could make a substantial difference to work incentives especially for lone parents who don't have access to affordable childcare. But it also serves to illustrate many of the trade-offs that exist within social security policy. By bringing many more people onto the taper, and by increasing the value of part-time work relative to full-time work, the WFTC will *reduce* incentives to work full time for many. This is especially true for secondary earners in couples. Now of course *there is no way round this type of trade-off*. We have little evidence to suggest what is the appropriate point on the trade-off. The childcare credit element of the WFTC also serves to illustrate an important trade-off. It creates the possibility that much childcare currently provided informally by friends and family will be 'marketized' to take advantage of the new subsidy. Indeed, some commentators have raised the spectre of two lone parents swapping children during the day such that each has a job as a child minder allowing them to claim both WFTC as a wage top up and the childcare credit to pay for the other to look after their children. Again creating a scope for gaming the system when the government intervenes with benefits and subsidies is an inevitable part of welfare policy.

In sum the Labour policy for those of working age is centred around work. The very large groups of disability benefit recipients and lone parents who are not officially unemployed represent a substantial challenge to this ideology. The response so far has been two pronged – to provide support in finding work and supporting incomes in work, while at the same time increasingly concentrating resources on the poorest of those not in work.

4.   The strategy for pensions

The other half of the social security system covers people of pension age. Here, to understand Labour's policy it is especially important to understand the legacy left by the Conservative government. For Labour did not inherit an over-large, over-expensive pension system in danger of imploding in the face of population ageing. The Conservative government had effectively done all that needed to be done to ensure the financial viability of the state pension system. They almost entirely undid the markedly generous 1970s legislation which saw the introduction of SERPS with, at the time, cross-party support.[14]

For very soon after implementation serious objections to SERPS, on both pragmatic and ideological grounds, became clear.[15] As with most social insurance systems it offered a great deal to the first generations but was only sustainable in the long run with ever increasing tax contributions. And the new Conservative government clearly had an ideological preference for the private sector, a preference set out in a government Green Paper of 1984 proposing the abolition of SERPS and its replacement with compulsory private provision. This plan was scuppered largely by Treasury opposition.[16] Instead a series of amendments was made to the formula for calculating SERPS reducing its eventual value, and cost, by about a half.[17] Note, though, that through all this, people retiring up to 1999 have been fully protected. It is at the end of the 1990s that the state pension system has reached its maximum generosity for many retirees.[18]

The same legislation also greatly encouraged the spread of private pensions through the creation of an option to 'contract out' of SERPS into a Personal Pension. In fact this was an extension of a novel feature that was included in SERPS at its birth. For, seen by its architects as a state alternative to occupational pension schemes, it was originally introduced in such a way as to allow defined benefit occupational pension schemes to *contract out*. In return for giving up (most) future rights to SERPS members of occupational pension schemes and their employers were able to pay lower rates of National Insurance Contributions. This proved to be an important model, and its extension to Personal Pensions had, by the mid-1990s, led to a situation in which nearly three-quarters of the working population had given up rights to SERPS in exchange for a private pension of some sort. Because of the distribution of their earnings SERPS had effectively become a system to provide future benefits for the low paid, but current subsidies towards private provision go to the better paid.

It is worth saying that, in opposition, Labour opposed all these changes. Most of all it did not become reconciled to the price indexation of the basic pension, which had been government policy since 1980s, until after the 1992 general election. At that election an increase in the basic pension and subsequent earnings indexation was at the core of the Labour manifesto.

So by the time of Labour's election the UK public pension system was in an unusual position internationally. It was solvent. Indeed, despite a substantial projected increase in the number of pensioners over the next 40 years (from 9.1 million people over age 65 in 2000 to a projected 14.9 million in 2040), the share of national income going on state pensions is projected to *fall* from an already relatively low base. This, of course, is reflected in a shortfall in incomes for future pensioners.

In its Green Paper of December 1998 (DSS 1998) the government recognized this problem. It proposed two major steps to remedy it through the state system. In the first place it committed itself (as resources allow) to uprate the means-tested minimum benefit for pensioners (Income Support) year by year in line with earnings – while continuing to increase the basic pension only in line with prices.[19] It is important to understand at this point that Income Support is *already* worth more than the basic state pension and, because it increases in value at ages 75 and 80, in the case of older pensioners it is worth considerably more. By 2050 the means-tested minimum will be worth about twice the basic pension on currently announced policies.

While one could argue that in some ways this is not a huge break with the past, since over time minimum benefit levels have tended to rise roughly in line with earnings, this commitment is certainly new. The increasing importance of means-tested benefits for lower income pensioners has been explicitly spelled out for the first time. It is fairly clear that both main political parties in the UK see a diminishing role for universal basic pensions.

Nevertheless the government is clearly ambivalent about means-testing. The Green Paper recognizes the problems of low take-up and the impact of means-tested benefits on incentives to save. That is where the second element of reforms to state pensions comes in. It is proposed that SERPS will be fundamentally changed (along with a name change to State Second Pension (SSP)) so that it offers substantially higher benefits to low earners than at present. In the medium term it is intended to turn it into a fully flat rate pension providing to anyone earning £9,000 a year or less double what SERPS currently offers to someone earning £9,000. This, the Green Paper states, would be enough to give anyone retiring in 2050, after a full working career, enough contributory pension to avoid reliance on even an earnings uprated Income Support.

So on top of the current flat rate basic pension we will have another flat rate pension. This looks odd at first sight. There will, though, be two very important differences between the current basic pension and the new SSP. In the first place it will still be possible to contract out of the SSP just as with SERPS. And while rights to the SSP itself will be accrued on a purely flat rate basis it is intended that contracting out rebates will remain earnings related. The idea is that this will give anyone earning more than £9,000 a year a substantial incentive to contract out of the SSP. One might, though, be forgiven for expressing scepticism regarding the durability of such an arrangement.

The second major difference between SSP and the basic pension will lie in its effective universality. In principle the basic pension is a contributory benefit receipt of which depends on a full, or nearly full, working life. In practice credits and allowances for periods of unemployment, disability and child-rearing will make it quite difficult to avoid accruing rights to a full or nearly full basic pension.[20] On the other hand rights to a full SSP will actually depend on working for a full 49 years from age 16 to 65 with only very limited exceptions for those with children under 5 or who are caring or disabled in particular circumstances. The upshot of all of which is, of course, that the combination of basic pension and the new SSP will not necessarily be enough to float people off means-tested benefits.

Without doubt there is some tension in the position with regard to means-testing. However, there is no doubt about the general direction of these reforms to state pensions. They are redistributive and leave the state focusing more on providing incomes to the poorest whilst providing yet more encouragement to even the very modestly well-off to leave part of the state system and join the private sector.

This is precisely where the other main element of government's proposals – the introduction of *Stakeholder Pensions* – comes in. These are new private pension vehicles intended to be simple, cheap and flexible, thereby providing a genuine option to many of the low and modestly paid. For the half of the workforce who do not have an occupational pension available, the only private pension vehicles currently available are Personal Pensions. These remain relatively expensive financial vehicles, and are probably not appropriate for many of the 25 to 30 per cent of the workforce who currently have no private provision, nor indeed for some of those on low incomes who currently do have a Personal Pension. There has been particular concern over the level of costs and the way in which much of the cost in Personal Pensions is 'front end loaded' such that much of the first year or two's contributions can be lost in charges.

Stakeholder Pensions are intended to get round these problems by having to meet strict criteria on costs, flexibility and governance. Employers will have to make them available to all employees who do not have access to an occupational pension and will be obliged to deduct any contributions an employee chooses to make direct from the pay packet. So what the government is doing is recognizing that the private sector is currently failing to meet the needs of many of those who the government would like to see with more provision of their own. While there is a clear belief that there is a bigger role for the private sector, there is no naive optimism that it will fill the gap appropriately if left entirely to its own devices. There clearly are substantial market failures in the provision of retail financial products and it is hoped that the new framework for Stakeholder Pensions will overcome most of these failures.

The pension industry in the UK has, of course, got itself a very bad name as a result of the mis-selling of Personal Pensions. This mainly involved the selling of Personal Pensions to people who were members of their employer's occupational pension scheme and who, by leaving it, lost their employer's contribution, and in many cases lost out because of the low transfer and preservation values of final salary schemes. In this area the Labour government is showing considerable public hostility towards the private sector, 'naming and shaming' companies that had been involved in the mis-selling scandal and which have not done enough to compensate their customers. The problems that surrounded mis-selling also indicate some important lessons to be taken account of in future welfare reform.

One should perhaps add to this discussion of Labour's sometimes ambivalent attitude to the private sector, that the biggest policy decision to affect pensions taken prior to the publication of the Green Paper involved a substantial tax increase on pension funds. The Labour Chancellor's first budget ended the system whereby pension funds were able to reclaim Advance Corporation Tax paid on dividends received. This was a tax rise designed to raise considerable sums – perhaps £5 billion a year – and yet to be invisible to the public. While the pension industry can cope with this, further policy changes of this type which might tip the balance against pensions with regard to the degree of fiscal privilege they enjoy relative to other savings products, and this would not augur well for the long-run security of private pensions in the UK. Returning to the main issues, the overall approach appears to be pragmatic. The state provides a universal basic pension on which to build. This rises with prices because, with the population ageing, anything more generous would result in an increasing portion of GDP being spent on a benefit much of which goes to an increasingly prosperous group of pensioners. So the basic pension is paid at low level, but means-tested assistance at a somewhat higher level is paid to the poorest pensioners. The level of this rises over time somewhat faster than prices. There is compulsory second-tier provision, with most people relying on the private sector, but with increased generosity to low earners within the state system. The exact boundaries between the public and private sectors in the provision of this second tier are up for negotiation on a largely pragmatic basis. The overall philosophy is not so different from that of the Conservatives – low-level state provision for those who need it, private provision for the rest.

5. Conclusions

New Labour's welfare policy is constructed very much within the UK paradigm. It is clearly distinguishable from the top-heavy social insurance systems of continental Europe. But there is little sign of a move down the truly minimalist American route – though if there is a clear direction of change it is towards less comprehensive provision and increased targeting of benefits. A number of other key points stand out:

1) On the whole there is a general pragmatism. There is little sign of concern about sacred cows. If it works do it. If it doesn't don't do it, or stop doing it.
2) In many areas there is more sign of continuity with the policies of the previous government than of dramatic change. But it may be too early to judge. We are only a few years into the new government. The Conservatives took at least a decade to impose a real and distinctive change on welfare policy.
3) The biggest and most important innovations have probably been in the field of welfare-to-work. The New Deal for young people, the Working Families Tax Credit and initiatives to help other marginalized groups into work have been implemented with urgency and have been backed by substantial resources. This, if anything, has been the defining feature of government policy. It is not just these particular policy initiatives, but the introduction of some form of work-related interview for lone parents and recipients of disability benefits as well, that indicates the overwhelming importance given to routes into work.

But as this paper makes clear it is certainly not *only* in the area of welfare to work that distinctive policy directions are observable. Here we have concentrated to a large extent on pension policy where conflicting attitudes to and problems of the roles of means-testing and of the private sector come into sharp relief. The need for the potential disincentive effects of targeting benefits through means-testing to be ameliorated by other policies is recognized. The need to regulate and direct the private sector rather more than in the past if more use is going to be made of it by lower income people is also clearly recognized. The set of policies that derives from these conflicting problems and priorities is, and is bound to be, complex. There is no simple ideology; there are no simple 'solutions'.

Notes

Much of this chapter was written while the author was at the Institute for Fiscal Studies. He is grateful for comments from participants at a conference at the Center for European Studies at Harvard in November 1998. Any views expressed are those of the author alone and should not be attributed to the IFS or to any other organization.

1   See, for example, Dilnot, Kay and Morris (1994).
2   For an assessment of some of the consequences of this see Giles, Johnson and McCrae (1996).
3   See Atkinson and Micklewright (1989).
4   Though replacing the old *Family Income Supplement* which had existed since the early 1970s.
5   This number was reduced from 30 hours a week, to 24, and then to 16.
6   See, for example Duncan and Giles (1996) for an assessment of Family Credit.
7   In real (1996/7 price) terms social security spending rose by £43 billion.
8   For details see, for example, Goodman Johnson and Webb (1997), Jenkins and Cowell (1994), and Hills (1995).
9   See, for example, Johnson and Stears (1995).
10   DSS (1998a).
11   DSS (1998b).
12   Again, see Oppenheim, Chapter 6, for more details.
13   The structure of the benefit calculation is just the same as for Family Credit, though the initial entitlement is more generous and the withdrawal rate less steep – 55 per cent rather than 70 per cent. Unlike the American EITC there is a simple structure of withdrawal as earnings rise rather than an initial rate of increase with rising earnings.
14   Note that the solvency of the UK pension system is almost entirely a result of policies implemented by the last government and hardly at all the result of a particular demographic situation.
15   On the expected costs of pre-reform SERPS see Hemming and Kay (1982).
16   Lawson (1992).
17   See Creedy and Disney (1988) for an analysis of the main 1988 reforms to SERPS, see Dilnot et al. (1994) and Johnson et al. (1996) for a more up-to-date and comprehensive analysis of reforms to SERPS.

18 Pension Provision Group (1998).
19 See, for instance, Rake, Falkingham and Evans (1999) for one analysis of the consequences of these proposals.
20 See the discussion in Johnson and Stears (1996).

References

Atkinson, A. and J. Micklewright (1989), 'Turning the Screw: Benefits for the Unemployed 1979–88', in A. Dilnot and I. Walker, eds, *The Economics of Social Security*, Oxford: Oxford University Press.

Creedy, J. and R. Disney (1988), 'The New Pension Scheme in Britain', *Fiscal Studies*, 9, no. 2, pp. 57–71.

Department of Social Security (1998a), *A New Contract for Welfare.* London: the Stationery Office.

Department of Social Security (1998b), *Partnership in Pensions.* London: the Stationery Office.

Dilnot, A., R. Disney, P. Johnson and E. Whitehouse (1994), *Pension Policy in the UK: an Economic Analysis.* London: Institute for Fiscal Studies.

Dilnot, A., J. Kay and N. Morris (1994), *The Reform of Social Security*, Oxford: Clarendon Press.

Duncan, A. and C. Giles (1996), 'Labour Supply Incentives and Family Credit Reforms', *Economic Journal*, 106, pp. 142–56.

Giles, C., P. Johnson and J. McCrae (1996), *Living with the State: the Incomes and Work Incentives of Tenants in the Social Rented Sector*, London: Institute for Fiscal Studies.

Goodman, A., P. Johnson and S. Webb (1997), *Inequality in the UK*, Oxford: Oxford University Press.

Hemming, R. and J. Kay (1982), 'The Costs of the State Earnings Related Pension Scheme', *Economic Journal*, June.

Hills, J. (1995), *Inquiry into Income and Wealth*, vol. 2: *A Summary of the Evidence*, York: Joseph Rowntree Foundation.

Jenkins, S. and F. Cowell (1994), 'Dwarfs and Giants in the 1980s: Trends in UK Income Distribution', *Fiscal Studies*, 15, no. 1, pp. 99–118.

Johnson, P. and G. Stears (1996), 'Should the State Pension be a Contributory Benefit?', *Fiscal Studies*, 17, no. 1, pp. 105–12.

Johnson, P. and G. Stears (1995), 'Pensioner Income Inequality', *Fiscal Studies*, 16, no. 4, pp. 69–94.

Johnson, P., R. Disney and G. Stears (1996), *Pensions 2000 and Beyond*, vol. 2: *Analysis of Trends and Options.* London: Retirement Income Inquiry.

Lawson, N. (1992), *The View from No. 11.* London: Bantam Press.

Pension Provision Group (1998), *We All Need Pensions – the Prospects for Pension Provision*, London: the Stationery Office.

Rake, K., J. Falkingham and M. Evans (1999), *Tightropes and Tripwire: New Labour's Proposals and Means-testing in Old Age*, CASE paper 23, London: London School of Economics.

6
Enabling Participation? New Labour's Welfare-to-Work Policies

Carey Oppenheim

1. Introduction: welfare reform and third-way themes

Welfare reform offers fruitful territory for exploring central themes of the so-called Third Way for it is here that the debates about how to rethink the traditional social-democratic vision are at their sharpest. The Green Paper, *New Ambitions for Our country: a New Contract for Welfare* (DSS 1998) conceives of the third way as a path between neo-liberal and traditional social democratic routes:

> The welfare state now faces a choice of futures. A privatised future, with the welfare state becoming a residual safety net for the poorest and most marginalised; the status quo, but with more generous benefits; or the Government's third way – promoting opportunity instead of dependence, with a welfare state providing for the mass of the people, but in new ways to fit the modern world. This is the choice for the nation. (Green Paper, *New Ambitions for Our Country: a New Contract for Welfare*, 1998, p. 19)

Three broad themes set the parameters for the debate on the specifics of welfare reform. First, in the view of third-wayers the globalization of markets and culture has had a profound impact on the capacity of national governments to shape their own macroeconomic policy, on the kinds of skills and mobility required in new labour markets and the scope for redistribution (Vandenbroucke 1998). This approach forms the backdrop to many of the specific welfare reforms – the emphasis on supply-side initiatives, the focus on the primary causes of poverty (education and skills) and the reluctance to pursue more transparent forms of income redistribution. Second, the roles of state and market, public and private sectors have been rethought entirely. The result is a pragmatic approach to whether the delivery and finance of welfare is in the public or private sectors, a positive emphasis on partnerships between public and private and a redrawing of the state's role as regulator, enabler, facilitator and financer. Third, associated with this approach to the public sector is the emphasis on accountable public spending and low taxation (Blair 1998). The Comprehensive Spending Plans, which review public spending over a three-year period, are the clearest attempt to tie spending to specific performance targets.

Turning the spotlight on welfare reform and the labour market, four narratives have dominated the debate: (1) equality of opportunity; (2) social ex/inclusion; (3) the importance of self-interest; and (4) the emphasis on obligation. The Chancellor of the Exchequer, Gordon Brown MP, has hammered out a revised conception of the social-democratic project with the goal of lifetime equality of opportunity (Brown 1996). It addresses the primary causes of poverty through *fostering human capital*. This has been the driving conception behind the government's New Deal programmes, its associated social security/tax changes and the introduction of Individual Learning Accounts (ILAs) targeted at those in work. Learning is seen as investment and the government's intention is that ILAs will become as widespread as home ownership and personal pensions.[1]

The corollary of this conception of lifetime equality of opportunity is a strong emphasis on social inclusion. As with lifetime equal opportunity, the route to social inclusion is via employment and employability. But the debate about social inclusion is differently nuanced; it is characterized by an area focus, a recognition of multi-dimensional forms of exclusion and the *importance of fostering social capital*. Social capital is inherently about *relationships* – between individuals, families, communities (Schuller 1999) – and about refurbishing civil society through democratic renewal in the form of local ownership and participation. In this vein, the third report from the Social Exclusion Unit (1998), *Bringing Britain Together: a National Strategy for Neighbourhood Renewal*, argues for consultation and participation by those in the locality. It is underpinned by the New Deal for Communities which provides £800 million for community-based initiatives. This is distinct from the traditional social-democratic approach, building on an understanding that the public sector cannot be equated with the public realm (Kelly and Gamble 1998).

A third crucial element in rethinking welfare is a shift in the conception of individual motivation.[2] Richard Titmuss, a dominant influence on British post-war social policy thinking, put altruism at the heart of the welfare state. The critique of this approach, in particular by public choice theorists, was taken up in the 1990s in a different form by Frank Field MP from the centre-left. Field (1997) argues that policies should not ignore self-interest, but should be formulated so as to harness self-interest for the public good.[3] Field also argues that the design of social security systems has a crucial impact on claimants' behaviour, pointing especially to the impact of means-tested benefits on honesty and willingness to earn and save.

A final theme of current debate on welfare reform is the emphasis on obligations to match rights: 'Our ambition is nothing less than a change of culture among benefit claimants, employers and public servants – with rights and responsibilities on all sides ... It is the government's responsibility to promote work opportunities and to help people take advantage of them. It is the responsibility of those who can take them up to do so' (Green Paper, *New Ambitions for Our Country: a New Contract for Welfare*, 1998, pp. 24, 31).

Arguably, this also marks an important shift from the Titmussian welfare paradigm, where unconditional, non-judgemental welfare was paramount. According to the new view, unconditional rights in the civil, political and social spheres do not themselves generate membership or inclusion. Active citizenship is required: 'receiving a giro through the post as part of welfare rights does not, in third way views, enhance a sense of citizenship' (Plant 1998). This reassertion of obligation not only reflects a more active notion of citizenship, but also helps legitimize welfare spending. Increases in taxes for benefit rises have to be tied to fulfilling obligations: 'Indeed I think that matching opportunity and responsibility is the only way to obtain consent from the public to fund the welfare state. It has to become the New Deal for 21st Century welfare' (Blair 1996, quoted in Deacon 1998).

The welfare-to-work programme explicitly draws on these four interlocking themes. The dominant idea uniting these themes is the centrality of employment as a tool to both foster equality of opportunity and social cohesion. This chapter returns to the themes and assesses them in the light of the government's programme.

2. The government's welfare-to-work strategy

There are three main components of the government's welfare-to-work strategy: (1) active labour-market measures – the New Deal, as it is known; (2) administrative changes in the delivery of benefits and programmes and (3) increasing incentives to work. There are other important aspects of the strategy which are not dealt with here – in particular the commitment to lifelong learning through the creation of Individual Learning Accounts (see Wood, Chapter 4 in this volume) and the improvement in the quality of the working environment through family-friendly policies and measures to increase employee security (Kelly and Oppenheim 1998).

The New Deal

The New Deal Programmes are the centrepiece of the government's strategy. The bulk of the £5.2 billion worth of spending on these programmes is focused on those 18- to 24-year-olds who have been unemployed for six months or more. The childless partners of the unemployed have also come within the scope of the New Deal. All are offered counselling/guidance by Employment Service advisers and independent career advice as part of the 'gateway' to the New Deal. Beyond the gateway, a four-pronged programme is on offer: employment in the private/public sector (through predominantly private) with a wage subsidy of £60 a week; work experience for 'benefits plus' (£15 per week) in the voluntary sector or as part of the Environmental Task Force; and access to full-time education/training on an approved course. The first three options require day release for an accredited educational/training qualification and last for six months on a full-time basis. The fourth may last for up to 12 months. Support is also given to those who move into self-employment. The New Deal is mandatory for the unemployed: there are sanctions for certain groups who refuse all the options. At the end of the six-month period further guidance and help are available. A follow-through service will monitor the progress of participants and offer further help if they return to unemployment. The 1999 Budget extended help to older people, introducing a New Deal for the over-50s who are either unemployed or economically inactive for six months or more (as well as their partners), backed up by an Employment Credit (see below).

For the very long-term unemployed aged over 25 there are two options available: either employment with private-sector employers subsidized by £75 a week for up to six months or access to an employment-related course leading to an accredited qualification for up to 12 months. Employment Zones, directed at people who have been unemployed for over a year, have been set up in five areas of the country. They are experimental, bringing together different streams of money from training and benefits, for use in a more flexible way to enhance job opportunities.

An important feature of the New Deal, however, is the inclusion of the economically inactive and not just those who count as officially unemployed. The New Deal for Lone Parents is especially noteworthy. Under this programme, lone parents with children over 5 have to attend a job centre interview to develop an individual plan of action combining job search skills, training and childcare with a personal caseworker. A New Deal for Disabled People is also being launched. It is linked to a reform of the work test, which places greater emphasis on capacity rather than incapacity for work. The Social Security and Pensions Bill introduces compulsory attendance for interviews at a job centre for all new claimants (see below). This rather modest change has been accompanied by the harsh rhetoric of tackling the 'something for nothing' society and emphasizing the toughness of the new regime (*Daily Mail*, 10 Feb. 1999, *The Independent*, 10 Feb. 1999).

Administrative reforms

The active labour-market initiatives are accompanied by an overhaul in delivery. Currently the New Deal is being delivered by the government's Employment Service in partnership with other organizations such as local authorities, Training and Enterprise Councils, voluntary organizations and private companies. The government's aim is to forge an entirely new culture which puts work first (DSS/DfEE 1998: 1). It proposes a single gateway, which will bring together the Employment Service, the Benefits Agency and other welfare providers at a single point of contact. All new claimants are to have a personal adviser. 'There is no question of forcing lone parents and disabled people into work. But we want to help people begin the process of becoming independent from benefit at the outset. That is why we believe it makes sense to make it a condition of receiving benefit that people should take part in a discussion about the kinds of support and incentives available to assist with the transition into work' (DSS/DfEE 1998: 3).

The consultation document makes it clear that the aim is to establish contact between claimant and adviser at the initial claim. However, it recognizes that for some groups such as the recently bereaved, lone parents with very young children, those with heavy caring responsibilities and the acutely ill, an immediate focus on work is inappropriate, but that future labour-market participation can be planned and followed up. A striking feature of the proposed changes is the inclusion of healthcare and housing services, recognizing the interrelated nature of many of the problems that claimants face on making decisions to enter work. Evidence about high levels of sickness/disability among lone parents which act as a barrier to paid work and about the mutually reinforcing spiral of unemployment, inactivity and poor health (Walker 1998) suggest that this will be a useful policy response.

Making work pay

The Chancellor has introduced a number of far-reaching changes, which aim to improve the work incentives for people at the lower end of the labour market. The first component of the package is Working Family Tax Credit (WFTC), a wage top-up which replaces family credit in October 1999. The tax credit is considerably more generous than its predecessor (withdrawal rates of net income are 55 per cent compared with the current 70 per cent for family credit). A similar Disability Person's Tax Credit replaces Disability Working Allowance. An Employment Credit for the over-50s will provide a £60 a week top-up (£40 for part-time work) for one year for the older unemployed and economically inactive. Strongly influenced by the US debate, the Chancellor took the tax credit route for a number of reasons, not least the political acceptability of improving the living standards of those on low incomes through more popular tax cuts than benefit rises. In response to criticism that the proposal will shift money from purse to wallet, the proposals have been modified to allow a choice as to whether the tax credit is received through the wage packet or as a direct payment to the mother at home. The Treasury estimates that a one-earner family with two children under 11 working a 35-hour week on £3.60 an hour would receive an effective hourly wage of £6.69 with the

WFTC. A lone-parent family with one child under 11 working similar hours and at the same wage rate would receive an effective hourly rate of £5.81 with the WFTC. The aim is create what the government calls a *minimum income guarantee* to all families with children in full-time work of £200 a week (£10,400 a year). The introduction of a statutory national minimum wage of £3.60 an hour for adults over 22 and a lower rate for younger workers provides an essential wage floor to underpin the welfare-to-work strategy.

A second element is the introduction of a generous Childcare Tax Credit, which will meet 70 per cent of childcare costs up to maximum specified ceilings. This refundable tax credit is available only for registered and not informal childcare. This proposal is part of a National Childcare Strategy, which aims to increase the supply of childcare and subsidize its cost. For the first time, childcare is at the heart of economic policy. Rather than providing a universal subsidy, the tax credit will reach middle and low income families and thus is more akin to a tax credit with an affluence test rather than a means test (Oppenheim 1998). The childcare proposals sit alongside an improvement in family-friendly employment measures with the extension of maternity rights and the adoption of the European Community's Directives on parental leave (albeit without pay), working time and pro-rata rights for part-time workers (*Fairness at Work White Paper*, DTI 1998). The government recognizes that reshaping the work environment is a central part of its welfare-to-work strategy.

A third strand of the proposals are changes to National Insurance contributions to lighten the tax burden on the low paid and employers of the low paid. For employees the lower earnings threshold is to be aligned with the single person's tax allowance at £83 a week and the 2 per cent entry fee is to be abolished.[4] The employer threshold is also raised to £83 a week and the staggered employer contributions above that level are aligned at a higher rate of 12.2 per cent. These changes are redistributive, shifting the tax burden from lower paid to higher paid employees. They may in turn create some incentives for job creation at the lower end of the labour market. A lower starting rate of income tax at 10 per cent has been introduced with a cut in the basic rate of income tax to 22 per cent from April 2000.

A fourth component is the package of support to families with children in recognition of particular hurdles this group faces in gaining a foothold in the labour market. The Chancellor has abolished the Married Couple's Allowance and redirected support in the form of higher universal child benefit and income-related support to families alongside a children's tax credit which will be tapered off from higher earners in April 2001. In the longer term there is a proposal to introduce a dual-track system of employment credits for those in paid work (for those with and without children), paid to the worker, and an integrated children's credit uniting all forms of child support, paid to the main carer: 'A seamless system, without disruption in financial support, would provide a secure income for children in the family's transition from welfare to work' (HM Treasury 1999a: 68, para. 5.13).

3. An assessment of the government's strategy

The New Deal is a substantial investment in the work experience and skills of those on low incomes. As such it should make an important contribution to improving the employability of the young and also make in-roads in this respect among lone parents and disabled people. As yet it is difficult to assess the policy against the tougher criteria of movement off benefits. An evaluation of the New Deal for Lone Parents shows that the effect of the programme was to reduce the number of lone parents on income support by an additional 1–2 per cent over an 8–9 month period between July 1997 to March 1998. This has increased over time and is expected to continue to increase. This effect is broadly in line with similar schemes in Australia and Canada. However, the impact of deadweight and substitution has not yet been estimated (Hales et al. 1998).

More difficult is lifting people beyond in-work tax credits/benefits or the marginalized sector of the labour market. White and Forth (1998) tracked the employment paths of the unemployed between 1990 and 1995 and found that three out of four jobs entered from unemployment were in temporary, part-time or self-employed jobs with low skill levels. And they found that people stayed in these jobs rather than move to different or better jobs. If the New Deal is to achieve more than churning of unemployment and low pay, strategies to help people to progress beyond the marginalized sector of the labour market must be explored. Possible options include targeting education and training credits via Individual Learning Accounts to those getting Working Family Tax Credit or those who have earnings below the National Insurance threshold (White and Forth 1998). More fundamental is the demand side of the question. Levels of unemployment appear to have been contained as growth has slowed and there has been considerable employment growth in some sectors. But there remain parts of Britain which are untouched by the growth of new industries and firms. It remains essential to explore new ways of creating employment whether though community enterprise, public–private sector partnerships or publicly funded part-time employment for the long-term unemployed in the Local Authority or third sector in areas of high unemployment and economic inactivity (Holtham and Mayhew 1996).

One criticism of the New Deal has been the rigidity of rules in the main schemes (although the pilots do allow room for experimentation). The amount of employer subsidy is fixed, for example, regardless of whether larger companies require the carrot of such a subsidy. An alternative approach would allow flexibility for the broker/administrator of the New Deal to use the subsidy where needed, for example to encourage small employers to take on new recruits. In some areas the groups most in need of help are the older long-term unemployed/inactive, and yet the rules of the scheme make it difficult to direct funds to this group. We know that among lone parents it is older lone mothers who have most difficulty in getting back into employment (Noble et al. 1998). Schemes should be free to focus resources on this particular group.

The measures to make work pay will improve incentives. A key remaining challenge for the government, however, is the reform of housing and council tax benefit and its interaction with Working Family Tax Credit (WFTC). In a recent survey 31–2 per cent of income support claimants identified help with housing costs as a key barrier to coming off benefit (Shaw et al. 1996). One option would be to roll up the WFTC and help with housing costs for the low paid into one tax credit (Oppenheim 1998). The greater generosity of the WFTC inevitably means extending means-testing further up the income scale and with it the poverty trap. The Treasury shows that the Budget measures lead to a fall in the numbers with marginal tax and benefit withdrawal rates of 70 per cent or more from 1,090,000 to 420,000 (due to the lower rate of withdrawal of WFTC); but the numbers with marginal rates between 60 and 70 per cent increase from 730,000 to 950,000 (HM Treasury 1999a).

The Childcare Tax Credit represents a major injection of cash into reducing formal childcare costs, and as such it will play an important role in enabling lone parents in particular to enter paid work. However, many lone mothers take jobs in the casualized and flexible parts of the labour market and use informal care, often unpaid: 'much of the discussion about lone mothers working may have assumed a full-time or part-time stable work setting, where lone mothers can break out of the benefits altogether, not a setting with erratic, unsocial hours and low pay, where the chances of working coming to an end are high' (Noble et al. 1998: 59).

Policies need to focus on incentives to provide flexible forms of childcare and increasing flexibility in employment in terms of hours, work-sharing, parental leave and term-time contract for men as well as women. Policies to pay for parental leave would be an additional element of flexibility particularly at the lower end of the labour market. The development of tax incentives, such as national insurance relief for employers who provide more flexible arrangements for parents, should be explored. Another approach would be to include the development of employer consortia for small and medium enterprises to pool initiatives in this area (Harker 1998, Kelly and Oppenheim 1998). Flexible hours and working arrangements will be essential to sustain long-term participation by lone mothers in the labour market.

Overall, the welfare-to-work strategy is likely to help people move off out-of-work benefits, although much here will depend on the macroeconomic context. The strategy is unlikely, however, to move people off in-work benefits/tax credits. Here there remains plenty of room for post-employment policies linked to education, training and the creation of a family-friendly working environment. The strategy should raise levels of employability and so help tilt labour-market demand incrementally in the direction of some of the disadvantaged. However, the policies on their own will not provide many new jobs; a recent analysis in the Bank of England's Inflation Report suggests that the WFTC will create between 10,000 to 45,000 new jobs (*Financial Times*, 11 Feb. 1999). The New Deals begin to recognize a broader conception of productive participation, one that goes beyond paid work, but this aspect could be developed further. However, access to paid work will remain central to social inclusion. We know that paid work reduces material hardship and has other non-pecuniary benefits (e.g., on health). Some of the most imaginative parts of the New Deal (the Employment Zones) are where policies attempt to combine increasing employability with the regeneration of local areas. Finally, welfare-to-work is often looked to as a source of savings in social security expenditure. Evaluation of Australia's Working Nation shows that in the medium term there were such savings, though these were offset by the costs of other parts of the work programme (Saunders 1995). We need to be cautious about significant savings from a welfare-to-work strategy.

The Treasury welfare-to-work strategy is complemented by the Social Exclusion Report *Bridging the Gap: New Opportunities for 16–18 Year Olds not in Education, Employment or Training* (SEU 1999). It develops an all-round approach to the engagement of young people with employment. It identifies crucial components of a successful welfare-to-work strategy: the importance of 'signals' to provide goals (they propose that all teenagers aim for a new 'graduation' target at age 19 with level 2 qualifications and some additional skills); a responsive institutional framework; coherent and accessible income streams (an enhanced Education Maintenance Allowance is being piloted); the control of costs (they suggest a youth card with discounts for particular services); and multi-faceted and personalized advice. This multi-dimensional approach conveys a sophisticated understanding of the mix of motivations that encourage people into paid work and provides a useful model for other groups.

4. Participation income: an alternative path?

While the welfare-to-work strategy of the present government has many strengths, it is important that we continue to consider possible alternatives and directions in which policy could perhaps move in the future. One such alternative is Participation Income: a flat rate benefit paid to adults who are 'participating', i.e., working, retired, unable to work through disability, caring for dependants, volunteering or unemployed.

IPPR and the Microsimulation Unit at Cambridge University modelled a Participation Income to examine its effects on income distribution, marginal tax rates and means-testing (Oppenheim 1998). The reform package consisted of a flat rate individual Participation Income of £20 a week for recognized activities running alongside existing national insurance benefits, and financed by abolition of personal tax allowances, mortgage tax interest relief and rises in national insurance contributions. The changes are highly progressive, lead to a rise in average marginal tax rates but a fall for those with the highest marginal tax rates, and lead to very substantial reductions in spending on means-tested benefits.

Participation Income can be seen as providing the social underpinning for flexibility in today's labour market. It allows greater choice over hours of work, and flexibility over working fewer hours is important in increasing the chances of moving into paid work (White and Forth 1997). Part-time work remains an important way of allowing parents to combine childcare and paid work, to maintain contact with the labour market and buffet women in particular from divorce and separation. As a non-means-tested payment, a Participation Income will reduce the incentive for people to hide their earnings. This should generate more tax revenue. By dramatically reducing means-testing it also encourages people to take greater risks about entering paid work or adding hours, as a substantial component of benefit income is not withdrawn. As an individually based benefit it will encourage independent work choices for men and women, helping to tackle the work rich/work poor divide.

Participation Income also rewards a wider range of desirable activities than paid work alone. It builds upon aspects of the New Deal which pay 'benefits plus' while claimants undertake education or participation in the voluntary sector. By introducing conditions of entitlement, it is likely to carry greater legitimacy than proposals for an unconditional basic income. Participation Income embodies a principle of reciprocity – the right to an income in return for the responsibility of contributing to society as a whole in a number of recognized ways. It thereby endorses a notion of active citizenship and has the potential to underpin social capital. It is of course possible to draw the boundaries of Participation Income more or less broadly than chosen in this particular version. For example, the definition of caring for a child full-time as participation could continue until the youngest child is at school full-time, thereafter the parent would have to participate in some other form, or availability for work could be reshaped along the lines of the New Deal.[5]

However, Participation Income does have important drawbacks. It is a sub-stantial change to the tax and benefit system and large changes clearly carry greater political dangers. A Participation Income would increase replacement ratios and this raises the question of the impact of a more extensive flat rate payment on decisions to enter work. While a Participation Income should encourage more people to experiment with paid work and declare earnings, for some with caring responsibilities (particularly women) a participation income may weigh in the other direction. The rise in average marginal tax rates also touches on a criticism frequently levelled at basic income – paying a much more extensive benefit comes with the cost of raising disincentives for the working population as a whole (Clinton et al. 1994). The question of what tax rise is acceptable for what level of Participation Income is clearly a political one, making decisions about redistribution highly transparent. This is in direct contrast to the proposals for WFTC, where it is precisely the lack of transparency about payments to those on low incomes which is regarded as attractive in policy terms.

Participation Income also raises a number of tricky administrative issues: the taxing of small amounts of earnings; and the definition, monitoring and enforcement of a broader range of activities. Administrative costs would continue to be substantial despite the reduction of means-testing as three systems would continue to be in operation – Participation Income, means-tested benefits and the national insurance scheme. Finally, there remains the question of transparency – while the number on means-tested benefits decreases dramatically, many people remain on participation income with a smaller top-up of means-tested benefits or national insurance benefits. How clear will it be to claimants with combinations of benefit what they can earn and against which benefit it counts?

The case for Participation Income has a strong theoretical appeal, particularly if the labour market continues to generate part-time, casual and temporary jobs. Importantly, a Participation Income could provide the underpinning for the enhancement of social capital both by supporting a variety of forms of engaging in public life and also by allowing people to work part-time, releasing time resources for social activities and improvements in the quality of life (Schuller 1999). However, there remain some difficult issues, in particular the transparency of the redistribution it entails. In the short-term, one option is to adopt a more targeted strategy by underpinning income support/job seekers allowance with a broader conception of productive participation. Interestingly, the appendix of the Social Exclusion Unit report on young people refers to the Australian Youth Allowance as a possible model for Britain. In Australia, young people between 16 and 25 who are studying, training, looking for work, in part-time work or voluntary work or some combination of these activities are eligible for a youth allowance which is subject to a test of parental or individual income depending on circumstances. Extra earnings can be stored in an Income Bank up to certain limits. While this is not a universal participation income model, it contains important elements of the participation strategy – financial support from the government for a wide range of activities. Moreover, the introduction of children's tax credits in Britain suggests that it may be possible to move in the direction of a participation income by extending the range of contingencies covered by such credits – caring activity and some forms of voluntary and part-time work alongside full-time employment. While it is hard to envisage these becoming fully universal, if they cover a substantial sector (two-thirds) of the population, we are much closer to the notion of participation income than might have been envisaged at the start of the reform process.

5. Conclusions

There is much that is compelling in the New Labour focus on enhancing skills, capacities and endowments as the route to tackling poverty at its source. The emphasis is on prevention, empowering individuals and on a lifetime perspective which offers a dynamic view of opportunities in which public policy is geared to reducing the duration of disadvantage. However, redistributing endowments does not come cheaply; it is a long-term strategy and there will always be a need to protect those who fail in the marketplace however good their education and skills. Thus maintaining a decent minimum living standard for those beyond the reaches of the labour market will remain an essential plank of policy. Indeed the research shows that this is one element of a strategy for encouraging people into paid work – that those who have a cushion of income to rely on are more likely to take risks of going into employment.

For all the talk of switching emphasis from the redistribution of incomes to the expansion of opportunities to learn and earn, income redistribution must remain deeply implicated in any credible picture of the justice society that New Labour wishes to create. Gordon Brown's vision of equality of opportunity is a demanding one, but it is not on its own sufficient as a vision of the just or good society. Miller (1997) rightly argues that social equality – equality of respect and status between individuals – captures another essential quality of the good society. But whether we take equality of opportunity or status equality as our goals, simple income inequality remains important. It is hard to envisage a more mobile, dynamic society where individuals have greater respect for each other in the context of an ever-increasing income gap between rich and poor. At the very least, the traditional social-democratic goal of improving the relative position of the worst off in relation to the average has to remain a crucial objective. The routes to achieving this are more varied – clearly skills and education will play a vital role over the longer term – but income redistribution must remain central. Interestingly, an analysis of the government's Budget measures shows that its strategy has been redistributive – the poorest 10 per cent of households gain on average by 9.2 per cent of their income (£7.90 per week) compared to the richest 10 per cent of households who gain on average by just 0.3 per cent of their incomes (£2.20 a week). In addition, households with children gain by a greater amount, particularly for those on lower incomes (Immervol et al. 1999). The Treasury estimates that its measures have lifted 800,000 children and 550,000 [**adults? families?**] out of poverty (HM Treasury 1999b). The challenge is to translate the cautious approach to redistribution by stealth into a more open-ended debate about the nature and principles underpinning different forms of redistribution.

The emphasis on social inclusion provides an important new dimension which is only beginning to be reflected in public policy. The tendency to equate social inclusion with employment is insufficient. If we value the important (albeit difficult to define) qualities of social capital, we have to ensure that public policy supports sustainable relationships within families and communities. This suggests a broader view of productive participation and contribution which looks very seriously at the redistribution of time resources over the life-span alongside more traditional notions of redistribution.

What of the third-way emphasis on self-interest as the driver of human action? This must find its place in a balanced picture of human motivation. Both the altruism and self-interest paradigms are implausible. Bowles and Gintis (1998–9) argue for two principles to underpin our thinking about human motivation and redistribution; the principle of strong reciprocity and basic needs generosity. They develop a 'homo reciprocans' model where individuals are not full-blooded altruists – they withdraw support from arrangements which they perceive to allow for free-riding. But nor are people full-bloodedly self-interested. They will contribute to welfare programmes which are redistributive, even if the net benefit to them is uncertain, if they can be assured that all other beneficiaries will 'do their bit' as contributors as well. People will accept redistribution provided that it is structured in a way that does not allow others to escape their responsibility to contribute. This suggests that we need to recast egalitarianism so as to tune in with people's notions of fairness which stop short of unconditional altruism.

Recognizing the mix of self-interested and altruistic motives people have enables us to perceive the variety of factors which shape people's ability to escape disadvantage. Policies need to pay attention to material, social, psychological and cultural dimensions of disadvantage and the interplay between them. For example, in some cases positive reinforcement of a person's identity may increase their sense of agency and in turn allows them to view the risk of entering employment differently. These insights must play a crucial role in developing a less mechanical approach to policy.

The third-way emphasis on balancing welfare rights with obligations raises a number of difficult questions that I have only begun to address here. The reciprocity of which Bowles and Gintis speak is all very well, but what do we do with people who refuse to fulfil their responsibilities? What, for instance, is the state's responsibility to citizens who fail to meet their defined obligations? Is it to withdraw support altogether, as embodied in the US time-limited access to welfare, or does it mean a series of penalties, as under our current social security system? The answer surely has to be the latter: the state has an obligation to provide a minimum income, albeit with penalties, for its citizens even if they fail to comply with their defined obligations. A different approach is to think about how to foster particular responsibilities or encourage certain kinds of participation through a system of bonuses rather than penalties. This could apply to activities beyond paid work such as attendance at ante-natal classes (the government has introduced a higher Sure Start Maternity Payment for those who make contact with a healthcare professional), parenting, literacy or a Citizens' Service.[6] An alternative approach is the introduction of civic education through citizenship lessons in schools in 2002 as proposed by the Crick Report (Advisory Group on Citizenship 1998). This in turn leads to a broader and neglected point – the obligations of the affluent. Much of the current debate over 'rights and responsibilities' is about the obligation of the poor rather than a more generalized understanding of universal obligations. If the 'politics of contribution' is to be explored further it needs to focus on the socially included as well as the excluded.

The government's strategy on welfare reform and the labour market does indeed represent a new and imaginative attempt to rethink strategies to tackle poverty and social exclusion in the light of a transformed economic, social and political context. But for it to be successful we need to retain a role for the government to foster employment actively; to improve the living standards of those on low income in relation to the average; and to develop a conception of social inclusion that is based on participation rather than paid employment alone.

Notes

1   The 1999 Budget introduced a number of incentives to promote ILAs: one million starter accounts with a government contribution of £150 per year, subject to a small contribution from the individual; a 20 per cent discount off the cost of eligible courses on spending up to £500 in each year; an 80 per cent discount off the cost of certain key courses, including computer literacy; and an incentive to encourage employers to provide contributions to ILAs for low paid employees (DfEE 1999).
2   For an excellent discussion of motivations in welfare see Julian Le Grand, 'Knights Knaves or Pawns? Human Behaviour and Social Policy', *Journal of Social Policy*, 26 (1997), pp. 149–69.
3   'No welfare system can function effectively if it is not based on a realistic view of human nature. Self-interest, not altruism, is mankind's main driving force. The view which exaggerated the place of altrusim ... was widely held by Labour activists during the latter part of the post-war period' (Field 1997: 19).
4   Under the current system employees pay no national insurance (NI) below the lower earnings threshold, but once they pass the threshold they pay NI on 2 per cent on all earnings below that level. Under the new proposals this will be abolished.
5   Proposals for Participation Income are consistent with improvements to National Insurance benefits, such as crediting in the low paid, extending coverage to new risks such as residential care.

6 Citizens' Service was suggested by the Commission on Social Justice. It would be a voluntary national service scheme for young people (McCormick 1994).

Bibliography

Advisory Group on Citizenship (1998), *Education for Democracy and the Teaching of Citizenship in Schools*, London: Qualifications and Curriculum Authority.

Atkinson, A. B. (1995), 'Beveridge, the National Minimum and its Future in a European Context', in Atkinson, A. B., *Incomes and the Welfare State*, Cambridge: Cambridge University Press.

Blair, T. (1998), *The Third Way: New Politics for the New Century*, London: Fabian Society.

Bowles, S. and Gintis, H. (1998/9), 'Is Equality Passe?', in *Boston Review*, 23, no. 6, Dec./Jan.

Brown, G. (1996), *New Labour and Equality*, The Second John Smith Memorial Lecture, 19 April 1996.

Bryson, A. and McKay, S. (eds) (1994), *Is It Worth Working? Factors Affecting Labour Supply*, London: Policy Studies Institute.

Bryson, A., Ford, R. and White, M. (1997), *Making Work Pay: Lone Mothers, Employment and Well-being*, London: Policy Studies Institute.

Clinton, D., Yates, M. and Kang, D. (1994), *Integrating Taxes and Benefits*, Commission on Social Justice, Institute for Public Policy Research, London.

Commission on Social Justice (1994), *Social Justice: Strategies for National Renewal*, London: IPPR, Vintage.

Deacon, A. (1998), 'Welfare Reform in the 51st State? The Influence of US Thinking and Experience upon the Welfare Debate in Britain', Paper presented to the Twentieth Annual Research Conference of the Association for Public Policy Analysis and Management, 29–31 Oct.

DfEE (1999), *Individual Learning Accounts, a Summary of Progress, The Learning Age*, HMSO.

DSS (1998), *New Ambitions for Our Country: a New Contract for Welfare*, Cm 3805, HMSO.

DSS and DfEE (1998), *A New Contract for Welfare: the Gateway to Work*, Cm 4102, HMSO.

Field, F. (1997), *Stakeholder Welfare*, London: Institute for Economic Affairs.

Gardiner, K. (1997), *Bridges from Benefit to Work: a Review*, York: Joseph Rowntree Foundation.

Giddens, A. (1998), *The Third Way: the Renewal of Social Democracy*, Cambridge: Polity.

Giddens, A. (1998), 'Equality and the Social Investment State', in I. Hargreaves and I. Christie, eds, London: Demos.

Hales, J., Shaw, A. and Roth, W. (1998), *Evaluation of the New Deal for Lone Parents: a Preliminary Assessment of the Counterfactual*, Social Security Research.

Hillman, J. (1998), 'The Learning Age – an Agenda for Lifelong Learning?' *The Political Quarterly*, 69, no. 3.

HM Treasury (1999a), *Budget 99, Building a Stronger Economic Future for Britain*, HC 298, HMSO.

HM Treasury (1999b), *The Modernisation of Britain's Tax and Benefit System, Number Four, Tackling Poverty and Extending Opportunity*, HMSO.

Immervol, H., Mitton, L., O'Donoghue, C. and Sutherland, H. (1999), *Budgeting for Fairness? the Distributional Effects of Three Labour Budgets*, the Microsimulation Unit, Dept of Applied Economics, University of Cambridge.

Jackson, P. R. (1994), 'Influences on Commitment to Employment and Commitment to Work', in A. Bryson, R. Ford and M. White, eds, *Making Work Pay: Lone Mothers, Employment and Well-being*, London: Policy Studies Institute.

Kelly, G. and Gamble, A. (1998), 'Ownership', *The Political Quarterly*, 69, no. 4.

Kelly, G. and Oppenheim, C. (1998), 'Working with New Labour', *Renewal*, 6, no. 3.

Marsh, A. and McKay, S. (1993), *Families, Work and Benefits*, London: Policy Studies Institute.

McCormick, J. (1994), *Citizens' Service*, Commission on Social Justice, Institute for Public Policy Research, London.

McLaughlin, E. (1994), *Flexibility in Work and Benefits*, Commission on Social Justice, IPPR, London.

Miller, D. (1997), 'What Kind of Equality Should the Left Pursue?', in J. Franklin, ed., *Equality*, London: Institute for Public Policy Research.

Oppenheim, C. (1997), 'The Post-Conservative Welfare State: a Framework for the Decade Ahead', Policy Paper 9, Sheffield: Political Economy Research Centre, Sheffield University.

Oppenheim, C. (ed.) (1998), *An Inclusive Society: Strategies for Tackling Poverty*, London: Institute for Public Policy Research.

Oppenheim, C. in J. McCormick and C. Oppenheim (eds) (1998), *Welfare in Working Order*, London: Institute for Public Policy Research.

Plant, R. (1998), *The Third Way*, Working Papers 5/98, Friedrich-Ebert-Stiftung.

Saunders, P. (1995), 'Improving Work Incentives in a Means-tested Welfare System: the 1994 Australian Social Security Reforms', *Fiscal Studies*, 16, no. 2, May, pp. 45–70.

Schuller, T. (1999), 'Individual Learning Accounts and Social Capital' (unpublished paper for IPPR seminar).

Shaw, A., Walker, R., Ashworth, K., Jenkins, S. and Middleton, S. (1996), *Moving Off Income Support: Barriers and Bridges*, DSS Research Report, no. 53, London, HMSO.

Social Exclusion Unit (1998), *Bringing Britain Together: A Strategy for Neighbourhood Renewal*.

Social Exclusion Unit (1999), *Bridging the Gap: New Opportunities for 16–18 Year Olds not in Education, Employment and Training*.

Vandenbroucke, F. (1998), *Globalisation, Inequality and Social Democracy*, London: Institute for Public Policy Research.

Walker, R. (1998), 'Unpicking Poverty', in C. Oppenheim, ed, *An Inclusive Society: Strategies for Tackling Poverty*, London: Institute for Public Policy Research.

Walker, R. and Wiseman, M. (1997), 'An Earned Income Tax Credit: Possibilities and Alternatives', Centre for Research in Social Policy, Loughborough.

Walzer, M. (1983), *Spheres of Justice*, Martin Robertson.

White, M. and Forth, J. (1998), *Pathways through Unemployment – Where Do They Lead?*, York: YPS and Joseph Rowntree Foundation.

White, S. (1995), 'Citizen's Income, Workfare and the Principle of Reciprocity', unpublished paper, Oxford University.

White, S. (1998), 'Interpreting the Third Way: Not One Road, but Many', *Renewal*, 6, no. 2.

Wilcox, S. (1997), 'Replacing Housing Benefit with Housing Credit: a Better Way to Help People with their Housing Costs', London: Chartered Institute of Housing.

7
A Third Way in Industrial Relations?

Colin Crouch

Analysing the idea of a third way between social democracy and neoliberalism is difficult, since social democracy itself has been a third way between socialism (seen as the removal of productive resources from private ownership to some form of collective control), and *laissez-faire* capitalism.[1] At the same time that social democracy in this sense was developing – broadly, from the 1930s to 1950s – conservative political forces were responding with their own middle way between these alternatives. As a result, in many advanced democracies political conflict in the first three post-war decades was played out in a rather narrow space. It is interesting to note that although both social democracy and reformist conservatism were compromise strategies, the policy mix they developed was not a mere central path between *laissez-faire* capitalism and socialism, but an original approach containing elements neither belonging to nor anticipated by either parent ideology: Keynesian demand management, neo-corporatist industrial relations, universal welfare states.[2] This was a true third way.

After the Keynesian inflation crisis of the mid-1970s, the political right moved back to *laissez-faire* or neo-liberal positions. On the face of it therefore any move on behalf of former social democrats to a new intermediate position, between their own former one and that of their rightward-moving opponents, would mark a mere camp-following move to the right, possibly even one leading to the right of former moderate conservatism. Perhaps partly for that reason, advocates of the new third way under discussion here prefer to see what they are doing as a complete escape from the cage of compromise between right and left, and as creating entirely new positions that do not refer principally to the old confrontation.

Given the example of the earlier compromise and the way that it created new positions out of original attempts at a middle way, such an aspiration towards novelty and innovation may well be realistic. Whether the hope of abandoning the confrontation between right and left is realistic is another matter. While the precise content changes with general social change, the basic formal conflict between right and left refers to the confrontation between those interests which, in the absence of any organized challenge, monopolize social and economic power, and those which challenge that monopoly and seek a redistribution. If the forces previously associated with the left no longer see the need for such a challenge, while power and wealth remain very unequally divided, there is simply a reassertion of the existing monopoly, not a transcendence of the conflict. It is notable that there is no equivalent move among those on the political right to find a central path between themselves and the left, as happened in the earlier period. If anything, at least in the UK and USA, they are shifting further to the right, adjusting the rigours of neo-liberalism with xenophobia rather than with characteristic social-democratic policies.

I shall return to the position of New Labour in relation to this situation at the end of this discussion, but it is not a question that can be resolved fully within this chapter. Our concern here is with the specific policy field of industrial relations and trade unions, while a discussion of the wider issue requires contributions from other areas of policy. For this specific study our attention is concentrated on the policies of the UK Labour government elected in May 1997, which has been clear and consistent in claiming its break from the social-democratic past and in pursuing a third way. I focus on the policy record, not ideological writings. The government itself, and particularly the Prime Minister, Tony Blair, has regarded the third way as something that has to be established, not something already existing as a doctrine. A plurality of voices has responded to the invitation to contribute to its formulation, hopefully trying to influence it in various ways. There is as yet no canon. It would therefore be possible to find formulations of a third way claiming many different positions for it. In this situation I shall follow the famous example of English empiricism set by Herbert Morrison's 'Socialism is what the Labour government does': 'The third way is what the New Labour government does' – within the policy area of industrial relations.

The evidence of the policy record

It is too early to do this conclusively, after only a few years. The rhythm of the government machine is still set in the neo-liberal mould of the preceding 18 years; the party is still fundamentally social democratic, in part even socialist. Emergence of a true third way might well expect to take considerably longer than this. Even five years after the neo-liberal turn of 1979 Britain had not changed so much from its moderate conservative and social-democratic past. This caveat is important, and we shall return to it.

The initial question must be whether there is evidence of policies which differ from either neo-liberalism or social democracy. Second, do any such differences take the form of straight middle ways between these two rival predecessors, or do they constitute a distinctive, *sui generis* political practice?

Establishing policy profiles

We must therefore first establish brief profiles of neo-liberalism and social democracy in industrial relations. We shall then examine the Labour government's record and try to allocate individual policies to one or other of these. Any item that does not fit either profile is a putative third way policy. Finally, we assess the overall fit to the models of the policy record. There are four possible outcomes of this: (1) that government policy fits a neo-liberal model; (2) that it fits a social-democratic one; (3) that it forms a compromise between the two, which might eventually evolve into a third way; (4) that it fits neither and already constitutes a truly new policy form.

Study of a policy record is more straightforward than that of an ideology, in that the identity of the subject of the action is clear – a government rather than a diffuse set of thinkers. It is, however, more difficult, in that whereas an ideology comprises its own preferences established in relation to specified constraints, real-life politics has to make daily compromises. When is a government's action an expression of its will and when a compromise? I shall tackle this in the following way. A particular policy stance (neo-liberalism, social democracy, etc.) of a modern mass party normally represents the interests of a certain core constituency, but attempts to do so through certain rule-following procedures which enable it also to claim to be governing in a general interest. Compromises with this stance are principally of two types. First, there are compromises with other political interests, the continuing existence of which has to be accepted. This is political compromise as normally understood, and the term compromise will henceforth be used here to mean this form alone. For simplicity, I shall here consider compromises made by neo-liberalism and social democracy only with each other as principal opponents, not with other interests (such as ecology movements).[3] Second, however, there are also compromises with the unprincipled interests of the core constituency, i.e. sheer self-interest that cannot be defended as the operation of a general-interest rule-following procedure. These are *déformations* or corruptions that come from the undue influence that the special interests have on the policy-maker's actions. They will here be called corruptions, though this is in no way meant in the legal, criminal sense.

In the case of neo-liberalism, the central policy principle is pursuit of free markets. This clearly favours a core constituency of the wealthy and those on high incomes, as they have more capacity than others to benefit from the operation of market forces. The market is, however, also a procedure to which the wealthy themselves must adhere; even the most powerful must buy rather than take. Also, those on modest incomes benefit from using the market's opportunities for free individual choice and purchase to the extent that their resources make possible. The market has important positive-sum components, and its operations are transparent and contain no 'dirty deals'.

Within the industrial relations field neo-liberalism primarily means reducing the role of organized action that seeks to interfere with market rules: in particular, collective bargaining by trade unions and employers' associations; attempts by either to influence government policy by imposing pressure; attempts to shift the distribution of income in ways other than those dictated by the market. Labour markets are to operate as freely as possible from interference by either government or organized interests, or indeed by monopolies and oligopolies. Where collectivities are unavoidable, they should operate locally and unpolitically, on the grounds that local action at least reproduces some of the unmanaged plurality of the free market, and that unpolitical industrial relations, even if collective, at least sustains the fundamental neo-liberal principle of a clear boundary between polity and economy. Government policy will aim to remove as much regulation and protective legislation as possible from interfering with the labour market.

A compromise with social democracy takes place when collective organization, political influence by trade unions, or regulation of the labour market are allowed to persist; or when new regulations favourable to trade unions in particular or organized interests in general are introduced despite the government's own preferences; or, more generally, when any items from the social-democratic agenda have to be adopted to ensure the government's survival or the maintenance of adequate social consensus.

A neo-liberal corruption is identified when wealthy interests are allowed to influence government policy or obtain special favours by privileged access to policy-makers.

In social democracy, the central policy principle is reconciliation of the operation of the market with a redistribution of resources and security towards those less favoured by it; and with the pursuit of collective and public goods which the market does not provide but which are indicated by the political process to be important. Beyond these constraints the market should be left to flourish. This clearly favours a core constituency of those on modest resources, but their interests are to be pursued in a manner compatible with a market economy and with the pursuit of wider public interests rather than their own client needs. Within industrial relations social democracy has in the past meant a prominent role for organizations, especially of employees (as the groups least favoured by the market), and for labour-market regulation. However, these organizations are expected to adhere to neo-corporatist self-discipline in order to avoid inflation and rigid labour practices, and regulation should be compatible with efficiency.

Compromises are difficult to identify in social democracy, as it already internalizes a balancing act between the market and both organization and intervention. Further compromise can be defined when, within the framework of such an industrial relations system, government acts to curtail redistributive action and labour regulation, or accepts any identifiable components of a neo-liberal strategy despite its preferences.

Social-democratic corruption is identified when trade union organizational interests are allowed to dominate policy at the expense of wider social redistribution, if inflationary policies are sustained in order to avoid confronting needs for wage restraint; or if social benefits are allocated to groups of political supporters without concern for the impact of such benefits on either the labour market or overall principles of social policy. A further potential problem area arises when there are large under-privileged groups who cannot be helped by trade-union action; unions are then in danger of representing the interests of labour-market insiders against those of outsiders. There has always been some tendency for this to occur – though to nothing like the same extent within western European industrial relations systems as in the USA. This is because in European countries there are usually mechanisms whereby gains in the unionized sector become extended more generally. However, workers in so-called atypical work – part-timers (who are primarily female), those with precarious employment, those in bogus forms of self-employment[4] – have often been beyond the reach of unions. One of the main changes in occupational patterns in recent years has been a major increase in these forms of work. Through no fault of their own, unions then find themselves representing insiders; if they fail to act to prevent this and to try to reach the outsiders but simply take advantage of the opportunities it brings, their activities become a kind of social-democratic corruption.

The policy stances of the Labour government

The principal policy actions of the Labour government in the industrial relations field can now be analysed within each of these heads: I: neo-liberal corruption; II: neo-liberalism (or neo-liberal compromises by social democrats); III: social democracy (or social-democratic compromises by neo-liberals); IV: social-democratic corruption; V: policy incapable of analysis under any of these – a potential third way.

I: Neo-liberal corruption

As discussed under section II below, one of the main distinguishing characteristics of this government compared with its various Labour predecessors in the UK and most of its contemporaries elsewhere in western Europe is its rejection of the use of organizations of business and labour for purposes of socio-economic steering. Among the processes which have emerged to fill what might otherwise be a 'consultation deficit' in relations between the government and the world of the economy has been a set of relations between firms, professional lobbyists, and government advisers, with considerable interchange of personnel between the last-mentioned two groups.

This may be normal practice in US politics, and it emerged in the UK during the previous period of Conservative governments, but it is a novelty for Labour. The work of insider lobbyists of this kind has extended across several areas of policy, including the industrial relations area. This is a field where formally organized interests had usually been very active until the Conservative governments of the 1980s gradually removed them from influence. Lobbying activities appear as a kind of functional equivalent for these, though one which largely excludes unions and which depends far more than do formal organizational links on patronage, personal connections, and occasionally party funding.

Given the novel character of this form of government consultation policy in the context of British labour history, this might be an initial candidate for consideration as a third way policy. However, I think it is more consistent with the idea of a corrupted neo-liberalism: firms which have grown rich through the market process use their strength to acquire insider influence with government. This is a breach of the rules of market transparency, free competition and clear separation between politics and business which are central to neo-liberalism, and therefore a corruption rather than an expression of that ideology. It is notable that, when the existence of these lobbying networks was first publicly discussed (in 1998), the government responded by dismissing some of the people involved and issuing a code of practice for lobbyists. Although the system remained largely in place, it was not claimed as part of a third way.

II: Neo-liberal policies

As indicated in the immediately previous discussion of lobbying, the Labour government has followed its Conservative predecessor in not making use of organizations of business and labour for purposes of macroeconomic management or social policy reform. Subject to any corruptions as already discussed, this is consistent with a neo-liberal insistence on separation of polity from economy and from organizational interests as opposed to those expressed through the market. It is a policy largely to be recognized by an absence of action rather than through specific acts, because the main work of excluding these interests and demolishing the institutions through which their former partnership with government was expressed had been carried out by the previous Conservative government. Examples were the abolition of such tripartite bodies as the National Economic Development Council, and the reduction of incomes policy to unilateral controls by government over the pay of public-sector employees. These policies have been fully maintained by Labour.

Within the general field of European politics, Labour has shown some significant shifts away from the pure neo-liberal direction of its predecessor (see below). It has, however, committed itself to the same fundamental line, regarding the flexibilization of employment as the central distinguishing feature of labour-market policy in the UK, imitation of which is actively commended to other European countries.[5]

II/III: Mixed neo-liberal and social-democratic policies

Some individual policy initiatives are difficult to analyse as either neo-liberal or social democratic, as they combine strong elements of both; rather than risk repetition by dividing discussion of them between two parts, I shall consider these 'mixed bags' as a separate group.

The policy for reducing unemployment and maximizing labour-force participation, *New Deal at Work* (HM Govt 1998), initiated in January 1998, is an interesting example of such a combination. Under the slogan 'from welfare into work' the government seeks to move as many unemployed people as possible from dependence on welfare support to participation in the labour force. The policy has several aspects:

i) welfare payments to single mothers without jobs have been reduced, and a number of measures introduced to provide both occupational training and childcare for these women to make it easier for them to secure jobs – a combination of sticks and carrots to encourage female labour-force participation;[6]

ii) all persons under 25 years of age who had been unemployed for six months or more have been given four choices, each of which is funded by government: to accept temporary subsidized employment; to take a course of up to 12 months' full-time study; to work for six months in the voluntary sector; to work for six months for a newly established environmental task force. Refusal to accept one of these offers will lead to reductions in welfare benefits; again a combination of sticks and carrots;

iii) persons aged over 25 and unemployed for over two years were subsequently also brought into this scheme.

This policy can be seen as neo-liberal in its 'stick' components of withdrawing welfare benefit and its toughening of incentives to enter the labour force. It is, however, also strongly social democratic in its use of public money to assist people's labour-market access through provision of childcare support, education and training, and subsidized work. It is clearly not a policy of social-democratic corruption, since it attacks one of the main forms of such corruption (benefit abuse). It resembles such major classic social-democratic initiatives as the Swedish active labour-market policy of the 1950s and 1960s, which used subsidies and other forms of public intervention to manage the movement of population from declining northern areas to the new industries of southern Sweden, and which later used such policies as the provision of childcare to assist women's labour-market participation. Initiatives in this area have therefore been a very interesting blend of important forms of both neo-liberalism and social democracy.

Similarly ambiguous has been the government's position on the so-called Social Dimension of European integration. Its Conservative predecessor had refused to participate in the Protocol on Social Policy of the Treaty of Maastricht, partly on neo-liberal grounds and partly those of national sovereignty. A major reversal of this policy was signalled by Labour when it announced early in its period of office a rejection of this abstention. It accepted existing agreements within the protocol (two rather weak ones on works councils in large corporations and parental leave), and there is no longer a special British opt-out. This enabled the Protocol to be incorporated into the main corpus of EU policy in the Treaty of Amsterdam, rather than being left as a special procedure for all other member states. The government has, however, continued to play a similar role to its predecessor in trying to limit the extent of any future initiatives in the framework of the Social Dimension. For example, it worked hard to ensure that no substantive measures were introduced to extend works councils to companies not having plants in more than one EU country, using the same combination of arguments about the sovereignty of both employers and nation-states the Conservatives would have used. It also did nothing to challenge or counteract the lobbying of the Confederation of British Industry (CBI), which ensured the failure of a draft directive on information rights for employees.

In similar fashion, in April 1998 the government accepted the EC Working Time Directive[7] (a matter in which it had in fact little choice), but announced its intention, when eventually framing legislation, to take advantage of all possibilities for flexibility and derogations within the scope of the directive to give more discretion to employers.

III: Social-democratic policies

Soon after taking office the government appointed a commission (the Low Pay Commission) to consider the feasibility of adopting a statutory minimum wage for the first time in British industrial history. Earlier opposition to a minimum wage had come as much from union as employer sources, as many unions often preferred to demonstrate their own bargaining power to workers on such issues. However, with the changing labour markets of the 1980s unions had started to shift their line on this considerably, and had sought commitment to a minimum wage from the Labour Party. The Commission duly reported positively on the idea, and the government early fulfilled its pledge to introduce legislation. The rate established (initially £3.60 per hour) was not high, and there are lower rates for workers under 21 (no minimum at all for those under 17), and a reduced rate for early trainees of any age. It might be argued that these dilutions follow a neo-liberal concern, but I would reject this interpretation. Neo-liberals are completely opposed to minimum wage policies, while it is entirely consistent with social democracy to bear in mind the implications of policy for the functioning of markets. (This is one of the respects in which analysis of social democracy in relation to alternative third ways is difficult.) It cannot be denied that wage levels among inexperienced and low-productivity workers are likely to affect demand for their services. This attempt to find a compromise between workers' security needs and market forces is entirely consistent with classic social democracy.

In the White Paper *Fairness at Work* (HM Govt 1998) the government announced its intention to introduce, again for the first time in Britain, a legal right of employees to trade union representation (see the detailed analysis in Taylor 1998). As in some other areas of its labour policies, the government has here been introducing an essentially American approach to union issues within an ostensible agenda of 'returning to Europe' and a constitutional approach to these issues after the years of Thatcherite exclusion.

As with minimum wage legislation, earlier opposition to this had come from unions as much as employers; only since their weakening in the 1980s had unions started unanimously to seek this legal assistance. The legislation will provide that workers will receive this right only if they work in firms with more than 20 employees and if 40 per cent of all employees (not just those voting) vote positively for union recognition. However, in firms where more than 50 per cent of workers can be proved already to be union members, no ballot will be necessary; recognition can be awarded as of right. All employees, regardless of size of firm and of any recognition of ballot outcomes, will receive the right to representation by a trade union official in any *individual* grievance with their employers. Under the same legislation existing provision for protection against arbitrary dismissal will be extended to all employees after one year of service, and existing ceilings (£12,000) on legal compensation for employees winning arbitrary dismissal cases against employers will be removed.[8] Further, rights to maternity leave will be extended to 18 months.

It is notable that these proposals were subject to heavy negotiation, and the CBI and the Trades Union Congress (TUC) had held informal meetings to try to reach a joint position. These had been largely unsuccessful, though the fact of the dialogue, after several years of virtually no activity of that kind in the UK, suggested a possible return to social partnership approaches. The unions had sought provision of simple majorities of those voting, while the employers had wanted the overall 40 per cent participation threshold. The Prime Minister adopted the CBI's position on this question, but conceded some other elements of the overall package (such as the right to representation in individual grievances) in order to win eventual acquiescence of the unions in the overall deal. The unions were unhappy, partly because they are required to achieve a threshold of support which few British national politicians ever secure in their own elections; and partly because the Prime Minister was so pointedly taking the CBI's line. However, they have achieved an important new right, and the Prime Minister's position was more consistent with a model of social democracy making compromises with neo-liberal objections rather than the other way round. Taylor argues (1998: 457) that this approach belongs with the core of European labour policy and not a new third way. There is, however, the possibility that, if British employers imitate their US counterparts and work aggressively to prevent their employees from voting for representation, the final outcome could be a loss of union legitimacy and a reduction of the size of the already declining union sector. This would certainly not be a third way, just a continuation of neo-liberalism, but it would also constitute Americanization rather than any European policy.

It is interesting to reflect that on the two questions of the minimum wage and union recognition rights, the present government has in fact been more social democratic than its Labour predecessors (1945–51; 1964–70; 1974–9), which had largely accepted British unions' long-standing previous *liberal* case that such rights are best won in economic struggle and not legislated for by governments.

Despite the generally negative approach taken by the government towards European and other proposals for measures generally to increase employees' rights to information, national legislation has been proposed (February 1998) to provide for the mandatory consultation of workforces before announcement of redundancies. Particular emphasis is placed on the consultation of trade unions in this process.

IV: Social-democratic corruption

None of the government's policies, or abstentions from policy, can be defined as social-democratic corruption, and some measures have been taken (as discussed above) to clamp down on what might be seen as past forms of such corruption. There is just one paradoxical point here. By continuing to accept the drift towards precarious work contracts and bogus self-employment, the government could be said (passively and even unconsciously) to be permitting unions to enter the trap of representing privileged insiders against a growing army of labour-market outsiders. There have been clear signs of union awareness of some aspects of this in their attempts to recruit and represent part-time women workers, but the possibility remains.

V: Putative third way policies

I do not think that any policies can so far be identified which cannot be fitted to one or other of the above categories, derived solely from the confrontation between social democracy and neo-liberalism. Again, such a fifth category is potentially operationalizable. This can be illustrated through the fate of the 'stakeholder' policy. Developed by a number of commentators close to the Party (e.g. Hutton 1995), and taken up enthusiastically by Mr Blair when Leader of the Opposition, this proposed legal recognition of the rights of a number of legitimate interests, including those of workers, within firms. The traditional position of English law has been to recognize only shareholders. This would have been analysable as a true third way policy, in that it can be assigned to neither neo-liberal nor social-democratic traditions.[9] However, these ideas were being developed at the time when the US model of capitalism as meaning the maximization of shareholder value as the sole goal of corporations began to dominate business ideology across the western world. The stakeholder policy became adjusted to a general advocacy of communication and consultation within firms, but left to employers' discretion – little more than human resource management within a neo-liberal frame.

An overall assessment: neo-liberalism with social-democratic compromises?

We can now attempt an overall characterization based on the above discussion.

The first point that can be established is that so far nothing has emerged from the British Labour government in the industrial relations field that cannot be fitted easily into either the neo-liberal or the social-democratic box or a mixture of both; there is no explanatory need for a concept of a third way. Attempts by some third way advocates to demonstrate the opposite depend on distortions of classic social democracy, or ignorance of what has been done within various forms of European, particularly Scandinavian, social democracy. For example, Raymond Plant (1998) has recently claimed that the New Deal at Work policy is not reconcilable with social democracy, which he seems to identify here as meaning an endless willingness to write welfare cheques. This is to mistake a corruption of a strategy for the strategy itself, and amounts to a gross distortion. Whether one looks at Scandinavian labour-market policies before the 1980s, post-war British ones, or 1930s US New Deal measures, the aim was always to use public spending, education and other government interventions to help people into jobs and increase labour-force participation. It was never to pay them to stay out of work. The latter emerged as a kind of desperate measure in the context of rising unemployment in the 1980s among governments of *all* colours; when social-democratic governments did it, it was a corruption of social-democratic policy aims, not their expression. An example of this would be the decline of Swedish active labour-market policy into a means of keeping people out of the unemployment statistics, where in the past it had enabled people rapidly to enter the workforce. However, the neo-liberal British Conservative government of the 1980s developed similar strategies.

We are therefore left with assessing the balance between neo-liberalism and social democracy, and with considering the likelihood that an unforeseen third way might emerge from the encounter between these two, as eventually occurred with social democracy and Keynesian economics in the first place.

The balance of policy *actions* of the government fall clearly within the social-democratic category. The majority of its legislative innovations reads like a social-democratic shopping list: a diversity of public measures to help people, especially women, enter the workforce; recognition rights for trade unions; consultation rights for workers and unions in the face of redundancy plans; a statutory minimum wage. These are offset by just a few neo-liberal measures in the punitive components of the 'welfare into work' incentives – fully consistent with the idea that social democracy has to make compromises in practice with neo-liberalism.

However, one must judge policy by what it does not do as well as by what it does. This is especially the case when a government inherits very strongly defined trajectories from its predecessor; to continue these requires no new actions. It is here that the neo-liberal continuities of New Labour need to be set alongside the social-democratic innovations: continued support for labour-market flexibilization and deregulation; support for the 'maximization of shareholder value' model of capitalism; no place for tripartite macroeconomic steering, or even for the active encouragement of bipartite action, in central tasks of economic governance.

Does the overall ensemble give us: (a) a social democracy which has to make concessions to powerful neo-liberal interests, for example the financial markets; (b) a neo-liberalism which has to make concessions to the social-democratic heritage and membership of the party; or (c) an unresolved mix of the two? It is at this point that the premature nature of this assessment becomes a serious problem; in particular, if one asks whether any of these three might eventually produce a validly original third way. This might in particular be inhibited for a lengthy initial period by both the neo-liberal inheritance of the government machine and the social-democratic inheritance of the party.

I would prefer to suspend judgement on the resolution of this question until more time has passed, as I consider that the answer might move in various ways. However, if required to give an answer, I would plump for (b), that is, that in the industrial relations field New Labour represents a continuation of the neo-liberalism of the Conservative government, but one required to make more concessions than its predecessor with trade unions and social-democratic policy preferences.

There is a number of reasons for this tentative judgement. First, while there has been no evidence that the government is vulnerable to corruptions of a social-democratic form, we have encountered evidence of distortions typical of neo-liberal corruption in the role of business lobbyists and the accessibility of the government to special pleading by business, but not labour, interests. This characteristic has not been limited to the industrial relations arena, but it has particular relevance here. One aim of New Labour is to reduce the party's former heavy dependence on trade unions for financial and ideological support. The main readily available alternative sources are business interests. This makes New Labour likely to offer insider relations with corporations of a kind which it is reluctant to offer to labour interests.

Second, and more important, the neo-liberal policy items, largely inherited from its predecessors, are central to core macroeconomic strategy: in particular the rejection of tripartite steering and of Keynesian demand management. The social democratic components, while very important, lie outside the frame of core strategy. The new rights for unions have the appearance of farewell concessions to allies from the past; as we have seen, some of these rights themselves leave unions vulnerable to employer attacks on the US model, or might permit them to become inward-looking representatives of insider interests of declining parts of the economy. There is nothing in the New Labour agenda to compensate this by offering unions a role in the construction of dynamic parts of the economy.

I would also rate as relatively weak the prospects for a distinctive third way emerging from this pattern of balances between neo-liberalism and social democracy. This is because the two aspects are kept distant from each other, in particular the way in which trade unions and indeed employers' organizations (as opposed to favoured firms) are not permitted to come near the strategic areas. If one looks at recent cases where industrial relations systems have produced important innovations, changing both social democracy and various conservative and neo-liberal legacies, organized interests have been drawn into core strategy. They have been forced to adapt to the challenge of change, and in turn have made their demands of the system. It is that kind of difficult interchange among governments, social partners and other interests that is likely to produce genuine innovation and 'third ways' in this field, not abstract advance reflection by academics and policy-makers. Well-known examples are the recent overhaul of some elements of industrial relations and welfare policy in the Netherlands (Visser and Hemerijck 1997, and this volume), or the novel mix of centralizing and decentralizing elements in the reshaping of Danish industrial relations (Due et al. 1994). New policies might also emerge from French and Italian welfare state reform, where there is both a financial imperative to make changes but also an institutionalized participation of trade unions in the management of the existing system.

Here past British experience with tri- or bipartite institutions inhibits creative development. Unions opted out of a formal involvement in the management of pensions and social security funds in the early twentieth century, and have therefore long been without what is now, in a period of welfare state reform, becoming an important key to influence in many other European countries. Further, apart from the decade of the 1940s, the British had a generally negative experience of neo-corporatist incomes policies: broadly, unions and employer organizations showed an almost American level of reluctance to become involved in sharing responsibility for public policy, while governments showed an almost French level of reluctance to allow them to do so anyway. New Labour thinking has absolutely no place for either neo-corporatism or its reform. In Anthony Giddens's analysis of the characteristics of political doctrines (1998), corporatism is listed as one of the five characteristics of social democracy, but is defined as 'state dominates over civil society'.[10] This shows little understanding of what neo-corporatist industrial relations meant in those countries where they were most practised.[11] It is unlikely therefore that a reshaping of neo-corporatist structures will play the same part in finding third ways in the UK that they do in a number of continental European countries – a fact which imposes major limitations on any wider European significance of the British experience, but which probably makes more viable a shared British/American agenda.

In a discussion full of reservations I must conclude with one more. I have here examined just one area of policy. We cannot extrapolate from this to others. It is possible, and I think likely, that a similar analysis of policies in fields of constitutional reform and law and order would find several elements in my empty box V: putative third way policies. In general I would expect third way politics to be easier to develop in such fields as these, remote from core issues of economic power. There are important reasons for this.

New Labour believes class conflict to be old-fashioned and claims to have transcended it, but is fearful of the responses to its actions of the financial markets, foreign direct investors, and employers in general. It either does not see these feared responses as expressions of capitalist power, or believes that it is powerless to do anything about them. What is really happening is that within the globalizing, deregulated economy many capitalist interests are able to act with fewer constraints on their autonomy and power than at any time since the 1920s; at the same time other social classes have lost both social and political identity. This is not a transcendence of class conflict but a particular turn in its development: a forceful reassertion of the dominance of one class. During the 1990s the Labour Party reformed itself so that it no longer represented a quixotic struggle on behalf of a lost working-class identity; but instead of identifying new bases of social criticism, it came to represent the logical consequences of class defeat. At least to date, it has shown no interest in forging new social solidarities and coalitions that would challenge the new capitalist hegemony; rather the reverse. For its own distinctive identity it therefore looks away from the classic battlegrounds of economic politics, talks of moving beyond right and left, and puts its creativity into areas not affected by these problems.

However, New Labour remains dependent on a party and a wider labour movement which retains many social-democratic concerns; and deregulated global capitalism and the financial markets may not indefinitely remain reliable alternative allies. Whether shaping up to the challenges of novelty and change will produce a third way or a gradual reshaping of social democracy also remains an open question.

Notes

I am very indebted to Mark Freedland (Professor of Law in the University of Oxford and Fellow of St John's College) for comments on an earlier draft of this chapter, though he cannot be held responsible for any of the points made herein.

1 The original use of social democracy was very different, being the name that both Marx and Lenin and their associates gave to early labour-movement organizations. It was then among the various terms in use to describe left-wing workers' organizations – others including socialist, communist and labour – without much sense of distinctions. It gradually acquired its meaning of a strategy of cooperation with, rather than transcendence of, capitalist economic organization after the Swedish and later the German parties which happened to be called social democratic became those most clearly associated with such a strategy. Especially as the Soviet Union adopted the word socialist to describe its brand of politics, social democratic became a useful designation for parties which did not believe in the concentration of all property ownership in the state. In the UK these designations never became clearly established, partly because British political thought is not very interested in labels, partly because socialism had in the late nineteenth century acquired a primarily moral rather than policy meaning in British debate. (A leading Liberal politician at that time famously declared in the House of Commons 'We're all socialists now!')

To some extent because of this British avoidance of precise terminology rather than because of any entrenched socialism in the policy sense, the British Labour Party was reluctant ever to resolve the question whether it believed in state ownership of most of the economy or not. Attempts in the early 1960s by the Party leader Hugh Gaitskell to imitate the German SPD and formally drop such a commitment were defeated at party conferences. However, in practice Labour governments were always social democratic rather than socialist in the sense meant here, but when the party in the country shifted sharply to the left in the early 1980s the old unresolved issue was raised again. There is therefore some lack of clarity whether New Labour is seeking a third way between social democracy and neo-liberalism, or between the latter and the resurgent socialism of the early 1980s.

Another early ambiguity concerning political forces which needs to be clarified is the fact that the dominant form of capitalism in Europe in the first half of the twentieth century was often protectionist rather than *laissez-faire*. This was, however, not the case in Scandinavia or the UK, which set much of the pace in the development of labour-movement politics at that time, and neither were these labour movements protectionist.

2   The welfare state has become so synonymous with the politics of the labour movement that we are today inclined to forget that early generations of socialists were contemptuous of it as a set of Bismarckian palliatives. Once capitalism was abolished, they would argue, insecurity and ill health would be banished from workers' lives, and state welfare support would be unnecessary.

3   The most interesting analysis would be to assess New Labour in relation to feminism. I think it would score highly on a feminist scale, which marks an important contrast with traditional social democracy – except in Scandinavia in the past 20 years.

4   Self-employment is bogus if the worker is *de facto* tied to a particular contractor, as occurs with many franchising arrangements or other situations where the principal motive for using self-employed status is evasion of payment of employers' social security contributions or observance of health, safety and security legislation.

5   Labour-market flexibility has several meanings. An indication of the fundamental interpretation placed on the idea by British governments can be gleaned from the official *Labour Market Trends* (HM Govt monthly) which measures progress in flexibilization by counting numbers on part-time and temporary contracts.

6   In May 1998 the government adopted a national childcare strategy in order to improve facilities for looking after young children. While this had a number of objectives, including educational ones, its main purpose was to ease mothers' labour-force participation – in this case, all mothers, not just those without partners.

7   The principal aim of the directive is to reduce the maximum working week for employees to 48 hours.

8   Service qualifications for protection against arbitrary dismissal have tended to oscillate between Labour and Conservative governments since the 1960s. In the past, Labour governments have established thresholds of six months, which subsequent Conservative ones have extended to two years.

9   It has strong precedents in German corporate law, the inclusion of labour among the interests recognized coming from a mixed Christian and Social Democratic legacy and therefore forming a genuine third way between those traditions in post-war Germany. Although not an original third way, it would have been original to the UK.

10 His neo-liberal counterpart of corporatism is the 'minimal state'; his third way counterpart is the undefined 'new democratic state', which tells us very little.

11 Governments did play a dominant role in neo-corporatist systems in Norway in the 1940s, the Netherlands until the 1960s, and in Belgium even today. Elsewhere, however, neo-corporatism has taken the form of the state sharing responsibilities with interest organizations, not 'dominating society'.

References

Due, J., Madsen, J. S. and Strøby, J. C., 1994, *The Survival of the Danish Model*, Copenhagen: DJØF.

Giddens, A., 1998, *The third way: the Renewal of Social Democracy*, Cambridge: Polity.

HM Govt, monthly, *Labour Market Trends*, London: HMSO.

HM Govt, 1998, New *Deal at Work*, London: HMSO.

HM Govt, 1998, Fairness *at Work*, London: HMSO.

Hutton, W., 1995, *The State We're In*, London: Cape.

Plant, R., 1998, *The Third Way*, Friedrich-Ebert-Stiftung Working Papers 5/98.

Taylor, R., 1998, 'The *Fairness at Work* White Paper', *The Political Quarterly*, 69, no. 4, pp. 451–7.

Visser, J. and Hemerijck, A., 1997, *A Dutch Miracle: Job Growth, Welfare Reform and Corporatism in the Netherlands*, Amsterdam: Amsterdam University Press.

8
Decentralization under New Labour: a Civic Liberal Perspective

Steven M. Teles and Marc Landy

1. Introduction: civic liberalism and the autonomy of the political

As Aristotle reminds us, constitutional reform is inherently dangerous.[1] It unsettles the polity, disturbs existing relationships and creates unanticipated consequences. Therefore it should not be undertaken lightly. It must have a profound rationale based on a recognition of serious defects in existing arrangements. This essay seeks to provide a philosophical framework for assessing the merits of reform based on decentralization, specifically in the British case. This framework enables us to examine the specific contributions which decentralization can make to improving public life as well as the preconditions which need to be in place for such improvement to actually take place.

How does reform of government and, in particular, political decentralization fit into a modern centre-left philosophy of governance?

Our exploration of this question is grounded in the philosophical tradition of civic liberalism. Our approach is *liberal* in that we take as given a multiplicity of interests, the necessity of fundamental rights, and limited, constitutional government. Our approach is *civic* in that we think these liberal commitments are best realized in a polity which has the following specific features: it enforces minimal civilities and civic attitudes, such as self-reliance, obedience to the law and respect for the rights of others; it provides sufficient opportunity for political participation so as to foster civic education and discourage servility; and, importantly, it draws upon, and perhaps cultivates, specific non- (but not anti-) liberal aspects of human personality. In the context of this chapter, the non-liberal aspect of personality that we shall primarily focus on is attachment to *place*. We take as given that human beings have a need to attach themselves to some grouping larger than themselves and their family. Place (as opposed to race or religion) is particularly valuable as an identity in a liberal society since membership is non-essentialist in nature: one can become a Mancunian much easier than one can become, for example, black. What also distinguishes civic liberalism is that it treats political institutions and their legitimacy as intrinsically valuable, not as valuable only in so far as they are instrumental to economic success. In the US, the economy is stronger than at any time since the early 1960s, but the level of distaste for the political system remains high.[2] This may also be true in Britain. Despite a very strong economy, the Conservative party was thrown out of office in 1997, and distaste for the mode of politics it represented was a key component of that defeat.[3] A centre-left political agenda that does not address this problem of alienation from political institutions would therefore be making a pragmatic as well as a theoretical mistake.

Thus, while politics is in some very important ways limited by economic factors, our account will focus on standards of evaluation that are intrinsic to political life, most critically *legitimacy*. Our primary question is: What set of arrangements will citizens feel has the strongest claim to rule them, and what set of supporting institutions is required to make these arrangements work? We will argue that over-centralized government saps power from lower-level political institutions that are potentially capable of attracting the attachment of citizens, and, that by doing too much, it draws down the legitimacy of central government as well. In developing our argument, we will discuss what is needed to make decentralization work; what should and should not be decentralized; and to what one should decentralize.

2.   The breakdown of the dual polity in Britain

Writing before the development of the welfare state, when the actual administrative functions of the British state, apart from defence and Empire, were few, the civic liberal *par excellence*, John Stuart Mill, could still perceive what we might call *the core geographical problem of modern government*: over-centralization leading to an overburdened central state. In Mill's words:

> It is but a small portion of the public business of a country, which can be well done, or safely attempted, by the central authorities; and even in our government, the least centralized in Europe, the legislative portion at least of the governing body busies itself far too much with local affairs, employing the supreme power of the State in cutting small knots which there ought to be other and better means of untying. The enormous amount of private business which takes up the time of Parliament, and the thoughts of its individual members, distracting them from the proper

occupations of the great council of the nation, is felt by all thinkers and observers as a serious evil, and what is worse, an increasing one.[4]

With the exception of describing British government as 'the least centralized in Europe' this description of the problem is still apt: how do you keep the central government from 'cutting small knots' and prevent it from being diverted from the 'proper occupations of the great council of the nation'?

Until the early twentieth century, this problem was solved in Britain, in large part, by the distinction between high and low politics. As Jim Bulpitt has argued, through the late nineteenth century Britain had, in effect, two polities.[5] The national polity was governed from London by a small elite whose primary concerns were national defence, the protection of Britain's overseas economic interests (and with them the power of the City of London), and the conduct of imperial affairs. While there were significant partisan splits between the Liberals and Tories on these high politics issues, the need to defend the division between the high and low was a significant area of consensus. In large part, this national elite wanted to protect these core state functions from democratic interference, but also to keep itself out of the mundane business of everyday domestic policy and administration. On the other side was a local polity, governed by provincial elites concerned almost exclusively with local affairs. This constitutional settlement held into the twentieth century, even as the nature of the political elites at both levels changed as a result of democratization and the rise of municipal socialism. The big exception to this constitutional settlement, of course, was Ireland, but there the question was not the balance of power between the centre and the periphery, but whether any such relationship should exist in the first place.

The early period of welfare state-building in Britain did not materially change this territorial constitutional settlement. Most of this process involved the state assuming powers that no one was exercising, or those exercised by private actors (such as Friendly Societies). Even the Attlee government's search for the New Jerusalem did not dramatically change the relations between the national and local governments. While hospitals were nationalized, for example, this was not a core local government function; many of the local hospitals were run as charities, not by the local council.[6] Councils were made the lead governmental unit in the great rebuilding campaigns of the 1950s and 1960s, and with it they took on what has continued to be their most important function: housing. But there was little in this relationship that was dictatorial in its nature.

However, the rise of the social-democratic state made Britain's dual polity inherently unstable. British Labourism was primarily concerned with equality, with delivering certain goods and conditions to all Britons as a condition of their citizenship. Welfare state-building went hand in hand with general state-building, with creating a homogenous, national citizenship. This is difficult to square with local autonomy, which leads inevitably to variation. Eventually, egalitarian nationalism, and then a reactive Thatcherite neo-liberal nationalism, would come to conflict with, and overturn, the dual polity.

If there was one crucial turning point in the loss of constitutional authority by local government this may well have been the policy of comprehensive schooling which dramatically accelerated under the 1964–70 Labour governments. Schools had long been the primary responsibility of local government in Britain. It had responsibility for the core institutional and curricular decisions, including the division between secondary modern and grammar schools. This latter division was seen by many in the Labour Party, however, as a bedrock of the British class system, the embodiment of inequality of opportunity. The traditional constitutional settlement in local affairs would have suggested central government encouragement or partnership in moving toward comprehensive education, but the pattern in practice was just short of dictation and a long struggle between the centre and local government over the speed, and indeed the desirability, of comprehensive education. In this battle, as in many others in the 1960s and 1970s, the Conservative Party played the part of the defenders of local autonomy, a role played throughout the post-war period primarily by whatever party was out of power at the time. Even so, the move to comprehensive education continued apace through the Heath government, under the control of that prize creature of grammar school education, Margaret Thatcher.[7]

If, however, the Labour government could be said to have made the initial breach in the territorial constitutional settlement, it was then torn to shreds under the Thatcher (and to a lesser degree) Major governments. In part this was a byproduct of the perceived monetarist need for centralized control over all spending and taxation. However, the Conservative government's war with local councils was also driven by a kind of egalitarianism, or perhaps simple uniformism. The poll tax, for example, was justified in part as a corrective to the widely differing and thereby 'unfair' levels of local taxation in Britain. Supporters of the poll tax argued that democratic elections were an insufficient protection against 'loony left' councils.[8]

The Thatcherite attack on local government was largely correct in its critique of local government, if not in its solution. Some councils were dominated by infantile leftism. Many more were corrupt, inefficient and incapable of holding much affection or attention from their own constituents. The initial response of the government was ever-increasing intervention in local affairs, culminating in rate-capping, the abolition of the Greater London Council, the transference of economic development functions to unelected quangos, and the establishment of a national curriculum in the schools. But intervention came at a cost: the deeper central government plunged into local government affairs, the further it got drawn down into the muck of day-to-day governance. It became ever more busied by the business of 'cutting small knots'.

The introduction of the poll tax was intended as a mechanism for cementing a new constitutional settlement, one that would permit central government to pull back from intrusive intervention in local affairs. By spreading the tax burden more widely, and making the connection between taxation and services clearer, it was hoped that the ordinary processes of local politics might be sufficient to control local government. But with the failure of the poll tax, the old centralizing approach reasserted itself. More and more functions were taken out of the hands of local government, reallocated upwards to government appointed quangos, or downward to self-governing hospitals and schools. Those powers that remained were more heavily controlled and regulated from the centre, subject to ongoing waves of 'reinventing government' through contracting out and compulsory competitive tendering. By the end of the Major government, local government in Britain had become just slightly more than an extension of Whitehall.

This, then, is the state of local government that Tony Blair's government faced upon taking office. Its policies toward local government can be grouped into two camps. On the one hand, there is a structural agenda, including Scottish and Welsh devolution, the establishment of a directly elected Mayor of London, and the creation of a tier of regional development agencies (which may in the future be brought under the control of elected assemblies) and the reform of the council system. The aim of these measures is to pave the way for some substantial decentralization of government authority away from Whitehall. On the other hand, there has been the heavy-handed Millbank involvement in the Scottish, Welsh and London elections, which suggests a basic suspicion of the diversity which goes hand in hand with decentralization. In the day-to-day business of the Labour government the great thrust of change, especially in the area of education, is still toward greater central control, with Whitehall 'naming and shaming' poorly performing schools, creating 'hit squads', 'action zones' and the like (see Wood, Chapter 4). This is to be expected. The natural flow of all governments, except where decentralization is their core mission, is toward accumulation of power at the centre. The purpose of constitutional reform is, quite simply, to keep governments from doing what comes naturally. But this begs the question of why one would want decentralization in the first place.

3. Why is some degree of decentralization important?

Decentralization has three important consequences, each of which comports favourably with the philosophy of civic liberalism. It encourages political diversity. It enhances the importance of place in politics. And it nourishes the cultivation of crucial citizenship skills and attitudes.

The values of diversity: choice and experimentation

From a liberal perspective, the choice and greater diversity of lifestyle promoted by a decentralized political system is of intrinsic value. In a decentralized system if one does not like the way a community is governed one can move elsewhere and, in all likelihood, find a community operating under governing principles, that, within limits, promote a very different conception of the good. Just as allowing different individuals to match their preferences to different packages of private goods maximizes individual utility, decentralization allows a closer fit between collective preferences and public goods.[9] But political decentralization is also a good because it can act as a shield against homogenization, against the tendency of centralized government and free markets to make all places alike. Local governments, with enough constitutional protection, can defend the peculiarities of place upon which people construct geographic identity.

Such diversity also permits experimentation. In a decentralized polity, innovative and risky reforms don't all have to squeeze through a single pipe. They can be tried even where no national majority exists for them. This permits policy to be improved through trial and error. To use Louis Brandeis' overused term, local governments can be 'laboratories of democracy'. Local governments provide each other with practical lessons in what works and what fails and this reduces the need to anticipate failure and success entirely through abstract reason.

The value of place as a basis for collective action

Local attachment and identity with place is an important potential source of collective action. Most people have only a spectatorial interest in national politics. They have a deeper attachment to their locality, and therefore perhaps a greater willingness to contribute to local than to national public goods. A partially decentralized political system can draw both on national and local attachment, and will thereby lead to support for a wider set of collective goods than a purely centralized system.[10]

Decentralization also provides a political focus for the cultivation and expression of civic spirit. Civic spirit is an impulse characterized by increasing returns: the more is asked of it, the more it comes into being. But it needs a visible outlet to become manifest. Good local government can serve as a mechanism for mobilizing, organizing and focusing this love of place. Such diverse objectives as the restoration of public spaces, fighting crime and improving economic opportunity can benefit from civic pride as well as an abstract commitment to justice.

Place is not unique in its ability to cultivate loyalty and energy. But, unlike kinship and ethnicity, place is non-essentialist. One can choose it. And place is relatively heterodox. One's townsmen are almost always a more diverse lot than one's professional peers or the members of one's religious denomination or ideological sect. Therefore, place lends itself better to the development of tolerance and moderation than do its essentialist or creedal competitors as sources of political identity.

The advantages of the small scale

A few decades ago, it was very difficult to find anyone who denied that bigger was better. Larger corporations could take on greater risks, could unlock synergies between different organizations, could spread fixed costs over a wider revenue base, and so on. A similar logic was applied to schools, hospitals, power plants, and just about everything else. The trend now seems to be in the opposite direction, with, for example, comprehensive high schools in the US breaking up into academies and large American universities creating specialized units within the university to alleviate its anonymity. Much of this effort may well prove as faddish and ephemeral as was the previous uncritical embrace of bigness. But certain forms of knowledge, certain types of efficiencies, and certain kinds of public attitudes and behaviours are best cultivated on a small scale. Here are just some of the advantages of governing locally on a small scale:

1) All large, centralized bureaucracies make decisions on the basis of abstractions, ideas about generalized humanity and typical conditions. This need to abstract and to homogenize may be a necessary part of statecraft, but it is also a dangerous one.[11] Variations in local practices often exist for very good reasons, as adaptations to localized circumstances or as unsystematic resolutions of conflicts between local groups or individuals. Of course, overturning local variation is necessary where such variation involves agreements to subordinate groups and the unrepresented. But most local variation is not of this kind.

2) Engagement in local politics is an indispensable form of civic education. Involving the local citizenry in the mundane business of everyday government inculcates the idea that government is in fact a difficult enterprise, dependent upon difficult trade-offs, sticky administrative questions and inevitable conflict. It can lead to a greater sobriety among citizens about the limits of politics. The development of a comparatively large group of citizens who have had a taste of administering the law is a civic resource, both for calling government to account and for defending it against unreasonable expectations.

3) Local control may enhance the legitimacy of onerous governmental activity. The police, in the everyday conduct of their job, require dozens of instances of voluntary cooperation. People either do or do not voluntarily

provide evidence, leads and tips to the police. They are either forthright or guarded in giving accounts of what they know. They either communicate to others the image of the police as protectors of the Queen's Peace, or as an occupying force harassing their community. Meaningful political control increases public trust in an institution such as the police and is therefore likely to raise levels of voluntary cooperation. This argument is especially compelling in ethnically diverse areas, where mistrust of police and unwillingness to cooperate with them can make improving order nearly impossible.

4) Local government permits policy coordination to be achieved on a more tangible basis than the abstract formalizations available at the centre. Consider the case of environmental protection, which encompasses transportation, urban planning, waste disposal, economic development and a myriad of other policy areas. It is almost impossible to create policies at the national level that will anticipate and account for the ways these various policy areas will interact at the point of implementation. To make them make sense together, there needs to be an executive authority at the local level to coordinate these various policies and ensure that the multiple and often contradictory guidelines established at the national level attain some coherence as they are administered. A polity with a single tier of executive authority at the national level is likely to be less efficient at the point of implementation than one with two tiers, one which sets broad goals and the other which integrates those goals into administerable plans.

5) Finally, local government is valuable as a training ground for higher office. At least one avenue for seeking higher office should be executive in nature in order that parliament contain a critical mass of MPs with substantial administrative experience. This can help correct the tendency of politicians trained in centralized legislatures to depend heavily on abstract reason and ideology, and thereby overlook the formidable obstacles to attaining any social goal through government action. It may also help create a more egalitarian legislature, by providing an avenue whereby those with less impressive educational credentials might prove their capacity for office, much as service in trade unions once did.

4.   What's suitable for decentralization?

The foregoing arguments do not justify wholesale devolution. While Britain has almost certainly gone too far in its zeal to centralize all important policy issues, there were very good reasons why it did so, and those need to be kept in mind in thinking about the scope and extent of future decentralization.

Consider first the conflict between decentralization and equality. If equality is defined as uniform treatment, decentralization will tend to make citizens' treatment more unequal. Some jurisdictions will be better administered, while some will choose to provide more of some goods at the expense of others. Two similarly situated citizens, in different parts of the country, will not receive equivalent services. Proponents of decentralization need, therefore, to distinguish between those policy spheres in which at least some degree of inequality is tolerable and those in which it is not. Questions which directly impinge on basic rights are not amenable to decentralization. However, if one defines rights too broadly, then virtually any political decision becomes a rights question. Any new territorial settlement must therefore include a realistic consideration of which goods and practices constitute the core of national citizenship, and a corresponding determination of which goods are desirable but discretionary.

Policies that are redistributive in nature are likewise poor candidates for decentralization. The American experience with decentralized welfare payments provides a useful object lesson in the problems that develop when cash transfers are the responsibility of many different constituent governments. Because states vary in the relative generosity of their programmes, potential beneficiaries have an incentive to migrate from the less to the more generous states. What is more, the fear of attracting 'welfare migrants' probably has a tendency to drive benefits below what they would be if they were nationally uniform.[12]

Much of the rest of government activity, which may be broadly characterized as the provision of public goods, is suited to decentralization, subject at most to very broad national guidelines or, even better, minimums. As the notion of a 'public good' implies, many of the things governments do benefit everyone, and are difficult to deny to those who do not contribute to their maintenance. Furthermore, as Thomas Schelling has argued, certain types of governmental decisions, which may be labelled planning, are intended to compensate for coordination problems in private markets.[13] These two large areas of government action, public goods and planning, are proper targets for almost complete decentralization. Local roads, public transportation, city planning, zoning, many environmental goods, economic development, parks, and the arts, are relatively free of intragovernmental pathologies, and are largely local in both their costs and benefits.

5. To what or whom do you devolve?

The desire for some form of decentralization begs the question of 'Decentralize to whom?' At least within the Department of Environment, Transportation and the Regions (DETR), there seems to be (as of mid-1999) very strong support for decentralization on a regional basis. In a recent interview, a junior minister in DETR observed that, 'Every advanced industrial nation organizes itself economically around a population limit of about five million. If you've got an identity it's helpful, but not a prerequisite.' The concept of an optimum size for sub-national government irrespective of attachment or identity appears in the government's policy of creating Regional Development Agencies as the first step toward democratically elected regional assemblies. The regions, which were originally created by the central government for the sake of bureaucratic convenience, are now being used as the building block for reshaping the democratic structure, indeed the political culture, of England.

This claim to have 'discovered' the optimum size for devolved jurisdictions appears, however, to rest on bureaucratic rather than civic principles. It reflects the technocrat's judgement of what is the best size through which to organize national government initiatives, or through which to attract EU regional development grants, rather than any of the civic liberal considerations discussed above. Perhaps there is a minimum viable size – large enough to permit suitable division of labour within government – and a maximum viable size – small enough that it isn't so bureaucratic that it differs only cosmetically from the national government. But that would still leave a wide range of alternative size options. Within those constraints, the specific size and boundaries of a governing body should be determined on the basis of extant citizen attachment and not bureaucratic convenience.

In some areas, like London, people seem to have a greater attachment to the metropolis as a whole than to particular boroughs, which suggests that the larger unit is to be preferred. Indeed, for most city-dwellers, it is the city rather than the region that people most closely identify with. There is still such a thing as a Yorkshireman, but the more predominant association is with Sheffield, Leeds or York, and certainly not with the wholly ahistorical unit called 'Yorkshire and Humberside'. The government knows this, but seems not to care. In its White Paper, *Building Partnerships for Prosperity: Sustainable Growth, Competitiveness and Employment in the English Regions*, the government observes that the south-west 'lacks a strong sense of common identity or effective regional institutions, and some consultees, principally Cornwall, Devon, Poole and Bournemouth, argued for different RDA boundaries. Nonetheless the RDA is seen as providing an opportunity to establish a level playing field between the South West and its competitors and to help make the region more competitive and more unified.'[14] This despite the fact that there seems to be little desire in the 'region' to become 'more unified', with the exception of those who see regionalism as a way of extracting more resources from the centre.[15] At least within DETR, the perceived economic consequences of decentralization seem currently to trump political concerns about the legitimacy of alternative ways of constructing jurisdictions.[16]

This way of approaching the subject of decentralization seems unlikely to produce anything lasting. Certainly, identities of any sort are in large part institutionally constructed, defined by lines drawn for reasons that, at the time they were drawn, typically did not reflect historically-rooted identities. But this fact does not mean that the current-day institution-maker can reshape jurisdictional identities with impunity. Identities take a very long time to readjust to new institutional structures, and in that transitional period resentment (or apathetic indifference) at being placed in an alien, unhistorical or unfamiliar political entity is likely to reduce willingness to contribute to public goods. Jurisdictions with a history, with a pre-existing store of attachment, are forms of social capital that cannot quickly be pulled down and built back up again at the will of the constitution-maker. The wise constitutionalist draws on what already is, rather than working from an abstract conception of the 'efficient' polity. One consequence of devolving on the basis of local attachment, rather than efficiency, is that jurisdictions will vary quite dramatically in size. There is no reason to think that this is necessarily a bad thing: in the US, for example, size and quality of state government do not seem to correlate in any obvious way.

6.   What do you need to make decentralization work?

Political decentralization requires wise determinations of what goods are to be devolved, and what size of jurisdiction to devolve to. It also requires a stable constitutional settlement to prevent renationalization, and strong supporting institutions, both at the national and the local levels. These provide the intelligence and the incentives needed to sustain local self-government. In their absence local government is likely to fail.

Acknowledge the conflict with equity concerns

The central obstacle to any system of decentralization is the hard fact of geographic inequality. A central challenge, therefore, is to devise mechanisms that redistribute resources without: 1) encouraging central government to encroach on devolved functions; or 2) reduce citizen interest in the conduct of local affairs. These goals are not wholly mutually attainable. The more revenue is centrally raised and distributed locally, the more that spending will be viewed by local citizens as 'free money', and the less responsibility they will exercise in spending it. Decentralization and equity conflict, necessarily.

Greater party competition

Viable decentralization in Britain is also hampered by the lack of effective political competition. In the US, the worst-managed cities are those where one party, and in the extreme case one individual, has had a stranglehold on the mayor's office. A similar phenomenon appears in Britain where cities such as Hull or Glasgow are effectively one-party states, with all the risk of corruption and unresponsiveness that monopoly breeds. We would argue that the best way to stimulate competition is for political parties to permit reasonably wide ideological diversity among their candidates for local office. For example, neither Richard Riordan in Los Angeles nor Rudolph Giuliani in New York could be elected as a national Republican candidate. If the standards for being a Republican were nationally uniform both of those cities would be one-party dominions. Variation in what the party label means in different places in the country makes local politics more competitive even where one party dominates in national elections. By maintaining the competitiveness of elections, and also by ensuring that there is some rotation in office, political interest and political accountability are both encouraged. This consideration may also suggest a rationale for proportional representation at the local level that does not exist at the national level.[17]

The importance of a vigorous local press

Tocqueville was neither the first nor the last student of democracy to point out the critical role of journalism as an extra-political check on office-holders. In England, the most prestigious papers are located in London and have an almost exclusively national focus. This is likely to be a major obstacle to effective decentralization. Mechanisms must be found to increase the quality and quantity of local journalism. One answer would be to accept that Britons are unlikely to buy provincial papers with anything like the regularity with which they purchase the major dailies (oh, for the days of the '*Manchester*' *Guardian*), and to encourage (possibly through subsidization of some sort), the production of local inserts, 'papers within papers'. In addition, the government should at least consider the effects of the concentration of journalistic power in a few (overwhelmingly conservative and foreign) hands on the ability of newspapers to serve their democratic, and particularly local, functions.

Links between local government and the higher education sector

In the US, there has always been a close relationship between state universities and state government. Many state universities have public policy programmes that funnel students into state government or local activism and help design policies to respond to state-level problems. British universities lack such a local focus. The old polytechnics are gradually losing their local flavour as a result of being transformed into universities. In planning the future of higher education, therefore, the government should consider not only the economic value of having a tier of educational institutions with a local orientation, but also their potential civic contribution.

Clear lines of accountability: the case for directly elected mayors

Most citizens know whether the place they live is generally well or poorly managed, but they have a hard time knowing who to praise or blame. They need a single person who can be held to account for the operation of government as a whole. This points in the direction of strong, directly elected mayors, with councils limiting themselves to approval of budgets, oversight and community outreach. The Labour government has been of two minds on the reorganization of local government, officially on the side of giving localities a choice of organizational forms in its White Paper *Modern Local Government: In Touch With the People*,[18] but with Number 10 publicly leaning toward elected mayors. This is a case where effective decentralization and local decision-making are in conflict, since the incentives are for councillors to preserve as much of their current power as they can rather than yield to a single politically accountable executive, even if it would strengthen local government in the long run.

Centrally set parameters on local tax policy

The decentralized system of the US creates opportunities for companies to play one jurisdiction off against another, each bidding with subsidies or tax benefits. The consequence is a classical downward spiral: every state is worse off than if they had simply agreed not to play the subsidy/tax cut game at all. Therefore, if substantial control of taxation is returned to local government in Britain, it should be accompanied by some centralized rules, the purpose of which would be to bolster the autonomy of local government, not to limit it.

Independent performance evaluation

Citizens need comprehensible measures of comparative performance with which to hold local government accountable, but which local government might not find it in their interest to collect or release. Comparative data denies citizens the ability to delude themselves that their government is performing better than it is and may encourage competition between local governments to provide high-quality services. As central government withdraws from policy areas, it should maintain a role in evaluation, preferably through the creation of an arm's-length Office of Evaluation and Statistics quite separate from the functioning departments of state, so as not to create incentives for renewed central intervention.

Protect local government at the centre: a new role for a reformed House of Lords?

Finally, there has to be some mechanism for ensuring that decentralized functions stay decentralized. A written constitution with clear division of functions between the national and local governments would be one possibility. However, parchment divisions are only as good as their enforcement either by courts, which traditionally have not had such a large political role in British politics, or by Parliament itself, which is itself an interested party. Perhaps a better way to provide a sturdy foundation for local autonomy would be political rather than legal. It would provide local government the power within national government to protect itself. Conveniently, Britain has an institution that might be up to the job: the House of Lords. The purpose of any second chamber in a parliamentary system is to serve as a check on the government in the name of some order or institution that is thought to be particularly vulnerable. For quite some time in British history, the House of Lords served this function in the name of the aristocracy, the Crown and the Church. The Labour government has rightly questioned the propriety of such an arrangement in a democratic system. But it has not adequately determined how the second chamber could continue to act as a check on central government, once its hereditary component is removed, without challenging the superiority of the House of Commons. Establishing a second chamber chosen at least in part by local government, possibly from the ranks of elected councillors or on their appointment (as the Senate in the US was once chosen), could enable local government to preserve its autonomy without threatening the supremacy of Parliament.[19]

7. Conclusion: why is this worth the trouble?

Some day the Labour Party will lose the general election. But Labour's constitutional reforms, if crafted carefully, will remain to reshape politics far into the future. Constitutions matter because they shape, over long periods of time, the character of citizenship. They communicate to citizens to whom they are obligated and how. In so doing, they serve as a kind of education, one with the potential to reshape preferences, to inculcate capacities and disciplines, and connect people to government. The great potential of constitutional reform, from the point of view of friends of activist government, is that if it is done intelligently it may make citizens more willing to contribute their resources to the pursuit of common objectives. And it is that willingness to contribute, in taxation but in so many other ways as well, that is the great resource upon which the welfare state depends. In our view, it is civic liberalism that takes the fostering of these social resources most seriously, and it is that tradition which can give to the Labour government the coherence which talk of a 'third way' never can.

Notes

1 Aristotle, *The Politics* (Oxford: Oxford University Press, 1995), Book V, pp. 178–228.
2 Joseph Nye, Phillip Zelikow and David King, *Why People Don't Trust Government* (Cambridge, Mass.: Harvard University Press, 1997).

3 David Denver et al., *New Labour Triumphs: Britain at the Polls* (Chatham, NJ: Chatham House Publishers, 1998), esp. chs 2 and 4.

4 John Stuart Mill, in *Utilitarianism, Liberty and Representative Government* (New York: E. P. Dutton), p. 346. (ch. 15, para. 1).

5 Jim Bulpitt, *Territory and Power in the United Kingdom: an Interpretation* (Manchester: Manchester University Press, 1983).

6 Nicholas Timmins, *The Five Giants: a Biography of the Welfare State* (London: HarperCollins, 1995), p. 113.

7 This account of the move to comprehensive education is necessarily compact, leaving out many of the complications in the story, among which is the fact that many local governments had already moved to comprehensive schools of their own accord before the Labour government came to power, with the support of the then Conservative government. It is also true that the Labour government stopped just short of dictating to local governments that they had to dismantle their grammar schools, but they did withhold funds for new school construction from local governments which did not do so. This was a substantial shift, in tone if not in letter.

8 David Butler, Andrew Adonis and Tony Travers, *Failure in British Government: the Politics of the Poll Tax* (Oxford: Oxford University Press, 1994), pp. 100–1.

9 This argument finds its strongest defenders among economists associated with the idea of 'fiscal federalism'. For a classic argument along these lines, see Wallace Oates, *Fiscal Federalism* (Brookfield, Vt.: Ashgate, 1993), and for a more recent treatment, Alice Rivlin, *Reviving the American Dream: the Economy, the States and the Federal Government* (Washington, DC: Brookings, 1992).

10 Note that localism can be expected to bring greater support for public goods, that is, those which are, to use the economists' definition, non-rival and non-excludable. For reasons we will discuss later in the chapter, localism can be expected to lead to less support for redistribution, which is the best reason for reserving much of the cash-transfer part of the welfare state to the national government.

11 James Scott, *Seeing Like a State* (New Haven: Yale University Press, 1998).

12 Paul Peterson and Mark Rom, *Welfare Magnets* (Washington, DC: Brookings, 1990).

13 Thomas Schelling, *Micromotives and Macrobehaviors* (New York: W. W. Norton, 1978).

14 UK Department of the Environment, Transportation and the Regions, *Building Partnerships for Prosperity: Sustainable Growth, Competitiveness and Employment in the English Regions* (White Paper, Released 16 Dec. 1997); *http://www.local-regions.detr.gov.uk/bpp/index.htm*

15 There is currently a 'movement' for regional government in Yorkshire, but it is funded by the Rowntree foundation with support from ministers in the Department of the Environment not exactly a grass-roots affair. See Martin Wainwright, 'Revolutionary Yorkshiremen Edge Towards Devolution', *The Guardian Online*, 18 March 1999.

16 See Steve Richards, 'An Evangelical DIY Salesman', *New Statesman*, 26 June 1998, Supplement IV.

17 We confess to being unconvinced of the merits of proportional representation, even at the local level. PR may lead to a situation in which elections lead only to shifting coalitions, rather than to true rotation in power. It is rotation that offers the surest protection against corruption.

18 Department of the Environment, *Modern Local Government: In Touch with the People*, 30 July 1998; *http://www.local-regions.detr.gov.uk/lgwp/index.htm*
19 This idea has been mooted for Scotland and Wales and perhaps for the English 'regions' as well. As stated before, we would prefer to have the body structured purely on a local rather than a regional or national basis. See 'FT Interview: Blair on Divided Loyalties', *Financial Times*, 14 Jan. 1999.

9
Feminism and the Third Way: a Call for Dialogue

Anna Coote

1. Introduction

There are now more than 100 women in the British parliament, as a direct result of special measures taken by the Labour Party to achieve a better gender balance. By introducing all-women shortlists for the selection of candidates in roughly half of the key 'winnable' seats in the 1997 General Election, Labour raised the proportion of women in the house from 8 to 16 per cent. There are also more women in the Cabinet than ever before – a consequence of Labour's introducing a quota system in elections to the Shadow Cabinet while the party was in opposition. The fact that women have been elected to more than one in three seats in the Scottish parliament and Welsh assembly is thanks to Labour's policy of 'twinning' constituencies, with each pair selecting a male and female candidate. In 1999, women accounted for 48 per cent of all Labour members of the Scottish parliament and 50 per cent of all Labour members of the Welsh assembly.

Positive action[1] was espoused by the Labour Party while in the process of modernization. It is not an 'Old Labour' strategy – indeed, it was passionately resisted by some traditionalists, who were more interested in defending the trade unions' powers within the party. But nor is it part of the Blair government's agenda. Those who campaigned to change the party from an old-fashioned bastion of white males into a more inclusive and egalitarian modern organization could be forgiven for assuming that New Labour would remain committed to their politics. How wrong they were. New Labour is acutely uncomfortable with promoting a pro-woman agenda. Like raising taxes and redistributing wealth, this is something it may do by stealth or sleight-of-hand, but never with pride or a positive spin.

What is it about New Labour and the 'third way' that makes it both a positive force for women and deeply antipathetic to the women's cause?

2.   A third way for women?

The third way is an attempt to fuse the liberal and social-democratic traditions. As Tony Blair wrote in a Fabian Pamphlet:

> Liberals asserted the primacy of individual liberty in the market economy; social democrats promoted social justice with the state as its main agent. There is no necessary conflict between the two, accepting as we now do that state power is one means to achieve our goals, but not the only one and emphatically not an end in itself ... The Third Way is a serious reappraisal of social democracy, reaching deep into the values of the Left to develop radically new approaches ... the Left is not returning to the old politics of isolation, nationalisation, bureaucracy and 'tax and spend'. We are acting afresh ...[2]

New Labour believes in work as the best way out of poverty and dependency. So it has put policies in place to ensure that the poorest and most dependent can get help to find employment. This is the main way in which women have benefited from the government's policies (for more details see Oppenheim, Chapter 6). It is not possible here to provide more than a brief catalogue, but the combined effect of the following measures could be momentous for women.

The welfare-to-work programme is New Labour's flagship policy for reforming the welfare state; it includes the New Deal for Lone Parents, which provides help to identify skills, training needs, childcare and routes into paid work for lone parents, the vast majority of whom are women. And because it became evident that a welfare-to-work programme could not work without tackling the childcare issue, for the first time in history, Britain now has a National Childcare Strategy, designed to stimulate diverse, local childcare provision and to offset the costs for low-income families.

Britain's first-ever national minimum wage is bound to benefit women disproportionately, as most low-paid workers are women. The minimum wage is part of a wider strategy to ensure that people find paid work more attractive than benefits, and this includes a new Working Families Tax Credit for low earners with dependent children, and a childcare tax credit supplement, which can provide up to £105 per week towards childcare costs, depending on the number of children in the family.

Measures to make working conditions more 'family friendly' will also benefit women disproportionately. These follow New Labour's decision to sign the social chapter of the Maastricht Treaty and include a right to up to three months' parental leave, available to fathers and mothers, limits on maximum hours, and new rights for part-timers. Finally, significant increases in Child Benefit, which is usually paid to the mother, will help raise the income levels of women with children, whether or not they are working.[3] All these measures, especially when taken together, can make a very substantial improvement to women's lives, especially those of poor, working-class and ethnic minority women.

New Labour claims to stand for fairness and social justice. On this basis, it is opposed to unfair discrimination and has signed up to equal opportunity. It has the right language to support gender parity. Tony Blair says the third way must engage fully with the implications of change, which includes a transformation in the role of women, questioning forms of social organization in place for centuries and at last offering half the population the chance – in the name of equality of opportunity – to fulfil their potential according to their own choices.

The government has made it clear that it wants to end social exclusion. This entails breaking out of entrenched patterns of poverty and deprivation, making sure that disadvantage is not handed on from one generation to the next. Women will probably benefit if they belong to any of the groups or neighbourhoods targeted for action under this agenda. So far so good.

3.   A third way against women?

Other characteristics of New Labour and the third way are less likely to help women. For example, New Labour needs to assert its newness and, to that end, repudiates anything that smacks of 'Old Labour'. This is likely to include redistribution, increased public spending and any calls for further state intervention to achieve equality. It may also include anything described by the media as 'politically correct' – a slur that has haunted Labour since the days of 'municipal socialism' in the 1980s, when Labour-controlled local authorities found themselves increasingly out of step with the burgeoning neo-liberalism of Margaret Thatcher's Conservative government. Some of the activity that attracted the slur was dire, didactic ultra-leftism that was, in its own way, oppressive. Much of it, however, was well-intentioned, egalitarian politics. Feminism, and the efforts of women to use positive action to gain more representation in parliament have been associated with the pre-New Labour era and tarred with the 'politically correct' brush. So it is one of the things from which New Labour seeks to distance itself.

New Labour wants 'opportunity for all'. However, it draws a line between opportunity and, in Blair's own words, 'dull uniformity in welfare provision and public services'.[4] New Labour is comfortable with the idea of rooting out pockets of disadvantage (this is the 'social exclusion' agenda). But it is not comfortable with any kind of systemic intervention to tackle entrenched patterns of advantage and disadvantage, such as those that sustain unequal power relations between women and men, and unequal pay. Accordingly, if women are a subcategory of a group targeted for help or improvement, they may do well out of it – for example, as noted above, as lone mothers in transition from welfare to work, or as members of families in receipt of the new childcare tax credit. But the specific disadvantages and imbalances of power that women suffer in relation to men are unlikely to be targeted by New Labour.

Absolutely central to the third way is the ambition to level up, not level down. New Labour wants to hold the balance between the disadvantaged and the advantaged, between the inner cities and middle England. This is the basis of its appeal to the electorate: better-off people must not lose out. However, while levelling up may work with economic inequalities (if only in times of growth), it does not work with gender inequalities, because so much depends on how time is used for paid and unpaid labour. If women are to boost their earnings there needs to be a redistribution of time between women and men, because time is a finite commodity. So is power. Women cannot increase their political strength unless men give up some of theirs. Gender parity requires a redistributive deal between women and men. But redistribution is an embarrassment to New Labour.

Tony Blair says the third way is about 'traditional values in a changed world'.[5] What are those values? Social justice is certainly one of them, opportunity for all another. Traditional values, in New Labour language, also take in family, community and responsibility. This has major implications for women. New Labour wants 'strong families' and 'strong communities'.[6] It is heavily influenced – as no other Labour leadership in British history – by Christianity. Tony Blair (who is known to be a devout, practising member of the Church of England, as are many prominent members of his government and inner circle) says that 'reconciling' changes in the role and opportunities of women 'to the strengthening of the family and local communities is among the greatest challenges of contemporary public policy'.[7] The policies that potentially liberate women are consequently caught in an undertow of traditional Christian values – evidenced by efforts to make divorce more difficult and strong endorsement of the family as 'society's most important unit'.[8] The latter is characterized as a stable marriage where parents supervise homework, prevent truancy, build social capital in the neighbourhood and convey appropriate values to the next generation. Family policy is treated as though it affected women and men indiscriminately. But guess which parent is expected to have time for all those tasks? What chance has she to enjoy equal opportunities if she encumbered with 'traditional' responsibilities?

New Labour wants strong government. As Tony Blair puts it, 'Freedom for the many requires strong government'.[9] That entails concentrating power at the centre. Here New Labour is on the horns of a dilemma: it needs to devolve power to show that it is not an old-left statist government, and it needs to engage others in partnership to implement policies because it is not a top-down, tax-and-spend government committed to direct action. It wants to 'steer more and row less'.[10] But it cannot easily tolerate the unpredictability and messy spontaneity of local action. It cannot accommodate the consequence of empowerment, because the empowered might want to steer as well as row. There are obvious implications here for sharing power between men and women. Women are acceptable as long as they remain 'on message'. If they start demonstrating independent or critical thought, they will cease to be considered suitable candidates for empowerment. (The same thing goes for men, but at least men are usually judged individually. When one woman steps out of line, she is readily judged as representing women as a category.)

The third way, by definition, is about reconciling opposites, squaring circles, having one's cake and eating it. Arguments about whether it is, or is not, an ideology will doubtless rumble on. Tony Blair has indicated that he is less interested in ideology than in knowing 'what works'. However, the hegemonizing force of New Labour as it seeks to be neither left nor right, neither liberal nor conservative, but always a bit of both, a synthesis to embrace opposites and end arguments, is beginning to feel remarkably like an ideology. As it radiates outwards from the centre, there is diminishing space even for loyal dissent. Either one is in and one buys the whole package, or one is in outer darkness.

An important part of the process shaping the third way has been Labour's commitment to understanding the nuances of voter opinion (see Norris, Chapter 3). Learning from the US Democrats, the Labour Party in opposition developed an expertise in profiling target groups in the electorate and identifying their interests and concerns. The idea that the party's electoral strength lay in consolidating and extending its traditional base, which was defined by economic interests, was no longer delivering results. Gradually, this gave way to a conviction that success lay in locating swing voters in key marginal constituencies and finding out what would make them cross the line on polling day. This has enabled New Labour to sideline old allegiances and rise above sectional interests. It can claim it is not about politics any more, but common sense, or what 'ordinary folk' want.

During the 1997 election campaign, the phrase 'Worcester Woman' emerged to describe the quintessentially middle-England swing voter who must switch from the Tories in order for Labour to win. (Her male equivalent was dubbed 'Sierra Man' – not a stubble-chinned cowboy from the high plains, but the upwardly mobile family man to be found washing his car in a suburban close.) Worcester Woman is in her thirties with a husband, a mortgage, a job, probably part-time, and one or two children. She is mainly concerned about the economy, schools and health services. Gender politics do not trouble her and she wouldn't call herself a feminist.

It is easy to see how a wedge can be driven between Worcester Woman and the cause of gender parity and its feminist protagonists. Feminism is, and has always been, ahead of popular opinion. That is one of its defining characteristics. Feminists called for the vote when most women didn't know they wanted it. Now they have won it, most women wouldn't do without it. The same could be said of equal pay and laws against sex discrimination, and possibly even the fact of having more than 100 women in parliament. Worcester Woman would not like to lose the vote, or the right to equal pay, or anti-discrimination laws; nor, I hazard to guess, would she like to see the numbers of women in parliament reduced. But she is unlikely to have thought much about getting more women into parliament, or onto local councils. In ditching its enthusiasm for a high-profile pro-woman agenda, New Labour can claim that it is on the side of 'real women', not those pushy (past-it) feminists who always want more.

New Labour was forged in highly charged, deeply embattled times. After its third and fourth election defeats the Labour Party had to rid itself of associations with the past, tighten discipline and close ranks against adversity on all sides. This has given rise to a close political culture of elite insiders. Predominantly they are young, male, white graduates who live and breathe and eat and dream in the same small biosphere.[11] They control entry and recruit those whom they trust, who speak their language, share their values and play to their rules. The Policy Unit at 10 Downing Street has been described as a 'football team' – and that is not just a metaphor. A few women are allowed in if they prove they can play the game (metaphorically if not literally), but they are not leading players. They cede rank to a generation of young males who grew up feeling that the gender issue was sorted and now think women are yesterday's problem. They enjoy power and do not want to give it up. They tend to be more comfortable with anti-racism than with anti-sexism. Anti-racism does not challenge their personal behaviour because they rarely meet black people. Anti-sexism is potentially more threatening, especially to those who go home to wives or girlfriends of an evening. And demands from women usually imply a need for changes in their own behaviour.

This elite enjoys a symbiotic relationship with the media, especially the political lobby, which tends to be peopled by similar sorts – men who are complacent about their masculine privileges, who disregard the women's agenda and denigrate feminism. Any woman who sticks her head above the parapet to call for a better deal for women is fair game for them. The young men at the political centre can justify distancing themselves from any pro-woman cause on the grounds that this sort of thing always gets a bad press. So the two groups reinforce each other's powers and prejudices.

It is hard for women politicians to fight for gender parity in such circumstances. If they are ambitious, they have got to try to keep in with the insiders, which means displaying their values and supporting their priorities. Its not easy to build and sustain solidarity among women in politics, especially in the House of Commons where the culture is profoundly indi-vidualist. Appointments are by favour. There are no codes of conduct, no procedures to ensure fairness in the promotions and sackings that punctu-ate political careers. Each woman has to fight for her own place on the greasy pole.

The terms of engagement are more complex than they used to be, because a lot of the more obvious goals have been reached (such as estab-lishing the principle of equal pay in law), and because, on the face of it, the government is doing a lot for women. But the gap between women's and men's pay still yawns wide (women earn 73 per cent of men's average weekly earnings[12]) and women remain pitifully underrepresented in most places where power is exercised (women account for only 27 per cent of local councillors and an even smaller proportion of senior civil servants).[13] The case has to be made for keeping up the momentum and finding more ways of creating conditions for genuine equality of opportunity. In the masculine undergrowth of New Labour, the tactics of passive resistance are skilfully employed. These involve agreeing with the need for equal oppor-tunity, but doing nothing about it, secure in the knowledge that nothing will change, since the men themselves hold the levers of power.

In short, there is a weak and ill-defined women's movement, fighting a close and powerful cadre of men in a hostile environment. It is slow and it is dirty. And it is not an equal contest.

4.   Conclusion: which way forward?

For all its faults, however, the third way is the only show in town at present and the New Labour government is best thing that has happened to any of us in Britain, including women, for decades. There doesn't have to be a per-manent stand-off between feminism and New Labour. The key to a *rap-prochement* lies in understanding that women's politics are integral to modern social democracy, not an add-on. They are an asset, not a threat: a key to the continuing process of political renewal, not a set of demands to be met in a one-off exercise and then forgotten. As women's lives continue to change, women's votes will remain volatile. Furthermore, a gendered perspective on politics points the way to addressing some of the govern-ment's most pressing social problems – which concern men and masculin-ity. New Labour appears to be increasingly concerned about young men not taking responsibility for their children, about boys underachieving at school, about the rising tide of young offenders, who are almost all male, about the failure of young men to get jobs, about older men disabled by work-related illnesses, and about the fact that men are affected dispropor-tionately by heart disease, suicide and premature death. All these factors are rooted – partly or wholly – in the ways in which time, power and responsibility are distributed between women and men, and the impact on male identities, lifestyles and opportunities. Gender politics and a redistributive deal between women and men are therefore necessary, not only to achieve a fair deal for women, but also, ultimately, to improve the health, well-being and life chances of men.[14] A one-dimensional third way, crafted almost exclusively by white males and reflecting their priorities, is intellectually frail and politically vulnerable. If Tony Blair wants to go on leading a modern, electable party, he can't afford to let his team slide into laddish complacency. Both sides need to get out of their bunkers and start talking.

Notes

This chapter was originally presented as a paper at a conference on 'Gender Parity and the Liberal Tradition' at the Centre for European Studies, Harvard University, 10 April 1999.

1 A term used to describe measures introduced to help bring about a 'level playing field' so that women can compete with men on genuinely equal terms. In the United States, it is known as 'affirmative action'.
2 Tony Blair, *The Third Way: New Politics for the New Century*, Fabian pamphlet 588 (London: Fabian Society, 1998), p. 2.
3 Child Benefit for the first child rose from £11.45 in 1998/9 to £14.40 in 1999/2000, with a further rise promised to £15.00 in 2000/1.
4 Blair, *The third way*, p. 3.
5 Ibid., p. 1.
6 Ibid., pp. 3, 12.
7 Ibid., p. 6.
8 Ibid., p. 13. See also *Supporting Families* (London: HMSO, 1999).
9 Blair, *The third way*, p. 4.
10 David Osborne and Ted Gaebler, *Reinventing Government* (Reading, Mass.: Addison-Wesley, 1992), pp. 25–49. See also Anna Coote, 'The Helmsman and the Cattle Prod', in Andrew Gamble and Tony Wright, eds, *The New Social Democracy* (Oxford: Blackwell, 1999).
11 M. Henderson and A. Sherwin, 'Revealed: the Whiz-kids Who Really Run Britain', *The Sunday Times*, 9 July 1999, p. 14. See also Helen Wilkinson, 'The Day I Fell Out of Love with Blair', *The New Statesman*, 7 Aug. 1998, pp. 9–10.
12 See Office for National Statistics, *Social Focus on Women and Men* (London: HMSO, 1998), p. 46.
13 See Harriet Harman, 'The Democratic Deficit: a Report on the Under-representation of Women in Local Authorities in Scotland, Wales and England', unpublished mimeo, 1999; and R. Scheider, 'Succeeding in the Civil Service: a Question of Culture', Cabinet Office, 1999.
14 See, for example, Anna Coote, ed., *Families, Children and Crime* (London: Institute for Public Policy Research, 1993); Royal College of Nusing Men's Health Fourm, *Men's Health Review* (London: RCN, 1999).

Part III
Comparative Perspectives

10
The Collapse of Bill Clinton's Third Way

Margaret Weir

1. Introduction: Clinton's legacy

In the waning years of his administration, Bill Clinton seized on the idea of the third way to frame his achievements in office, anxious to be remembered for something other than scandal. The notion of a third way – a policy and politics threaded between the market and old-style social democracy – is inherently ambiguous. But in the United States, which never embraced many of the main tenets of postwar social democracy, charting a third way is especially murky. Some versions of the third way envision a more ambitious role for government than that of the American federal government even in the heyday of postwar liberalism; others propose that government do considerably less.[1]

Part of Clinton's political genius – his election in an era when Democrats appeared doomed to lose presidential contests and his against-all-odds reelection and impeachment survival – lay in his ability to be many things to many people. His initial electoral rhetoric excited the hopes of both traditional Democrats and the self-proclaimed new Democrats. In the end, however, Clinton presided over the implementation of very constricted version of the third way whose short-term political and market successes mask the limits of its institutionalized policy achievements. With the exception of the expanded earned income tax credit and the increased minimum wage, the administration did little to address the sharp inequality that has become the hallmark of the American road to prosperity. Despite much talk about job training, it failed to create elements of the 'intelligent and active' welfare state described by Frank Vandenbroucke in Chapter 12 in this volume. Indeed, it is striking how much the administration ultimately drew on only two policy tools – tax expenditures and minor regulation – for all its initiatives after the healthcare debacle.

Likewise, Clinton's longer-term political accomplishments – coalitional as well as ideological – remained sharply circumscribed. Clinton's greatest political contribution was to block the Republican right's bid for power. But he did not press forward with a new inclusive social agenda. By moving to the right on welfare, crime, and urban issues, he helped inoculate Democrats from attack around these racially-driven wedge issues – but this rightward movement came with significant costs to racial minorities and the poor. Nor was Clinton successful at revitalizing a new public philosophy. After twelve years of Republican attack on government, at best the portrayal of government as menace has been replaced by the sense that government is largely irrelevant.

This chapter assesses the Clinton administration in light of third-way approaches toward a new progressive politics. I begin by defending the claim that such progressive aspirations can be discerned amidst the inchoate but often deliberately hybrid approach to politics and policy embodied in the administration's early initiatives. I then examine how basic features of American politics and institutional organization made progressive strategies so difficult to pursue and made a tepid centrism such an attractive alternative. I conclude by identifying the strategic approach that progressive politics now needs to pursue and I consider some steps that move in that direction.

2.   The eclipse of the progressive path

Clinton's campaign rhetoric and early policy proposals can be read in two ways. One is a centrist approach designed primarily to inoculate Democrats against criticism on issues of values 'big government.' But a more ambitious and transformative strategy can also be discerned, one that embraced activist government but sought to establish new premises for public action and to create new mechanisms to achieve its goals.[2]

This transformative strategy had three components: (1) To counter distrust of the federal government, policy would work through market mechanisms or the states and it would 'reinvent' government. (2) To counter racially-charged 'wedge' issues, such as crime and welfare, policy would set clear expectations for individual responsibility and impose sanctions on bad behavior. It would, however, provide resources to assist people if they lived up to their part of this bargain. The President encapsulated this bargain in the aphorism, 'If you work, you shouldn't be poor.' (3) To counter arguments that social spending was too expensive, policy would highlight the long-term benefits of 'investing' in people so that they could be productive workers and citizens.

This approach to policy can be distinguished from two Democratic alternatives. It most visibly departed from 'old Democratic' policy orientations in its forthright embrace of responsibility and expectations for individual behavior as conditions for beneficiaries. But it also envisioned a different relationship between government and the market than traditional New

Deal policies. 'Old Democratic' policies had combined a social strategy of strengthening labor plus providing compensation (such as unemployment insurance) for market losers. Growing difficulties with these policies, their inability to improve the lot of most workers, and their failure to reconnect workers to the labor market lay behind Clinton's alternative. Clinton adopted an aggressive market-oriented internationalism, evidenced in his support for the North American Free Trade Act (NAFTA). And instead of passive compensation, Clinton championed policies that would actively assist individuals in making the transitions that markets made necessary.

This approach also differed from the centrist 'new Democratic' orientation of the Democratic Leadership Council (DLC). Formed by a group of moderate southerners in the mid-1980s as an alternative to the 'big government' of northern liberal Democrats, the DLC embraced themes of individual responsibility and advocated using market mechanisms rather than government wherever possible.[3] But its agenda did not emphasize public investment or the need to increase benefits along with responsibility. The DLC was concerned with repositioning the Democrats on the existing political and policy spectrum, not with changing existing conceptions of 'left and right.'

The expansive version of Clinton's strategy aimed to reinvigorate the Democratic coalition by shifting the axes of debate to overcome the recurring divisions over race and values that had blocked major Democratic social policy initiatives since the 1960s and to revamp government programs to address widespread public concern about new economic and social conditions. The broad social programs would promote a commonality of interests among the poor and the middle class while the emphasis on values would remove a crucial wedge issue dividing them.[4] This underlying political aim is evident in the central priority given to health reform, which was designed as a popular security-oriented program that would benefit both the poor and the middle class and secure an ongoing role for government.

With the failure of health reform and the election of the Republican Congress in 1994, Clinton effectively dropped the transformative agenda, while retaining much of the rhetoric. Under the guidance of his new adviser Dick Morris, the administration instead pursued a centrist 'triangulation strategy' to paint Clinton as a reasonable middle between the extremes of congressional Democrats and Republicans. Politically, this meant appealing to the middle class on terms that limited the government role. It essentially ignored the inclusive aspect of the earlier approach, eliminating the less well-off and bothersome questions about inequality from the political equation. In policy, this switch was evident in such crudely transparent ploys as the 'Middle Class Bill of Rights' announced soon after the 1994 election – tax credits designed to assist the middle class in sending their children to college. Clinton's second term was far more noted for what his Labor Secretary Robert Reich called 'tiny symbolic gestures' (TSGs), such as backing school uniforms, than for new third-way initiatives.

3. Political and institutional barriers to a progressive third way

In crafting a third-way approach, the Clinton administration faced distinctive institutional and political barriers that make it particularly difficult to move onto the path of an expansive third way in the United States. Three factors stand out as obstacles. The first is the meager institutional legacy of American liberalism, which left few building blocks from which to launch active and intelligent state action. Second, is the difficulty in the American political system of striking the kinds of legislative bargains that third-way approaches often entail. Third, the political temptations of a diffuse centrism aimed at the middle class are especially strong in the American context. The atrophy of political organizations capable of mobilizing popular support left Clinton – and Democrats more broadly – with the uncertain power of public opinion as a key political resource. When public opinion proved unreliable during Clinton's first two years in office, the President retreated to a defensive, nonactivist centrism as the least risky course.

The limited reach of New Deal liberalism left few institutions on which to build the new approach. In contrast to Britain, where Tony Blair could make renewed commitment to the National Health Service a key aspect of his program, Clinton spent all his early political capital trying to fashion a public framework for universal health coverage. Although the widespread criticism of the process he chose is largely deserved, the limited institutional structure on which to build made the task inherently risky. Most of the American middle class receives its key social welfare benefits through the 'shadow welfare state' of employer-provided healthcare, supplemental pensions, sick days and other benefits.[5] These privately provided benefits are publicly subsidized through the tax system but because they are part of the private employment contract, there is little public politics that surrounds them. Moreover, the extensive reliance of the middle class on the shadow welfare state creates a sharp institutional divide with the less well-off who rely on public benefits.

Likewise, in the area of job training and retraining, the New Deal left a paltry institutional legacy. One of the striking features of postwar employment policies in the United States was the narrow definition of the problem toward which policy should be directed: unemployment measured by a single statistic was the problem, economic growth was the remedy. Employment policy reflected the triumph of this particularly narrow form of Keynesianism. The pubic employment service remained a small state-run agency focused at the bottom of the labor market. In the absence of a strong public role, private job placement services came to dominate the market. Nor did public training ever become institutionalized. Despite the regular creation of 'manpower programs' from the 1960s on, retraining never played a significant role in American economic policy and job training programs remained remedial and isolated from the labor market.[6] Extensive evaluation studies showed that these programs did little to improve the job prospects of the participants.

Without an institutional base on which to build, the Clinton administration found it difficult to devise effective programs and nearly impossible to arouse strong support for a greater government role in employment and training. Public opinion polls generally showed support for training but few workers had actually had experience with public training programs and, given their track record, had no reason to believe that such programs would be effective. Business and organized labor voiced support for improved training but neither saw these programs as essential to their interests. In the face of this broad but shallow support, Clinton did not expend much political capital on job training despite its centrality to his initial policy strategy. Instead, like Blair, he began to focus on education. But in this domain, the US federal government, in contrast to Britain, has quite limited influence. At all levels of schooling, states play a much greater role in the financing and delivery of education. Thus, despite the prominence of rhetoric about education in the last years of the Clinton administration it could not easily or directly chart a progressive third way strategy for education.

In addition to these institutional handicaps, Clinton's quest to chart a third way faced formidable political obstacles. One of the serious political problems that most third-way initiatives confront is the lack of a natural constituency. Reich has argued that the fundamental challenge of third-way strategies in Europe and the United States is to build political support from two naturally opposing interests, the winners and losers from globalization. Many third-way approaches involve complex two-step processes that roll back some protections, requiring some groups to face more risk in return for other kinds of government assistance. This type of process requires building alliances of opposing interests, enacting policies that draw only tepid support, or passing programs that some interests deeply oppose.

Such political tasks are difficult everywhere but they are especially troublesome in the United States. The lack of party discipline, the remarkable power of narrow interest groups, partisan budget wrangling, and the limited resources that presidents have to enforce bargains all make such two-step approaches particularly difficult to enact. Many of Clinton's early policies envisioned these types of complex policy trades. For example, welfare reform initially sought to combine time limits with the promise of subsidized work for people who were unable to find work in the private sector. The market-opening NAFTA was to be combined with a much-enhanced system of job training. A proposal to create 'high performance workplaces' envisioned a trade-off between business and labor in which business would make employee organizing easier and unions would agree to allow non-union forms of representation in the workforce.[7] None of these bargains was ever struck. In the first two cases, the market half of the initiatives were ultimately put into place with very little of the complementary governmental assistance. The third initiative, the high performance workplace, became the province of a commission whose report, issued after the 1994 congressional elections, failed to attract serious political attention. The opposing parties in these cases had no incentive to compromise nor did the President have any power to sanction them or induce them to bargain. The expanded earned income tax credit, the President's greatest legislative success in promoting his promise that 'if you work, you shouldn't be poor,' was an exception to these political dynamics. It passed as part of a complex budget package during Clinton's first year, backed by only Democrats. As a significant but low-visibility program implemented through the tax system and rolled into a larger budget package full of desired legislation, the EITC benefited from a rare instance of Democratic Party unity and interest-group indifference.[8] Other successful initiatives linked to a progressive third-way position tended to be small, low-budget programs that involved little federal action, such as the very modest 'school-to-work' grants to the states.

In addition to these institutional and political obstacles, progressive initiatives suffered from the very demobilized political environment in which they had to be enacted. Clinton's political strategy was fashioned with this demobilized polity in mind. Rather than aiming to rally broad support for proposed initiatives, the strategy sought to use public opinion polling to discern which policies a majority would likely support. This strategy made Clinton's policies popular in the abstract but it created problems for enacting them. The complex policies balancing right and left approaches in new ways were popular but their complexity made them harder to enact in the American political system. Moreover, public opinion turned out to be an unreliable political resource. Public support as measured by public opinion polling often proved shallow or subject to persuasion based on other considerations. Majorities for such issues as universal healthcare evaporated when narrow, well-financed interests from the insurance industry tapped into public fears about losing what they had.

Third-way approaches everywhere suffer from the lack of a natural constituency, much less a universal agent, as social democracy claimed to have in the working class. But in the United States, the problem is more severe. Within the American political system, there is very little organizational infrastructure for mobilizing grass-roots constituencies of any kind. The atrophy of local political party organization and its replacement with a politics driven by consultants, polls, media, and money has reached its apex in the United States.[9] The mainline incentives surrounding political competition are not linked to building organizations that incorporate citizens into political life in a regular way nor are they connected to efforts to mobilize broad groups of citizens to participate in elections. Instead, as Marshall Ganz has argued, the goal is simply to win over swing voters among those already likely to participate in elections.[10] The liberal political forces most likely to support a progressive third way were no exception to this pattern and, if anything, were less likely to mobilize popular support than the right. Decades of a Democratic Congress and sympathetic court system had provided liberals with political channels that did not require grass-roots mobilization. The result of this style of politics is a well-documented skewing of political participation and political power toward the upper middle class.[11]

The importance of public opinion and the absence of mobilized political organizations gave many policy battles during the Clinton administration a virtual cast. Political elites referred to opinion polls but, with the exception of the Christian right, there was very little mobilization. In some instances, public opinion provided a good resource to defend existing programs; for example, in 1995 when Republicans backed away from budget balancing plans that would have reduced spending on healthcare for the elderly. But only in rare exceptions did it provide sufficient force to take positive action. One such occasion was the passage of the increased minimum wage in 1996. Undoubtedly the very high public support for the increase helped push some Republicans, fearful of being tagged as a do-nothing Congress, into supporting the measure. In general, however, the uncertain links between public opinion and election results made the impact of polls on political elites tenuous.

These institutional and political obstacles to a progressive third way meant that much of what the President did succeed in accomplishing reflected the conservative side of his agenda. In exchange for NAFTA and time limits on welfare, some compensating spending did occur, but it fell far short of the kind of job system so integral to the third-way vision.

4. The social consequences of the path not taken

In the face of these obstacles, Clinton's policies and his politics tacked toward a bland centrism that did little to chart new approaches to using government. Politically, it focused on the broad middle class, defending existing programs that serve them with much less attention to including the poor.

This political approach was particularly prone to symbolic initiatives that only provide the form of third-way approaches. The first bill Clinton signed – the Medical and Family Leave Act of 1993 – provides an example. Available only to workers in companies employing more than 50 people, the law provides only unpaid leave for valid family and medical reasons.

Workers in low-wage jobs, least able to afford private help to manage family and medical concerns, are also the least likely to benefit from the law. Likewise in 1996, Congress enacted a new law to increase the portability of health insurance from job to job. The measure did nothing to limit the cost of the insurance that a new employer could charge, much less address the problem of those who lacked healthcare altogether. Even for much of the expanded American middle class, such measures are of limited assistance.

The long stretch of economic growth since 1994 has stripped the urgency from many of the concerns that sparked interest in progressive third-way approaches and brought Clinton to power in the first place. Even the wages of those at the bottom of the income spectrum have begun to rise under sustained economic growth. Yet several kinds of challenges remain unmet even in these prosperous circumstances. First is continued inequality. The recent uptick in wages for those at the bottom makes barely a dent in the growth in inequality over the past two decades. Americans have always accepted relatively high levels of inequality, reflecting widespread beliefs in opportunities for mobility. But the levels of inequality – the highest in the postwar era – may be large enough to undermine the American self-understanding as a broad middle-class society. Access to good jobs not only determines wage levels, it also determines access to the shadow welfare state benefits, greatly compounding the impact of inequality. The wage and benefits gap between male workers with college education and those with only high school has grown so large that higher education is increasingly becoming the only route into middle-class economic security. This restriction on opportunity channels comes at a time when, in contrast to the 1960s, public systems of higher education are constrained by state budget limits.[12] During the Clinton administration, the Earned Income Tax Credit and the increased minimum wage helped to counter low wages, but far more ambitious measures are needed to moderate inequality and to open opportunity.

The second challenge are issues related to gender and the family. Third-way approaches – even at their most progressive – prize market activity, a framework in which caring work fits uneasily. In the United States, welfare reform is only the most egregious example of public policy that fails to adequately confront the tensions between caring work and the market. Childcare, long-term care for the elderly, and other tasks related to family life are disproportionately performed by women. Unwilling to substantially increase the public responsibilities for these tasks but anxious to reduce 'passive' assistance, the American policy strategy puts the pressure on women to privately reconcile the tensions between markets and families. Obviously household economic status determines what options are open to them. This policy orientation is particularly harsh for households headed by women. Reliance on a single breadwinner has become difficult for most

American families; for households headed by women the problems are compounded by the significantly lower wages of women. The inability of American politics to make the problems of single-parent households a public concern plays a significant role in child poverty rates that hover at 20 per cent even at the height of the economic recovery. Conservative moralism about unwed motherhood and divorce are part of the story but so is a broader reluctance to take onto the public ledger issues that have been addressed privately. A progressive version of third-way policies has to move beyond its preoccupation with markets to acknowledge that these gender and family issues are social concerns, not simply the problems of private individuals.

Finally, the United States faces the challenge of entrenched, racially linked, concentrated urban poverty. High levels of growth reduced African-American poverty to its lowest level ever in 1998. But at 26 per cent, that rate was still double the national average. Economic growth may be a precondition to reducing such poverty, but, alone, the impact of growth will be limited. Urban poverty has a strong racial geographic element that public policy has more often abetted than mitigated.[13] Longstanding efforts at community development have had to swim against the tide of incentives sending jobs and middle-class people out of cities.[14] The pattern of job creation over the past two decades – with the majority of entry-level jobs created in suburban areas – has exacerbated the isolation of the urban poor from emerging opportunities. The lack of affordable housing in the suburbs and poor public transportation systems create ongoing obstacles for those who try to cross these geographic divides. The great variation in local school systems and the deterioration of urban schools presents a further barrier to the urban poor. Immigrants, who have scaled some of these hurdles though use of ethnic networks, are often held up to show that such problems can be solved without government assistance. Yet, the experience of immigrant groups is far from uniform and it is unclear how the distinctive resources of ethnic solidarity survive into the second generation. Moreover, as the high rates of black segregation attest, distinct groups confront different racial barriers as they attempt to cross those boundaries.[15]

The Clinton administration did very little to confront this set of problems. Its centerpiece strategy for addressing cities – urban empowerment zones – envisioned an 'in place' remedy to the problems of the urban poor. Yet, like its predecessor, the enterprise zones launched both in Britain and in many American states, this market-incentive strategy has not evidenced much success. Other efforts to address residential segregation more directly proved controversial and were dropped after white protests. The urban social problem that has declined most dramatically during the Clinton years is crime, although the contribution of public policy to this outcome is hotly contested. This success is tarnished by the very high rates of incarceration – especially of African-American males – that accompany it. The limited strategy of local development and incarceration constitute containment-type strategies that are out of step with third-way ideas about breaking down barriers to market participation. Geographic separation of races into distinct political jurisdictions is a central barrier that a progressive third way must address.

5. The future of progressive strategy in the United States

The political divisions and institutional difficulties that hindered movement toward third-way policies are deeply ingrained in the American polity. There is little reason to believe that much more can be achieved by pursuing the political and policy strategies that animated the Clinton presidency. Instead, the experience of the Clinton years points to the importance of two long-ignored activities for progressive forces. The first is to build a progressive presence in state-level policy-making, where many of the key decisions about institutional design are now lodged. The second is to rebuild grass-roots organization that facilitates the emergence of a common agenda among the liberal interest groups, which have for too long gone their separate ways.

Since the New Deal, liberal forces have concentrated their political and policy activities at the federal level. The power of rural interests in state legislatures, the limited administrative capacities, and the restricted policy agenda in the states all focused liberal interests on the federal government. But key institutional decisions relevant to third-way strategies now rest in the hands of the states. The meaning of welfare reform depends on what kind of assistance states offer and on the systems they do or don't build for opening opportunity to former recipients. Likewise, job training now consists largely of block grants to the states and vouchers for individuals. Education has always been predominately a state function and is likely to remain so. Only 6 per cent of expenditures for primary and secondary education come from the federal government. While the federal government plays a greater role in financing higher education, states are in charge of the public systems of colleges and universities. This division of responsibility in the federal system means that the states bear responsibility for building institutions that deliver the services of the active and intelligent welfare state. The federal role is still significant, but for the foreseeable future it is likely to be restricted to block grants, assistance through tax expenditures, and limited forms of regulation.

In addition to focusing on institution building in the states, progressive forces need to build grass-roots organization and arenas in which diverse interests can fashion common agendas. The top-down approach of the Clinton administration – its attempt to sell policies assembled on the basis of public opinion polls – was crafted for the demobilized context of

American politics. But the conservative bias in the interest group world and the over-representation of high income voters in elections makes policy strategies based on public opinion very risky. The only way to counter this handicap is by rebuilding a grass-roots progressive presence, capable of making plausible electoral threats and organized to intervene in policy conflicts. The renewed efforts of unions to emphasize organizing and to mobilize politically are an important step in this direction. But the low levels of unionization make it essential that ongoing links across groups – such as community-based groups and environmental organizations – be built as well.

Clinton's political genius got him elected and allowed him to hang onto office under extraordinary pressures. Those same political skills led him to accept policies that elevated markets without defining a new role for government. Unless policies can be crafted to ensure that the benefits of markets are more broadly shared, the third way will remain little more than a justification for capitulating to the conservative agenda.

Notes

1 Contrast Anthony Giddens, *The Third Way: the Renewal of Social Democracy* (Cambridge, UK: Polity Press, 1998) with the much more straightforwardly pro-business Democratic Leadership Council's *Mandate for Change*, eds. Will Marshall and Martin Schram (New York: Berkley Books, 1993).

2 See Bill Clinton and Al Gore, *Putting People First: How We Can All Change America* (New York: Times Books, 1992).

3 See the DLC Manifesto, *Mandate for Change* (note 1 above).

4 For an elaboration of this strategy see the arguments of the President's pollster, Stanley B. Greenberg, *Middle Class Dreams: the Politics and Power of the New American Majority* (New York: Random House, 1995).

5 Christopher Howard, *The Hidden Welfare State* (Princeton, NJ: Princeton University Press, 1997).

6 See Margaret Weir, *Politics and Jobs: the Boundaries of Employment Policy in the United States* (Princeton: Princeton University Press, 1992), chs 2–3.

7 See Commission on the Future of Worker–Management Relations, Fact Finding Report, Report and Recommendations (Washington, DC: US Dept of Labour, US Dept of Commerce, 1994).

8 See Bob Woodward, *The Agenda: Inside the Clinton White House* (New York: Simon and Schuster, 1994).

9 Margaret Weir and Marshall Ganz, 'Reconnecting People and Politics,' in *The New Majority: Toward a Popular Progressive Politics*, eds. Stanley B. Greenberg and Theda Skocpol (New Haven: Yale University Press, 1997), pp. 149–71; Manuel Castells, *The Information Age: Economy, Society and Culture*, vol. II, *The Power of Identity* (Oxford: Blackwell, 1997), pp. 309–53.

10 Marshall Ganz, 'Voters in the Cross-Hairs: How Technology and the Market are Destroying Politics,' *The American Prospect*, 16 (winter 1994), pp. 100–9.

11 See Sidney Verba, Kay Lehman Schlozman and Henry E. Brady, *Voice and Equality: Civic Voluntarism in American Politics* (Cambridge, Mass.: Harvard University Press, 1995).

12 See, for example, Roger Benjamin and Stephen J. Carroll, *Breaking the Social Contract: the Fiscal Crisis in California Higher Education* (Council for Aid to Education, 1998).

13 See Kenneth T. Jackson, *Crabgrass Frontier: the Suburbanization of the United States* (New York: Oxford University Press, 1985), ch. 11.

14 See Alice O'Connor, 'Swimming Against the Tide,' in *Urban Problems and Community Development*, eds. Ronald F. Ferguson and William T. Dickens (Washington, DC: Brookings Institution Press, 1999), pp. 77–121.

15 Douglas S. Massey and Nancy A. Denton, *American Apartheid: Segregation and the Making of the American Underclass* (Cambridge, Mass.: Harvard University Press, 1993).

11
Prolegomena to the Third Way Debate
Michele Salvati

1. Introduction: third ways, old and new

Talking about 'third ways' in Italy is like bringing coal to Newcastle.[1] Of course, the third way we Italians have been talking about for thirty years, from the first centre-left government in the early sixties to the collapse of communism in the late eighties and early nineties, was of a quite different kind from the one we are talking about now: it was a third way between communism and social democracy, or, more generally, between a radical or revolutionary programme and the actual experience of social-democratic governments in the rest of Europe.[2] Such a third way was also meant to be a reformist way, but the reforms to be implemented were different from the conventional social-democratic reforms: they had to be 'structural' reforms, aimed at the core of the capitalist mode of production; they even had to be 'destabilizing' reforms, aimed at disrupting key capitalist equilibria and setting in motion a process of almost revolutionary change. Not only the communists talked this way. In fact Italian communists had always been suspicious of the radical overtones of the 'old' third-way debate, which was mainly fuelled by left-wing socialists and *gauchistes* of various brands. But, of course, plain social-democratic policies could not be fully recognized as a legitimate goal by the leaders of the communist party (CP), who coined subtle distinctions between *riformista*, a bad thing, a weak, merely social-democratic platform, and *riformatore*, the good, communist, truly transformational platform. In the Italian CP there was a right wing which increasingly saw the social-democratic experience as a source of inspiration. Its members were recognizing – in private or in guarded, diplomatic public speeches – that the split between social democracy and communism had been a disaster and that the arch-revisionist Eduard Bernstein had been perfectly right all along. Not surprisingly, it is these people (and members of what remains of the Italian Socialist Party) who are most distrustful of the 'new' third way. At last, they say, after a long and painful historical process, the Italian communist party has changed its name (*Democratici di Sinistra*,

Democratic Left), has come to embrace a real social-democratic platform, frankly admits that social democracy was right and communism wrong, has become a proud member of the Socialist International. But at this very moment, along comes this new nuisance: these silly people who are talking again about a third way, this time a way that is not intermediate between communism and social democracy, but between social democracy and liberalism. To hell with them!

Things look different, however, when they are pulled down from the heaven of theory to the specifics of national politics. They look different from abstract theoretical statements, and they look different from one another. The 'third way' is shorthand for different political programmes in Britain, Germany and Italy, not to mention the United States or Brazil. As a consequence, there is not one, but a veritable plurality of 'new' third ways: they are culturally specific, national programmes, sometimes little more than catchphrases in electoral platforms. The question I would like to address is whether there is something more than this, whether all this talking about a third way in different national contexts points to an underlying common problem for the left, and a problem serious enough to be seriously considered. My answer is yes. A qualified yes, however, since the 'serious' problem has to do not so much with a comparison between socialist and conservative policies, the 'third way' being a kind of *tertium genus*, presumably intermediate between them. This comparison wouldn't lead us very far and isn't really necessary once the real questions at stake have been identified and addressed. The real questions, which refer only to the space of progressive political practice, are these: is it sensible, today, to draw a neat dividing line between progressive policies adopted (and which proved successful) in the past and those that are suitable and desirable in the present situation of advanced, post-industrial societies? Is such a dividing line a deep, epochal shift, similar to that between the liberal-democratic left in the century after the French Revolution and the socialist left in the following one? If the answer is yes, what has changed to warrant such an epochal shift in the character of the left? I won't be able to answer these questions fully here. What I can do is to sketch a rough map of how we might search for an answer, and, on the basis of a preliminary and admittedly sketchy survey of the terrain, offer some tentative and provisional conclusions.

2.   The three dimensions of the left's political practice

The three main places where one must look for an answer, where one might check whether there is real discontinuity, are the following: (a) the value system of the left: its understanding of the values that must be realized in the good society; (b) the 'world' (the society) in which those values should be pursued; (c) the world-view and the theoretical tools by means of which the left both tries to make sense of that world and to devise policies for changing it, in the light of the values it upholds. A sharp distinction between these analytical dimensions is provided only for purposes of logical clarity. As a matter of fact they are deeply intertwined, and it is difficult to imagine a big change in one dimension that does not affect at least one of the remaining two. The space covered is exhaustive, however. An important shift in the nature of the left and in the policies it pursues (a third, a fourth or an *n*th way) must follow either a change in values, or a change in the 'world', or a change in the tools adopted for understanding the world and the consequences of political action; or, no matter where the epicentre of change is located, a change in all of them. Thus for Anthony Giddens,[3] the epicentre of the third-way earthquake is firmly set in the 'world' dimension, but the value and the theoretical dimensions are deeply involved in the new social and economic situation that the left is now allegedly confronted with. And likewise for major changes in the strategies of the left, for the real epochal shifts that the left has experienced in the two centuries for which we can talk of left and right in the modern meaning of these terms.

Let us briefly survey these past epochal shifts. Doing so will help to establish a benchmark against which to pit the current third-way debate and assess whether the order of magnitude is comparable. Leaving aside national variations and concentrating on the real turning points of the left as an international political movement, only two of them deserve to fall in this category: the transition between the liberal-democratic century of the left and the socialist one, and, within the socialist century, the split between the social-democratic and the communist way. The first one is more relevant for a comparison with the contemporary third way, both because the kind of social and economic change (our 'world' dimension) that prompted the shift in strategy is somewhat analogous in the two cases, and because there is some reason to define the third way (in its British version, at least) as a modern variety of liberalism. So, I will be not only brief, but painfully schematic on the second.

3. The great historical phases of the left

The social democratic/communist divide has more to do with the theoretical-ideological and the value dimensions than with the 'world' dimension: social democrats and communists, Mensheviks and Bolsheviks, were looking at the same world, but they were looking at it through different theoretical, ideological and value spectacles. It is true that material conditions for a successful revolution varied a great deal between Russia and central-western Europe. But there were Mensheviks in Russia as there were communists or revolutionary socialists in the rest of Europe. Differences in social and economic conditions may help to explain the success of revolutionary attempts or the prevalence of either wing inside the socialist movements of different countries, but not the radical split between them. In order to explain this division, the theoretical, ideological and value dimensions are of critical importance. The main theoretical tool that the continental labour movement was using, Marxism, and the way in which successive theoretical and ideological developments framed the goals, both intermediate and final, of the socialist parties, inexorably led, in the turbulent social conditions around and after the First Word War, to a split that had been brewing for decades. Everybody accepted as an article of faith, even in the right wing of social-democratic parties, that the remedy to the exploitation of the working class necessarily consisted in the abolition of private property and markets and in the substitution of a collectivized economy; and since it was rather difficult to envisage such a radical change occurring through peaceful means and within the 'bourgeois' legal order, everybody admitted that sooner or later a revolution was inevitable: always later, obviously, for the right-wing social democrats. In order to escape these conclusions it would have been necessary to completely reshape the theoretical-ideological-value framework from which they followed: only Eduard Bernstein, deeply influenced by the British labour (and liberal) traditions, made a sustained attempt in this direction. As a consequence he became an outcast in the German (and continental) labour movement.

Possibly more relevant to our argument is the previous epochal turning point in the history of the modern European left. It occurred much more slowly, between the last decades of the nineteenth century and the First World War, and it gradually led to labour and socialist parties replacing liberal-democratic or bourgeois-radical ones as the main parliamentary representatives of the left. After the First World War, almost everywhere in Europe (both in parliaments and even more in society, where it was backed by increasingly powerful trade union organizations) the left had become the labour and socialist movement: the former liberal-democratic parties had lost most of their weight and had been pushed towards a more central position on the political spectrum.

All the dimensions of the left changed deeply in this transition. In the value dimension the pendulum shifted from a formal-legal definition of equality of civil and political rights to the social and economic ('material', as it was said) conditions that had to accompany and underpin those rights: a decent level of welfare, education and job security had to be assured to all citizens, both as an end in itself and so that citizens could exercise their civil and political rights effectively. This new category of rights – T. H. Marshall's social rights – is a late theorization,[4] but a demand for social rights was there from the beginning and the breadth and subtlety of today's discussions on equality would be unthinkable if such a shift in the value dimension of the left had not occurred.

The shift in the value dimension was inextricably intertwined with a parallel shift in the theoretical dimension, in the analytical tools and in the world-view through which the European left tried to make sense of the society it was living in and to define policies for transforming it. It is hard to overestimate the break in the theoretical continuity between the bourgeois and the socialist left brought about by Marx and Marxism in continental Europe. But everywhere, even in those countries in which Marxism never became the predominant theoretical reference of the left, a clear shift in emphasis and concepts was perceptible. Everywhere socialists (and proto-socialist radical liberals) were claiming deep reforms in the working of the economic system: the word 'capitalism' was not used only by Marxists, and with its adoption came the idea that it was a historically contingent way of organizing the economy and that it could be changed. Everywhere socialists, Marxists or not, were convinced that the values they proclaimed could be attained only by a strong limitation of the role played by private property in the organization of production and a stricter public regulation of markets. Such a concern with the fundamentals of economic organization followed necessarily from the concern to secure the material basis of citizens' rights. It is the hallmark of all socialists.

But the underlying shift, the one that prompted them all, was a shift in the 'world' dimension, in the economic and social conditions of Europe in the mid-nineteenth century. The deeper change was mass industrialization and the emergence of a new, ominous economic cleavage in society; it was the sufferings and the exploitation of millions of people, pushed away from stagnant agrarian and artisan trades and melted together in the new condition of an industrial proletariat. Without this gigantic social change, without so strong a disruption in the previous social conditions, the reshaping of the value system of the left would have quietly rested in the writings of a few radical utopians, and the new theoretical instruments would not have had any clout. The liberal and bourgeois-radical left of the previous century, at least in Europe, was gradually pushed aside by a socialist left which differed from the former in three aspects, which are all important for the definition of a political force. (i) It differed in the nature of its basic political demands: to the civil and political aims of the enlightened bourgeoisie new and more radical demands about social and economic conditions were added. (ii) It differed in the social strata to which it referred and which it tried to represent: common industrial workers instead of bourgeois and petty-bourgeois. (iii) Finally it differed – and this is perhaps the crucial difference – in its characterization of the political foe: the enemy of the liberal and bourgeois-radical left was the Church, aristocracy and landed classes, the traditional supporters of the *ancien régime*. These continued to be enemies for the socialists, but the socialist left also identified the capitalist class as a major foe, and this put a serious strain on the relationship between the two strands of the left.

Since we are looking for turning points in the history of the left, under-lining the big differences between the century of the liberal left and the century of socialism is perfectly justified. For the sake of historical balance, however, one should also stress the elements of continuity. These can be found, above all, in the value system, where the socialist views on equality can be seen as an enlargement of the previous ones. In particular, the demand for civil and political rights, the main historical objective of the liberal left (e.g., rights of free association, universal suffrage) was taken up by the socialist movement. When the socialists succeeded the bourgeois-radicals as the main representatives of the left in the first decades of the twentieth century, such rights were far from being secured and, as a matter of fact, in most European countries they were obtained in their present, complete form only after the Second World War, almost simultaneously with the 'social' rights advocated by the socialists. This point is important and highly relevant for the contemporary third-way debate for it indicates that today's social democracy is already a kind of 'third way', a blend of liberal and socialist theories, practices, principles and values.

4. Social democracy is already a third way

My excuse for the brutal schematism of my historical references is that I wish to move as quickly as possible to the key question we should consider: how does the purported transition from traditional social democracy to the new politics of the 'third way' compare with the grand transitions we have sketched? In order to answer this question we should return to the 'dimen-sions' of the left ((a) to (c)) and to the characteristics of the left as a political force ((i) to (iii)) we distinguished above. Do the value, theoretical and 'world' dimensions significantly differ? Has there been a socio-economic change of an intensity comparable with the industrial revolution? A change to which the left must respond with radically new objectives and political strategies? Are there new social groups to which the third way refers and to which social democracy does not? Is there a new definition of the political foe?

There are two big difficulties in answering these questions. One has to do with a quantity/quality judgement: at which point, exactly, are differences in our dimensions and characters big enough to warrant the judgement that we are witnessing qualitative change? The second has to do with the muddled and eclectic nature of our standard of comparison: the contempo-rary social-democratic left. The first difficulty is certainly serious and, however solved, will always give rise to controversies: but it can be solved in the way that is usual for this kind of difficulty, i.e., by defining, either theoretically or conventionally, a threshold condition after which our change can be considered 'big enough'. It is the second, however, that is almost intractable and leaves little hope, I fear, for a meaningful dialogue between those who have already taken sides in the debate between social democracy and the third way.

The reason why such a difficulty cannot be easily overcome is that, in the years since the Second World War, as we noted above, social democracy has itself become a kind of third way: i.e., a rather muddled and unprincipled array of theoretical tools, ideological references and actual practices; a political compromise shifting in time and varying according to national contexts. More emphatically: *today's social democracy is already a liberal-socialist compromise*. The main goals, and above all the tools, that led social democracy to the heyday of the sixties and seventies – the welfare state and demand management for the maintenance of full employment – were pioneered by two great, self-avowed liberals, Beveridge and Keynes, and in a thoroughly liberal spirit.[5] Ecology and feminism have been more or less easily digested in the ideological compromise of most national social democracies. And when a few typically socialist demands emerged – the more principled and best-known is possibly the Meidner plan in Sweden – they were utterly rejected. So, when we venture comparisons between social democracy and the third way, we are not taking as our benchmark the social democracy of Karl Kautsky or Otto Adler, or not even the social democracy of the Bad Godesberg programme (a far cry from today's statements and practices), but the hyper-revisionist, contemporary programmes of the European social-democratic parties, all of which represent slightly different compromises between socialist and liberal principles. This is also why I cite Eduard Bernstein, since it is in the *Voraussetzungen*[6] that one can find the first and extremely conscious statement of this compromise. We are already in a third way and we have been for some time: why, then, all this new talk about third ways?

The reason is twofold, I think, and has to do with two of the dimensions of left political practice we distinguished above, the theoretical-ideological and the 'world' dimensions. The first is less important, but still significant: the traditional tools of the socialist left, its characteristic analysis of society, have received a heavy blow to their credibility by the bankruptcy of that tragic social experiment – Communism – that self-avowedly relied on a strong and principled version of those tools. The second, and most important, is that capitalism has changed and this has provoked serious difficulties in the actual policies the social-democratic left has recently relied on in advanced countries: the Keynes–Beveridge strategy that worked so well up to the 1970s doesn't work any more and the left is desperately looking for a new, viable political strategy, always remaining within the framework of the post-war socialist-liberal compromise. And here, at last, we reach the nub of the matter: in the search for such a strategy, those who want to strengthen the liberal aspects of the compromise usually talk about a third way; those who want to defend its socialist aspects stand on the social-democratic side of the debate.

This statement is so rough that it almost risks a misrepresentation of the debate. It should at least be added that taking sides is not only motivated by reasons of principle but also by very mundane electoral reasons. On the one side, the previous phase of the compromise has created a thick web of interests and expectations that makes a sharp change rather costly and painful for the established parties of the left. This gives politicians of the left a strong motive to stick to traditional social-democratic policies. On the other, profound changes in the social and economic environment have given rise to new demands that traditional social-democratic policies cannot answer. This has produced a growing reservoir of voter discontent which the right is strongly placed to exploit and calls for a change of policies from, and in the very image of, the left. In all essentials, however, our statement gets to the heart of the matter. We could and should discuss the problems that the left is facing in advanced, post-industrial countries bypassing the concept of third way, at least to begin with. After we have analysed in depth the nature and the dimensions of the change in the 'world' and in the theoretical dimensions of left political practices, their possible repercussions for left values and the consequences for the strategy of the left on both the parliamentary and social levels, we could ask ourselves whether it is useful to introduce a new name for whatever new model of the left emerges. For the reasons just mentioned, 'third way' is probably a misnomer for this new left, as the political strategy has long been a liberal-socialist compromise, a 'lib-lab' experience. If the changes in the dimensions and defining characteristics of left political practices turn out to be big enough, if we find it useful to draw a distinction between the Keynes–Beveridge phase and the one we are living in, it will probably be a further step within the liberal-socialist compromise, a 'lib-lib-lab' mixture, and not a totally innovative third way.

5. What is the third way, then?

This is true, of course, if the third way is located in the value and political space already covered by the historical experiences of the left, the liberal and the socialist left, in their innumerable varieties. But in assuming this are we not putting the cart before the horse? Perhaps we still do not yet know enough about the values, the world-views, the theories that third-way ideologues are advancing. Perhaps they will eventually turn out to be of a completely different nature from the two great historical traditions of the left. If so, perhaps 'third way' would not be a misnomer. But I frankly confess my prejudice: from what I have read about the third way, and seen of the policies pursued by the main political leaders of the putative 'Third Way International' (Blair, Schroeder, Clinton, Cardoso, Prodi-D'Alema), I cannot spot anything of real importance that falls outside the domain of the two great traditions.

True, in some of the more theory-oriented writings there is a serious and unusual concern for environmental, feminist and world-level problems, which are often (but not always) marginal in the programmes of both the liberal and the social-democratic left. This doesn't show up with the same quality and intensity, however, in the electoral platforms and in the actual policies of the leaders I mentioned. Indeed, it shows up instead in the programmes of other European social-democratic parties, especially in the Nordic countries, that would not dream of talking about third ways. These parties are perhaps following a third way without knowing it, like that Mr Jourdain of Molière when he was talking in prose. Apart from mundane policies, I also doubt whether the stress on these important themes is sufficient to put the third way in a category that cannot be obtained by selection, rearrangement and differential weighting of items already contained in the two great traditions: 'lib-lib-lab' (left-wing critics would add a few other 'libs') is a superficial and slightly abusive characterization, but until third-way theorists have proven the radical otherness of this political strategy *vis-à-vis* the old traditions, a judgement in these terms cannot be escaped.

Things may look a bit different when seen from a particular national rather than an international perspective. For whereas at the international level the two great traditions of the left are the socialist and the liberal ones, at the national level other cultural and ideological streams may flow into the river of a 'new' or enlarged left and it may be important to pay attention to this confluence. In Italy, for example, the tradition of social Catholicism was situated until recently on the left-wing border of a big centrist party, Christian Democracy. Now that this party has disappeared, the left-wing Catholics have become a part of the Olive Tree (centre-left) coalition, but they want to underline the religious motivation that leads them to stand with the left, and they want their outlook (on family, education, bio-ethical questions) to be explicitly taken into account in the programme of the coalition. This is not a problem for Blair, or Jospin, or Delors, or other European social-democratic leaders with profound religious motivations, but it is a problem in Italy, where social Catholicism must be recognized as one of the ideological ingredients of the new left, next to liberalism and socialism. Other national examples could be found of different ideological mixtures. In such 'national variants', however, I do not see anything that would lead me to change the judgement that I have passed on the relationship between the 'third way' and the two great traditions of the left at the international level. And as far as Britain is concerned, as things stand, Tony Blair's own words would seem to bear our analysis out. According to Blair: 'The third way ... draws vitality from uniting the two great streams of left-of-centre thought, democratic socialism and liberal-ism.'[7] Blair treats 'democratic socialism' as interchangeable with 'social democracy' in the paragraph from which the quotation is taken, and if we bear in mind that for much of the century the social democracy to which he refers was itself the focus of a liberal-socialist compromise, it becomes clear that the third way he advocates is a renegotiation of that compromise characterized by a strengthening of the liberal element: a 'lib-lib-lab' politics indeed.

6. Four concluding thoughts on the future of progressive politics

I shall end this 'prolegomena' with a brief round-up of some of the more important points I think we need to bear in mind as we consider the options for the future of progressive politics.

First, like the third-way theorists, I believe that there has indeed been a significant change in the situation of the left, a change that I would locate in the 'world' and the theoretical dimensions of left political practice as I defined these above. As a consequence, the political strategies of the left in advanced, post-industrial societies must change. More specifically, they should incorporate greater input from the liberal-democratic tradition, as is already happening, and address new and urgent issues relating to gender, the environment and systemic risks at the world scale (and this is not happening, or happening enough, unfortunately). On the whole, however, I do not think that such a change has the same epochal nature as the ones I described above, but I admit that a full assessment of this point needs an enquiry that I cannot provide here.[8] Both because of the nature of this change, and because the ideology and practice of the main social-democratic parties in Europe has already gone a fair way towards the incorporation of liberal-democratic values and policies, if we find a better expression than 'third way' to describe the new post-Keynes/Beveridge form of left politics, we would do well to adopt it.

Secondly, having recognized that there has been an important change, we need to analyse carefully its nature and repercussions on our 'analytical dimensions' in order not to throw the baby out with the bath water. At the 'world' dimension it is easy both to underestimate and overestimate the nature, size and novelty of economic change. Internationally, globalization and technological revolution are very real things, but the talk about them is often full of nonsense and ideology. Common national problems, new demographic trends, changes in the structure of employment and the function of labour markets, increasing difficulties with previous welfare arrangements are often real enough, but here also ideology and unjustified generalizations creep in. At the theoretical level, the deficiencies of the established socialist traditions should not lead to an uncritical embrace of 'neo-liberal' and libertarian ideas. The fact that we have to live in a market economy (more: that we have to appreciate its positive contribution to innovation, growth and liberty) should not hinder us from recognizing that capitalism is still a pretty rough beast – especially at the international level and in institutionally underdeveloped national contexts – and has not lost those negative characteristics that prompted socialists and liberals alike to devise policy instruments in order to tame it. More specifically, the reaction against Marxism has probably gone too far. Conceived as a toolbox of potentially useful ideas, rather than as an encompassing ideology, Marxism can still produce precious insights on the working of a market economy.[9] Finally, on the value dimension of left political practice, I do not see any reason to depart from the discussion that was already taking place within the framework of the 'old' liberal-socialist compromise. I have a few problems, in particular, about the substitution of the discourse of 'social inclusion' for 'equality' which is taking place *du coté de chez* Third Way. Taken in earnest, social inclusion is just as demanding as equality and should not be used as an excuse for abandoning demands of solidarity that are electorally costly, but that the left cannot but address.

Thirdly, there is a need to keep in mind the very real dangers of falling into opportunistic and unprincipled versions of both 'old' social-democratic politics and 'new' third-way politics. I have already hinted at this dilemma above, and explained how different sorts of electoral considerations might incline particular social-democratic parties in one of these two directions. A course must be steered, if possible, between the danger of opportunistic innovation on the one hand (ditching the demands of solidarity so as not to be outflanked by the right) and opportunistic conservatism on the other (talking boldly about innovation while actually defending the producer and consumer clients of the established welfare state).

Fourthly, following on from the previous point and going a further step down the ladder of abstraction, one should always keep in mind the great variety of situations in which national left-wing parties are operating: I started from this point at the beginning of this chapter and would like to end with it. The great problems that social-democratic parties are facing, the ones we have described until now, are common to all; but the ways to respond to them cannot but be different, since they depend on historical (social, political, cultural, institutional) legacies that vary profoundly even among countries as close as the European ones. Blair and Schroeder may well sign a common manifesto, but then will face very different problems when trying to implement it and will have to explore rather different institutional roads in order to reach similar political aims. Just to mention the most obvious diversities: Schroeder is the head of a *coalition* government in a *federal* state and the secretary of a *traditional* social-democratic party in which the *influence of the unions* is powerful; none of these constraints impair the freedom of action of Tony Blair. But sometimes constraints may turn into opportunities, liabilities into assets. Who would have predicted in the early eighties, when the Dutch economy was universally considered as one of the most serious *malades d'Europe*, that the Netherlands would have become in the nineties a model both for economic performance and social justice,[10] and this would have happened also through a skilful use of just those corporatist institutions that were considered the cause of the illness? This is not to say that 'traditional' social democracy, strong unions, coalition government, even corporatism are good, in general, for tackling the problems of change the left is facing. They are not. It is only to say that institutional path-dependency and historical viscosity force European social-democratic parties to operate within contexts that they cannot change at will. And that there can be surprises for those who equate the third way – or, more generally, an economically successful and socially progressive adaptation to the present phase of economic growth – with the post-Thatcher, 'New Labour' strategy of Mr Blair.

Notes

1 This paper was originally prepared for a joint workshop of the journals *Dissent* and *Reset*, Abano Terme, 16–17 Oct. 1998, and a shortened version has already been published in *Dissent*, Summer 1999.
2 This is a much older story, since there was a discussion on the 'third way' in this sense between the two World Wars, especially within the Austrian and the German labour movements. The best single source of information for this and the following references to the history of the labour and socialist movement is D. Sasson, *One Hundred Years of Socialism*, (New York: The New Press, 1996).
3 A. Giddens, *The Third Way: the Renewal of Social Democracy* (Oxford: Polity, 1998).
4 See T. H. Marshall, 'Citizenship and Social Class', in Marshall, *Citizenship and Social Class* (Cambridge: Cambridge University Press, 1950).
5 In the British context, the post-war welfare state owed much to the blueprint provided by William Beveridge's wartime report, *Social Insurance and Allied Services*. John Maynard Keynes is the greatest economist of this century and the pioneer of the theory of demand management. Keynes was a committed liberal, and Beveridge also joined the Liberal party in the 1940s.
6 An edition in English of Bernstein's famous book (originally published in 1899) is *Evolutionary Socialism* (New York: Shocken Books, 1961).
7 Tony Blair, *The Third Way: New Politics for the New Century* (London: Fabian Society, 1998), p. 1.
8 A short but very balanced assessment of this crucial point and a thoughtful discussion of the main literature are provided by Frank Vandenbroucke, *Globalization, Inequality and Social Democracy* (London: Institute for Public Policy Research, 1998). See also, of course, Chapter 12 below.
9 A good example is the recent essay by Robert Brenner, 'The Economics of Global Turbulence', Special Issue of *New Left Review*, 229, 1998.
10 See J. Visser and A. C. Hemerijk, *'A Dutch Miracle': Job Growth, Welfare Reform and Corporatism in the Netherlands* (Amsterdam: Amsterdam University Press, 1997).

12

European Social Democracy and the Third Way: Convergence, Divisions, and Shared Questions

Frank Vandenbroucke

Introduction: convergence within the European left

Taking a long-term view of social-democratic history, Donald Sassoon argues, convincingly, that we witness 'an unprecedented, Europe-wide convergence of the parties of the Left' (1998: 92).[1] There is convergence of a short-term nature too. Read a sample of the European literature on the welfare state published over the last five or six years by centre-left policy institutes, parties and scholars. You may start with the report issued by the British Commission on Social Justice (1994), and end by reading the chapters on the German welfare state in the report of the 'Zukunftskommission' of the social-democratic Friedrich Ebert Stiftung (1998). Despite important national differences, you will be struck by the recurrence of the following fixed points:

1) Welfare policy cannot be reduced to employment, but employment is the key issue in welfare reform. Moreover, the nature of the employment objective has changed. 'Full employment' as it was conceived in the past in most European countries, underlying traditional concepts of the welfare state, was full employment for *men*. The social challenge today is full employment for men and *women*. This is linked to the transformation of family structures and our conception of women's role in society.

2) The welfare state should not only cover social risks as traditionally conceived (unemployment, illness and disability, old age, child benefits) but also new social risks (lack of skills causing long-term unemployment or poor employment, lone parenthood) and new social needs (namely, the need to reconcile work, family life and education, and the need to be able to negotiate changes within both family and workplace, over one's entire life cycle).

3) The 'intelligent welfare state' should respond to those old and new risks and needs in an active and preventive way. The welfare state should not only engage in 'social spending', but also in 'social investment' (e.g., in training and education).

4) Active labour-market policies should be higher on the agenda and upgraded, both in quantity and in quality, by tailoring them more effectively to individual needs and situations. Active labour-market policies presuppose a correct balance between incentives, opportunities and obligations for the people involved.

5) It is necessary to subsidize low-skilled labour by topping up low-skilled workers' pay, or by subsidizing employers, combined with decent minimum wages.

6) Taxes and benefits must not lead to a situation in which individuals (or their families) face very high marginal tax rates when they take up a job. This problem of 'poverty traps' is particularly acute with benefit systems that are too selective, as in the UK. Yet 'unemployment traps' exist in other welfare systems as well, although to a lesser extent.

7) People who work part-time or in flexible jobs should be adequately integrated in and protected by the social security system.

8) Such an 'intelligent welfare state' needs an economic environment based upon both a competitive exposed sector and the development of a private service sector which is not exposed to international competition and in which low-skilled people find new job opportunities. Continental Europe typically lags behind in the development of the private service sector. Wage subsidies for low-skilled people can also be instrumental in this respect.

Delors (1997) has written an excellent short paper for the Party of European Socialists on a 'new model of development', in which the foregoing points – concerning the family and the distribution of work, wage subsidies for the low-skilled, development of the service sector, etc. – fit very well. One finds the same core insight – that tackling unemployment and reforming the welfare state requires a new European social and *economic* model – in many social-democratic documents. The Friedrich Ebert Stiftung's Zukunftskommission proposes a 'new German model' along the same lines, stressing, for instance, the need to create a market for low-skilled labour in services.

These fixed points mark an area of useful convergence of views on the welfare state among European social democrats, at least on the level of general diagnosis and general policy guidelines (Vandenbroucke 1997). Of course, a consensus on such guidelines need not entail close convergence of national social models or policies within the European Community. But even so, this theoretical convergence has practical import as demonstrated by the way it facilitated discussion of the elaboration of European Guidelines for Employment Policies at the 1997 Luxemburg Job Summit, an event that, contrary to what many sceptics feared, turned out to be a substantive exercise. (See the account by the European Commission, 1998; and remarks by the former French Minister Employment Minister, Martine Aubry, 1998.)

Of course, establishing the potential for convergence of views on the welfare state entails much more than what I have said so far. A comprehensive approach to welfare reform requires positions on the future of pensions, healthcare, and the much-debated issue of universality versus selectivity in social security. It is possible to specify some common points on these issues, similar in terms of generality to the fixed points on employment and employment-centred welfare reform described above. Moreover, I believe that, if formulated on a suitably foundational level, they stand a good chance of representing much of European social-democratic thought and practice today. Consider, for instance, the following statement on universalism, which I would add to my list of fixed points:

9) Neither selectivity of benefits nor universalism are social-democratic dogmas: these are not foundational values, but methods to be judged on the basis of efficiency in the short and long term. Long-term efficiency requires legitimation of welfare state provisions in the eyes of the public at large. In some sectors universalism can lead to visible 'waste' of money, and so undermine legitimacy. But in other sectors (e.g., health) universalism can be the precondition for a broad base of support for the welfare state. Selectivity – in the form of an 'affluence test' rather than a 'poverty test' – can serve short-term efficiency. However, too much selectivity typically catches people in poverty traps and reduces efficiency. Social democrats should find an appropriate balance. The foundational value in this endeavour is the idea of a fair distribution of burdens and benefits, and the political challenge is to find majority support for a distribution that is accepted as fair.

Again, it has to be stressed that convergence of view on this level of thinking will not necessarily lead to convergence on practical measures between countries due to their very different starting-points. Greater selectivity may make good sense in the context of Belgium, for example, but less sense in the British context given that there is already considerable reliance on means-testing. Social democrats need to be careful not to generalize from their respective national situations but should focus on the general principles that properly inform choices over degrees of selectivity. (See Ferrera 1998 for an explanation of why arguments on selectivity mean different things in different countries.)

So, there has been some real and significant convergence in policy thinking on the European left in the late 1990s. However, this convergence leaves open some basic normative questions. It also conceals some important divisions and differences in emphasis within the European left. It is to these divisions, differences in emphasis, and unanswered normative questions that I now turn.

2. Divisions and differences in emphasis

Keynesians versus supply-siders?

Confronted with the 8 or 9 fixed points listed above, many social democrats would add that the emphasis on employment for low-skilled workers must not lead to a one-sided approach. To be successful, they would say – and I would concur with them – targeted employment policies require a sufficient overall pressure of demand for labour. Hence macroeconomic policy is important. More precisely, as the French, the German, and the Italian governments argue: Europe needs macroeconomic policy coordination, *a fortiori* in the context of EMU. They thereby appeal to some basically Keynesian insights.

This appears to be one important division between the British 'third way' and continental social democracy. Particularly worrying, I think, is that the intellectual arguments presented as inspiring New Labour's third way seem incapable of grasping this division; or, more precisely, do not provide the intellectual resources needed to engage in fruitful dialogue about it. The alleged demise of Keynesianism is essential, for instance, to Anthony Giddens' explanation of the *need* for a third way. As he puts it in *Beyond Left and Right*:

> Keynesianism became ineffective as a result of the twin and interconnected influences of the intensified globalization and the transformation of everyday life. ... Keynesianism worked tolerably well in a world of *simple modernization*; but it could not survive in a world of *reflexive modernization* – a world of intensified social reflexivity. Reflexive citizens, responding to a new social universe of global uncertainties, become aware of, and may subvert, the economic incentives that are supposed to mobilize their behaviour. Keynesianism, like some forms of policy which helped structure the welfare state, presumes a citizenry with more stable lifestyle habits than are characteristic of a globalized universe of high reflexivity. (Giddens 1994: 42)

Since we are not given a shred of empirical support for the supposed link between lifestyle instability and the demise of Keynesianism, this remains a rather vacuous statement (see Vandenbroucke 1998). More fundamentally, this way of thinking overlooks the *real* difficulties social democrats have encountered with Keynesian policies in the past, and it makes it hard to engage in an intelligent and productive dialogue with continental social democrats today.

I cannot go through all the arguments here, but let me put it as follows. The identification of 'classical social democracy' with 'effective Keynesianism' relies on hidden but rather questionable assumptions. Once, so it is assumed, we lived in a 'golden age' during which, first, the appropriate policy for social democrats confronted with unemployment was *in all circumstances* some mixture of fiscal and monetary demand expansion organized by governments, and second, Keynesianism, so conceived, was essentially unproblematic in less open economies. Neither of these assumptions is true. In his important work, *Crisis and Choice in European Social Democracy*, Fritz Scharpf neatly identifies various economic problems for which fiscal or monetary demand management has never offered the sole solution. Stagflation, fuelled by cost-push inflation, is one example. Incomes policies were the key additional instrument needed to tackle stagflation, for which close cooperation between governments and unions was necessary (Scharpf 1991: 25–37). Even when confronted with the usual swings of the business cycle successful economic policy depended on the voluntary cooperation of unions and employers. The policy instruments directly available to governments are not sufficient to cope with all economic problems, not even in a closed economy.

I stress this point to eliminate the bizarre idea that 'in the golden era' – pre-globalization, so to speak – social democracy could always successfully rely on the single track of fiscal and monetary demand management by governments to fight unemployment, whatever the problem causing it. Returning to contemporary discussions, the real issue may be formulated as follows. Successful macroeconomic policies require coordination and mutual trust between at least three actors, or sets of actors: budgetary authorities (governments), monetary authorities (central banks), and employers and trade unions who negotiate wage increases. The requirement facing the latter is, more precisely, the acceptance of some discipline concerning the growth of the average wage level in both slack and tight labour markets. The difficulty of achieving coordination and trust between these actors is exacerbated now on the European level, where we will have a multitude and layers of governments, layers of employers and trade union organizations, and one monetary authority. The French, following long-standing pleas by Delors, have a project designed to overcome this difficulty, which they summarize by the idea of '*un gouvernement économique*' – an economic government for Europe. Within the Euro-zone, close economic coordination between governments should create 'un pôle économique', i.e. a point of reference for the Central Bank, and this should, ideally, be supplemented by some forms of Europe-wide collective bargaining. This generates a complex agenda, to which specific proposals concerning coordination between the various Councils of Ministers are added. The former German Minister of Finance, Oskar Lafontaine, referred to the same ideas (Lafontaine 1998: 105), but his rather simplistic and provocative approach to the European economic policy debate has not been helpful.

A sensible reading of this approach, which I cannot pursue in detail here, is that it is structural. Its aim is to create the institutional conditions for a sustainable mix of demand and supply policies, in particular for the kind of flexibility in monetary management exerted by the Fed in the USA. The approach clearly relies on Keynesian insights. But there is no question of encouraging any 'dash for growth' or of 'Keynesian fine-tuning'. In addition, the emphasis is on monetary over fiscal policy. The aim is to create enough trust and coordination between the main actors so that the European central bank can confidently relax monetary policy when it is economically indicated. The essential difficulty in this approach is the perception of an irreversible decline in the coherence and cohesion of collective bargaining and corporatist institutions in Europe. The challenge in that respect is to create new forms of successful national corporatism, and to design a European model that can incorporate the variety of national models. Although optimism of the will should, in these matters, be counterbalanced by pessimism of the intellect, all-out pessimism on the future of collective bargaining is not warranted: the Netherlands provides a well-known example of the possibility of successful neo-corporatism.

Here, then, we have a defining issue for the longer-term future of European social democracy, and a matter for serious debate. The report on European economic policy, presented by the Portuguese Prime Minister, Antonio Guterres, and adopted by the Party of European Socialists in March 1999, illustrates that progress is possible and that potential divisions can be bridged, thanks to open-minded discussion. However, the intellectual framework underpinning the British third way – or at least, the framework that Giddens presents – offers no purchase on this debate. It declares itself uninterested. It asserts that the world has changed so dramatically that textbook macroeconomic analysis and steering have become *irrelevant*. I believe this is not only wrong, but it also hampers New Labour's capacity to engage thoroughly in key debates within European social democracy, such as the management of the Euro, the future of European collective bargaining, the future of budgetary politics, the future of the European model *tout court*.

Social investment replacing social spending?

Convergence on employment-centred welfare reform, centred around the fixed points 1 to 8 given above, also conceals important differences in emphasis within European social democracy. The third fixed point listed above holds that the intelligent welfare state should not only engage in 'social spending' (on benefits), but also in 'social investment' (e.g., in training and education). But I would emphasize that we are not confronted with a principled choice between social investment and social spending. The distinction highlights a pragmatic trade-off between two tracks of redistribution in society, which are both necessary, and we should avoid creating false dichotomies.

It is often suggested that spending on benefits instantiates 'redistribution', while social investment is something entirely different. An intuitive and politically attractive argument supports such a dividing line. It holds that social investment makes everybody better off, while spending on social benefits makes some people better off at the cost of others; hence, the latter is 'redistributive', and the former is not. Although it may be politically convenient, and often analytically correct, it is difficult to maintain that social spending *always* embodies redistribution, so conceived, while social investment *never* does. First, social investment does not come cheap, certainly not in the short run. Even in the longer term, some people may be permanently worse off, as a consequence of reallocating the resources invested in society. To put the same idea in other words, even if social investment raises economic efficiency sufficiently to generate a macroeconomic return, there is no guarantee that each individual citizen will be a net beneficiary. Secondly, some key policies are difficult to classify using this taxonomy: wage subsidies entail both an investment (in human capital because people get work experience thanks to the wage subsidy) and a direct form of redistribution (because some people's taxes are funding an increase in other people's net wages). The reality is that much of social spending and much of what we call social investment appeals to our willingness to redistribute resources, often from identifiable, high-skilled, high-income people, to identifiable, low-skilled, low-income people. And, in setting priorities, we face an inevitable trade-off between those two tracks of redistribution – between increasing benefits for poor people who cannot improve their situation via employment (the retired, the disabled) and investing in jobs and skills for those who can escape poverty by means of employment.

Important changes in the world necessitate important changes in welfare states (cf. fixed points 1 and 2). But the claim that social investment will allow a significant decrease of aggregate social spending reflects a view that, if pursued in practice, can only be achieved through real retrenchment of welfare provisions and social security. It is not consistent with a genuinely social-democratic agenda. This is not to say that we cannot improve the structure of social spending, or that all existing social spending is sacrosanct. But sweeping assertions about the 'inefficiency' of social spending made in the early stages of the British third way debate mistake problems specific to the British welfare state for general defects in all contemporary welfare states. And this, too, hinders meaningful dialogue with modernizing European social democrats on the future of the European model.

3. Shared normative questions

Perhaps it is not only, or even primarily, the world that needs to be reconsidered, but the values of social democracy. Modernizers on the left typically speak of the need to work out new ways of applying 'traditional values in a modern context'. But however reassuring this may sound, it is not necessarily a true reflection of what is going on in the debates on social democracy and the third way. Between foundational values and practical implementation lie standards of justice, that is, normative criteria that indicate in ideal terms what our society must achieve if it is to be just. Many social democrats may now be in the process of reviewing, if not their deepest values, at least their standards of justice. *A priori* I do not consider this a problem. Maybe we *should* revisit and review settled ideas on justice in society. Therefore, I find Tony Blair's insistence on the importance of the discussion of ideas and values most welcome. Although he stresses very much the unchanged character of social-democratic values, he simultaneously makes it quite clear that the discussion is 'about ideas' (Blair 1998: 1).

Participation and social inclusion

One idea which recurs in debate over the third way is that of social inclusion, which is, in turn, linked to that of participation. I propose to begin our discussion of values and standards of justice with this concept of participation, however vague it may at first sight appear.

If we take it that participation is the value underpinning employment policies, we can formulate one cluster of questions, concealed by fixed points 1–8 above, as follows: *what* is it participation *in, why* is that so important, and how do we want to distribute the *benefits and burdens* of the drive towards participation – if we really mean to achieve an inclusive society, that is, a society in which *all* participate?

In practice, references to inclusion and participation focus on a narrow definition of participation, that is, participation in the labour market (see also Oppenheim, Chapter 6). More precisely, for Britain's New Labour government, increasing participation is essentially increasing participation in the private sector of the labour market. (Other European social-democratic governments give a significant role to public sector jobs too.) This reflects a morality of 'supported self-reliance', i.e., a morality stressing both the importance of self-reliance and the need for governments to support the individual's effort to achieve it. Why this focus on paid labour? In part, perhaps because of the beneficial effects it has on the way people structure their lives and integrate into society. More importantly, one should certainly not dismiss the value of non-monetary rewards from participation in the labour market.[2] Labour-market surveys show that many people willingly pay a monetary 'price' – having less overall net income than they would if they were to live on benefits – to obtain the esteem and self-esteem provided by self-reliance. Edmund Phelps' argument for a massive programme of employment subsidies to boost the income of people with low economic productivity explicitly refers to the idea that achieving self-esteem in a market economy can be valuable but quite costly for individuals:

> The measure of cash reward for the *work* supplied by the disadvantaged to the market economy is only their *earnings*. And the *net* reward from this work is only the *excess* of these earnings over the entitlement benefits for which these workers become ineligible as a result of their wage income. Our self-esteem from being self-supporting, not dependent upon the state or kin, hinges on our sense that what we have provided ourselves and our families is largely due to our own efforts. If the net reward is actually negative and large, those low-wage workers with comparably low private wealth may feel themselves too poor to be able to afford the pecuniary sacrifice necessary to 'buy' the self-esteem of being self-supporting. (Phelps 1997: 21–2)

If we really mean it, the inclusive society is not a cheap option. It requires not only extensive investment in education and training, massive subsidies to increase the net income of low-productivity people as Phelps proposes, but also, as Solow (1998) emphasizes, the effective supply of jobs via which people can participate in economic life.

If paid labour is reasonably seen as central to participation and social inclusion, however, we should be wary of identifying these ideas too closely. First, comparative figures on poverty in the working age population make it clear that high employment rates are by no means a sufficient condition of social inclusion. The relative poverty rate for the working age population in the USA is almost twice as high as in Germany or France, and almost four times as high as in Belgium, although a far greater proportion of the working age population has at least one job in the USA. Likewise, poverty at working age appears to be more widespread in Australia, Canada and Britain, all of which are countries with much better employment records than most of the continental European countries (Marx and Verbist 1997: 5; fig. 2 and table 1).

Secondly, if participation is to be a central and overarching value for social democrats, it cannot be limited to participation in the labour market (see Oppenheim, Chapter 6). Constructive participation in the community can be pursued by activities outside the labour market – think, for example, of the role of parents in local schools. In general, care should be regarded as a valuable form of participation in society. A comprehensive view of active participation implies that more be done to allow people to combine work and family life, not only by providing professional childcare, but also by means of flexible systems for short- and long-term parental sabbaticals. Pursuing a comprehensive view of participation suggests even more ambitious propositions. The Dutch social democrats considered introducing an overall 'participation law' in their social security system, covering various activities, ranging from training, job search, to specified socially useful work outside the market (PvdA 1997: 29–30). Anthony Atkinson's proposal for a participation income is a yet more radical proposal of this kind (Atkinson 1995: 301–3; see also Oppenheim, Chapter 6, for a brief account of advantages and drawbacks). If participation or inclusion is to have any meaning for the increasing number of elderly, or for those who cannot contribute productively to society, it must also include a notion of participation in consumption (cf. Atkinson 1998: 24 and 27), hence, decent income levels.

Hopefully these summary remarks show that the goals of participation and inclusion inevitably put both the ideals and the practical politics of redistribution high on the agenda. They do so because huge burdens and benefits are to be distributed in the process of achieving participation and inclusion. Social democracy has to define itself both by its ideals of distributive justice and by its pragmatic capacity to build coalitions between 'winners' and 'losers', as the Dutch social democrat Ad Melkert writes in an interesting contribution on the future of social democracy and the third way (Melkert 1998).

Responsibility and equality

A further, related normative issue confronting the European left concerns our conceptions of citizenship and responsibility. Today, even more than in the past, social democracy needs a moral programme if it is not to become hostage to the conservatism of an 'affluent majority'. I believe a coherent moral programme has to be built around an ethic of responsibility (Vandenbroucke 1990). Although personal responsibility regularly surfaced as a theme in social-democratic discourse during this century, it would be disingenuous to claim that it has always been prominent in our thinking. Blair is right when he says: 'In recent decades, responsibility and duty were the preserve of the Right ... it was a mistake for them ever to become so, for they were powerful forces in the growth of the labour movement in Britain and beyond' (Blair 1998: 4).

I think four features distinguish a responsibility-sensitive conception of social democracy from a market-exchange conception of responsibility. First, in a responsibility-sensitive conception of social democracy the government not only levels the playing field and equips and helps people to confront the market, it is also prepared to change the result of the market reward structure in a more egalitarian direction by means of taxes and subsidies if differential market reward is *not* a true reflection of personal responsibility and effort. Second, in a responsibility-sensitive conception of social democracy the government accepts that it is part of its responsibility to ensure that sufficient opportunities for participation in the labour market do emerge. Third, a responsibility-sensitive social-democratic government takes it that citizens display social responsibility in various forms of participation, not only in the labour market, but also in caring and other social activities that the market does not remunerate. Fourth, 'the easy rhetoric about the moral responsibilities of the poor and the powerless should be more than matched by a more difficult rhetoric about the social obligations of the rich and powerful' (Wright 1996: 147).

It is crucially important not to see the issue in terms of a choice *between* equality and responsibility. Rather, the two ideas must be integrated: distributive justice obtains when – and only when – we reward responsibility in a manner that acknowledges the foundational value of 'equal concern for all'. The development of an appropriately responsibility-sensitive conception of equality has been a major preoccupation of analytical political philosophers in the last two decades. This project has been the focus of many exchanges amongst philosophers like John Rawls, Amartya Sen, Ronald Dworkin, G. A. Cohen, Richard Arneson, John Roemer, Serge Kolm and Brian Barry. Julian Le Grand captures one of the central ideas of modern egalitarian philosophy as follows:

> [O]ur judgements concerning the degree of inequity inherent in a given distribution depend on the extent to which we see that distribution as the outcome of individual choice. If one individual receives less than another owing to her own choice, then the disparity is not considered inequitable; if it arises for reasons beyond her control, then it is inequitable. (Le Grand 1991: 87)

Equality, so conceived, is *not* uniformity, for instance uniformity of income imposed independently of people's personal choices and personal effort. But it is more demanding than meritocracy because it calls into question the fundamental legitimacy of inequalities in 'choice sets' attributable to unequal endowments of natural ability as well as to that attributable to inequality in educational opportunity and in initial endowments of external wealth. Personal skills are the combined result of individual talents and effort to develop those talents. Hence, the market value of your skills is the combined result of luck and choice:

(i) *luck*, first with regard to your original talents, as determined by the genetic endowments with which you are born; and secondly, luck with regard to the market for your skills, i.e., the interaction between the demand for your skills, which is influenced by other people's preferences, and the competing supply of the same skills by other workers;

(ii) *personal choice*, regarding the kind of skills you choose to develop on the basis of your talents, and the effort you put into it.

That these issues are intrinsically difficult does not mean that they can be assumed away. Political discussions about the relevance of personal skills to just rewards necessarily raise basic philosophical questions about the relationship between talent, choice and just desert, questions that lie at the heart of contemporary theorizing about egalitarian justice (cf. Cohen 1989; White 1997; White 1998: 25–6; Chapter 1, this volume).

4. Conclusion: the poverty of theory?

Social-democratic action needs a moral programme nourished by empirical theory (Wright 1996: 51). Having painted his picture of long-term social-democratic convergence, Donald Sassoon concludes on some pessimistic notes, one of which he labels 'the poverty of theory':

> A further negative aspect of convergence is the practical end of an intellectual framework able to guide or inspire the parties of the Left. The European Left can no longer rely on theoretical instruments – such as Marxism or Keynesianism – to find a way out of the present impasse. Here the fault lies not with the politicians but with the intelligentsia. (Sassoon 1998: 96)

I am not sure that the references to Marxism and Keynesianism constitute the best way to illustrate the contemporary intellectual challenge. True, once the idea prevailed that social-democratic action could and should rely on a self-contained body of scientific theory, clearly separated from 'bourgeois' thinking. And it may be the case that after Marxism, some social democrats have embraced Keynesianism as if it were the new social-democratic *passepartout*, to the effect that any criticism or nuance *vis-à-vis* traditional Keynesianism came to be seen as 'neo-liberal'. If so, that was simply a mistake. Does the demise of the belief in a separate, self-contained domain of socialist theory mean that, today, we lack intellectual resources? Not at all. The intellectual resources required to develop both the moral programme and the empirical theory which social democrats need are available in contemporary political philosophy and in social, economic and political theory. They are not available as a neat, unified programme. Connecting with them requires grasping complex and conflicting arguments and empirical evidence. Building bridges between practice and theory is a painstaking exercise. The endeavour is not well served by sweeping generalizations which all too often prevail in our discussions, by the 'glib rhetoric that appeals to those who want to sound sophisticated without engaging in hard thinking' (Krugman 1996: ix). The intellectual challenge, nowadays, is to confront rhetoric – on a variety of subjects such as 'globalization', 'the end of Keynesianism', 'the end of welfare as we know it', or, indeed, 'the coming crisis of capitalism' – with clear thinking and hard facts. The challenge is also to revisit, critically and constructively, our core values. The intellectual resources required to do this are abundantly available. Social democrats are not in want of intellectual resources, even less are they in want of political power today. Two conditions might hamper our common action: lack of open-minded communication across national borders, and reluctance to engage in a thorough debate on ideas. We never had fewer excuses for failure, on any of these accounts.

Notes

1 An earlier version of this essay appeared in A. Gamble and T. Wright, eds, *The New Social Democracy* (Oxford: Blackwell, 1998), whose kind permission to reprint we here acknowledge.

2 Note, though, that one can construe the argument for taking labour-market participation as the central policy objective quite differently. As already indicated, a typical argument in Dutch public discourse, as I read it, holds that increasing labour-market participation is crucial in an ageing society if we want to be able to maintain a certain parity between the benefit levels for the inactive and the average wage of the active. The latter is a much more down-to-earth argument for increased labour-market participation, focusing on the economic viability of a generous welfare state. (See Wetenschappelijke Raad voor het Regeringsbeleid 1997 and van der Veen 1998 for a critical account; but see also WRR 1996 for a combination of economic and other arguments supporting the *'participatieparadigma'*.)

Bibliography

Atkinson, Anthony B. (1995), *Incomes and the Welfare State*, Cambridge University Press, Cambridge.

Atkinson, Anthony B. (1998), *Poverty in Europe*, Blackwell, Oxford.

Aubry, Martine (1998), Intervention au Colloque 'Quelle gauche pour le XXIe siècle?', organisé par 'Action pour le Renouveau Socialiste', Samedi 10 Octobre.

Blair, Tony (1998), *The Third Way: New Politics for the New Century*, Fabian Pamphlet 588, Fabian Society, London.

Cohen, Gerald A. (1989), 'On the Currency of Egalitarian Justice', *Ethics* 99, pp. 912–44.

Commission on Social Justice (1994), *Social Justice: Strategies for National Renewal*, Vintage, London.

Delors, Jacques (1997), *Réflexions et propositions pour un nouveau modèle de développement*, May, Party of European Socialists, mimeo.

European Commission, Direction générale, 'Emploi, relations industrielles et affaires sociales', Direction V/A (1998), *Des lignes directrices á l'action concrète: les plans d'action nationaux pour l'emploi*, May, Luxemburg.

Ferrera, Maurizio (1998), 'The Four "Social Europes": Between Universalism and Selectivity', in Rhodes, Martin and Meny, Yves (eds), *The Future of European Welfare: a New Social Contract?*, Macmillan, London.

Giddens, Anthony (1994), *Beyond Left and Right: the Future of Radical Politics*, Polity Press, Cambridge.

Guterres, A. (1999), *A European Employment Pact for a New European Way*, report adopted by the PES Congress, 2 March, Milan.

Krugman, Paul (1996), *Pop Internationalism*, MIT Press, Cambridge, Mass.

Lafontaine, O. and Müller, C. (1998), *Keine Angst vor der Globalisierung: Wohlstand and Arbeit für alle*, Dietz, Bonn.

Le Grand, Julian (1991), *Equity and Choice: an Essay in Economics and Applied Philosophy*, Harper Collins Academic, London.

Marx, Ive and Verbist, Gerre (1997), *Low-paid Work, the Household Income Package and Poverty*, paper presented at the Lower Conference, Dec. 12–13, London.

Melkert, Ad (1998), 'Over de sociaal-democratie in Europa', *Socialisme & Democratie*, 55, no. 10, pp. 419–25.

Phelps, Edmund S. (1997), *Rewarding Work: How to Restore Participation and Self-Support to Free Enterprise*, Harvard University Press, Cambridge, Mass.

PvdA (1997), *Sociale Zekerheid bij de Tijd: Op weg naar het Congres van 14 en 15 februari 1997*.

Sassoon, Donald (1998), 'Fin-de-Siècle Socialism: the United, Modest Left', *New Left Review*, 227, Jan./Feb., pp. 88–96.

Scharpf, Fritz W. (1991), *Crisis and Choice in European Social Democracy*, Cornell University Press, Ithaca (trans. from German edn, 1987).

Solow, Robert M. (1998), 'Guess Who Pays for Workfare?', *New York Review of Books*, 5 Nov., pp. 27–37.

Van Der Veen, Robert J. (1998), *Participate or Sink: Threshold Equality Behind the Dykes*, paper presented in the ECPR Workshop, *The Uncertain Future of the Welfare State in Europe: Normative Foundations and Sustainability*, Warwick ECPR Joint Sessions, 23–8 March.

Vandenbroucke, Frank (1990), *Over Dromen en Mensen*, Davidsfonds,/Socialistische Standpunten, Leuven/Brussel.

Vandenbroucke, Frank (1997), 'De nieuwe centrum-linkse tijdgeest en zijn beperkingen', *Socialisme & Democratie*, 54, no. 6, pp. 257–65.

Vandenbroucke, Frank (1998), *Globalisation, Inequality, and Social Democracy*, Institute of Public Policy Research, London.

Wetenschappelijke Raad Voor Het Regeringsbeleid (1997), *Van verdelen naar verdienen: Afwegingen voor de sociale zekerheid in de 21ste eeuw*, Sdu Uitgevers, Den Haag.

Wetenschappelijke Raad Voor Het Regeringsbeleid (1996), *Tweedeling in perspectief*, Sdu Uitgevers, Den Haag.

White, Stuart (1997), 'What do Egalitarians Want?', in Franklin, Jane (ed.), *Equality*, IPPR, London, pp. 59–82.

White, Stuart (1998), 'Interpreting the "Third Way": Not One Road, but Many', *Renewal*, 6, no. 2, Spring, pp. 17–30.

Wright, Tony (1996), *Socialisms, Old and New*, Routledge, London.

Zukunftskommission der Friedrich-Ebert-Stiftung (1998), *Wirtschaftliche Leistungsfähigkeit, sozialer Zusammenhalt, ökologische Nachhaltigkeit: Drei Ziele – ein Weg*, Dietz, Bonn.

13

The SPD and the Neue Mitte in Germany

Andreas Busch and Philip Manow

1. Introduction: Schroeder and Blair, birds of a feather?

When on 27 September 1998, Helmut Kohl, a Christian Democract, was voted out of office after 16 years and a Social Democrat, Gerhard Schroeder, took his place, many things pointed to this being an historic event. It was, for example, the first time a sitting Chancellor had been *voted* out of office and the previously governing coalition sent to the opposition benches.[1] After its biggest loss of support ever (6.2 percentage points), the CDU/CSU was left with their smallest share of the vote since 1949 at 35.2 per cent. By contrast, the SPD enjoyed its largest increase ever (4.5 percentage points) and became, at 40.9 per cent, the strongest party in the Bundestag for only the second time since 1972 (Forschungsgruppe Wahlen 1998). A parallel with Labour's landslide victory in May 1997 under Tony Blair naturally comes to mind. And yet it was not only the scenes of jubilation comparable with those in London's Downing Street on 2 May 1997 that were missing from the streets of Bonn and Berlin.[2] The more time passed after the federal election, the clearer it became that – despite pre-election vows to the contrary and subsequent attempts to appear as birds of the same feather (Blair/Schroeder 1999) – there remain substantial differences between Blair's New Labour and Schroeder's New Centre or Neue Mitte. What explains these differences? And what are the prospects that the Neue Mitte will move beyond a campaign slogan and become a real programme of progressive government?

These are the questions we address in this chapter. First, in section 2, we chart and explain the shifts in the SPD's political strategy during its period in opposition. In section 3, we outline some key features of the German party and political systems which must be taken into account in any realistic assessment of prospects for reform and in any realistic comparison of the SPD under Schroeder with the position of New Labour under Tony Blair. Section 4 explains how differences in institutional contexts between the two countries made for very different degrees of programmatic reform in these two parties during their respective years of opposition, and how the SPD was accordingly obliged to adopt a different, and fundamentally ambiguous, strategy for communicating change in the party (or the appearance of change) to the electorate. One of the main challenges now facing the new Schroeder government is to resolve the 'crisis of inactivity' in the German welfare state. Having explained the basic nature of the problem in section 5, in section 6 we discuss the prospects for reform in this area. Given the various constraints posed by the party and political systems, as explained in the earlier sections of the chapter, we conclude that at present the prospects for fundamental reform are poor. We conclude, in section 7, with some speculations on possible future developments of the Neue Mitte government.

2.   The uncertain strategy of the SPD in opposition

The Labour Party's dominance of the centre-left of British politics was challenged in the 1980s by the SDP/Liberal Alliance, a force to its right. By contrast, the SPD was confronted with an emergent party to its left, namely the Green Party, a development that signalled the appearance of a new 'post-materialist' cleavage in the West German party system.[3] This put the SPD at a severe strategic disadvantage. With a portion of their vote moving to the Greens, the Social Democrats lost their capacity to form a winning two-party coalition (with the exception of a 'grand coalition' with the CDU). Three responses were open to the SPD in this new situation. First, it could try to reintegrate the groups of the New Left which centred mainly around so-called post-materialist issues like ecology and peace; secondly, it could focus, and try to broaden its appeal, on its old materialist core issues (jobs, welfare and so on); thirdly, it could seek a division of labour with the Greens with the aim of forming a coalition with them. During its 16 years in opposition, the SPD tried all three strategies and switched uncertainly between them.

The SPD first tried to integrate the post-materialist left. It revised its defence policy and, in 1986, rejected nuclear power. It advocated a so-called reconciliation between labour and the environment so as to bridge the gap between the unions and the partisans of the 'new politics'. But the latter half of the 1980s also saw an attempt by the 'old' SPD under Rau to emphasize the concerns of the trade unions and the interests of old industries such as steel and coal. At the same time, the 'new' SPD under Lafontaine launched a discussion around economic modernization characterized by calculated attacks on the trade unions and their perceived immobility.[4] While gaining a lot of publicity, however, Lafontaine did not move the SPD's economic programme beyond an emphasis on shortening of work hours. Meanwhile, the party laboriously sought a replacement for the 'Godesberg' programme of 1959. It finished this work in December 1989 only to find the Berlin Wall coming down and the political context completely altered.

After a disastrous election result in 1990, a weak party leadership (first Engholm, then Scharping) tried to refocus the SPD as a party of economic modernization, emphasizing fiscal probity and lower taxes. Following Scharping's fall at the Mannheim party conference in 1995, the new chairman Lafontaine maintained this focus while at the same time paying tribute to traditional party concerns to defend the generous German welfare state and maintain encompassing state responsibility for 'social justice'. Gerhard Schroeder, in the meantime, sharpened his profile through confrontation with the party, criticizing the party leadership, and posing as the 'Genosse der Bosse': the bosses' comrade. He gained his reputation as a reformer primarily in the role of the outsider who loves to provoke the traditional SPD rank and file by continuously putting into question core beliefs of German Social Democracy. In this way, he underscored how little programmatic reform the SPD had undertaken during its long years in opposition.

Schroeder could play this role because he did not depend on the central party machine for his political survival – he had his own power centre in Lower Saxony.[5] In addition, he was adept in his handling of the mass media. As a consequence, the SPD approached the 1998 federal elections with a 'Doppelspitze' (twin leadership) featuring Lafontaine as party chairman and Schroeder as candidate for Chancellor. While many thought that Schroeder–Lafontaine relationship would be a major liability for the election campaign, this dual leadership turned out to be a neat solution to the dilemma of strategic placement between traditional SPD voters and the pool of moderate votes to the right whom the party needed to woo (Alemann 1999: 42). Lafontaine could please the core party clientele, while Schroeder attracted the voters of the centre. The SPD was thus able to fully mobilize their traditional voters and, in addition, to appeal to a significant number of swing voters.[6] This was a crucial precondition of electoral success for a party that usually – given the socio-economic composition of the German electorate – represents a 'structural minority'.

And yet this success has come at a price. Those who voted SPD in September 1998 are now split into two electorates with clearly distinct policy preferences, different socio-economic, age, and gender characteristics, and different degrees of party loyalty (Falter 1999). It seems almost impossible to please one group without disappointing the other. While the younger, less orthodox portion of the SPD voters are smaller in number, their lower level of party loyalty means they can threaten the SPD more credibly with 'exit' than traditional SPD supporters. And this is one constraint that might force the Schroeder government to deliver on the reform promises spelled out in the Neue Mitte campaign platform.

3.   The SPD: a decentralized party in a decentralized political system

Sixteen years of opposition did not deprive the SPD of significant influence in the German political system, and its existence as a viable national party was never really threatened. The main reason is that in these years the SPD managed to expand its power-base in the Länder – Germany's tier of devolved state government. In 1982, the SPD was represented in 4 of 11 Länder governments; at the beginning of 1999, in 13 of 16 Länder governments. As a result of its local strength, from 1991 the Social Democrats continuously held a majority in the second (federal) chamber, the Bundesrat, giving the party considerable influence on most of the bills that passed parliament.[7] The broad administrative responsibilities and exclusive political control of the German states in several policy fields like education, policing and culture, also gave the SPD considerable influence on German public policy at this time. On the other hand, such a situation may create problems of its own. During these years, the SPD never felt obliged to undertake a programmatic rethink comparable to the 'policy review' process that the British Labour Party underwent under Kinnock, Smith and Blair in the years after 1987. Its electoral failure was simply never as evident precisely because there were always limited successes on the Länder level to compensate for failure at the federal level.

Apart from this, it is doubtful whether a policy review process comparable to that in the Labour Party could have been organized within the SPD, for it is a Party without a strong and recognized centre.[8] The contemporary SPD is characterized by organizational decentralization and fragmentation, resting on a high level of local autonomy, exacerbated by the considerable autonomy of the various *Arbeitsgemeinschaften* (e.g., the party youth organization, the women's organization, the various organizations along profession lines, and so on). In addition, left-wing, centrist and right-wing party activists are organized in their own networks. All these different groups act like intra-party interest groups and compete for influence. As a result, the SPD, historically the ideal type of the hierarchic, centralized, bureaucratic, monolithic, ideologically coherent organization (Michels 1927 [1989]), today rather resembles a 'federation of federations of federations of local groups' (Lösche 1993).[9] In addition, the party's social base is now very heterogeneous, encompassing skilled and unskilled workers, academics, small businessmen, managers, students and old-age pensioners. Relatedly, the party now exhibits considerable ideological diversity. This makes it hard to agree on anything except very abstract programmatic generalizations that paper over immediate disagreements but which are difficult to translate into specific policy positions once in government.

Shifting alliances between the various power centres within the party has also resulted in a high level of discontinuity in the party leadership since

the early 1980s. After more than 23 years of Brandt's continuous chairmanship, the quick succession and short-lived chairmanships of Vogel
(1987–91), Engholm (1991–3), Scharping (1993–5) and Lafontaine (1995–9)
are indicative of a lack of direction. A tendency towards programmatic conservatism was the natural outcome of this situation, for leaders who have
to establish their support continuously cannot embark upon a fundamental
reorientation of the party program.

Even if one gets elected to office, what one can do there is constrained by
other features of the political system. Here a fundamental contrast between
Tony Blair's position and that of Gerhard Schroeder lies in the federal character of the German political system, already alluded to in our discussion of
the SPD's relatively decentralized structure. Manfred Schmidt has constructed an indicator measuring the institutional constraints on central government (Schmidt 1995, 1996). On Schmidt's scale, which varies from 0 to
5, the latter indicating the most powerful constraints, Germany scores 5,
while the United Kingdom is among the countries with the fewest constraints, scoring only 1. In such a system, much obviously depends on negotiations and compromises with the other power centres. The same argument
applies to the non-state sector, where trade unions and employers' associations are stronger and have more influence in Germany than in Britain.
Both have traditionally played an important role in coordinating not only
collective bargaining, but also more generally in the sphere of economic
policy. While the trade unions are not as influential in the SPD as they were
in the old Labour Party, they are an important part of it and, especially
under the conditions outlined above, enjoy the status of a blocking minority when it comes to major shifts in (especially economic) strategy.

4. The 'Neue Mitte': a slogan in search of a programme?

But isn't the existence of the Neue Mitte proof that the programmatic
blockage within the SPD has been overcome? We would argue that it isn't.
The 'Neue Mitte' was merely the slogan of the SPD's 1997 campaign platform and *not* one of deeper programmatic dignity. It should therefore not
be overrated. Let us quote the SPD's own definition of the 'Neue Mitte':

> the 'key players' [*Leistungsträger*] in society, who are highly qualified and
> motivated; who bear responsibility in families and schools for education
> and training of children; the far-sighted and committed managers and
> entrepreneurs, the innovative craftsmen and professionals, those who
> dare to start up new companies, the highly qualified computer scientists,
> physicians and engineers, the inventive technicians and scientists, and
> the responsible German trade unions. These are the men and women
> upon which we build. Together with these key players of our society, we
> are the New Centre of Germany. Men and women who look for their

place in employment and society in order to make their contribution also belong to this New Centre, as well as the young people who look for training and employment and all the others who will not accept unemployment and injustice.[10]

This definition is rather unspecific; hardly anyone is excluded. While this creation of the campaign headquarters seems to have been successful in attracting the German electorate (perhaps through the combination of two positively associated words, namely the dynamic 'New' with the dependable, non-extremist 'Centre'), the SPD has not been through a process comparable to New Labour's revision of Clause IV and its commitment to public ownership, which was so crucial in communicating the fact that the party had changed to the British public. In the German case, signalling a new beginning was instead achieved through symbolic personnel decisions. For example, the reformist trade unionist Walter Riester, former deputy head of the IG Metall, was appointed as shadow minister for employment and social affairs early in the campaign, ending the domination of this policy area by the conservative Rudolf Dressler. This was to communicate that new flexibility in employment and social policy was clearly part of the Schroeder agenda. Other such signals included the appointment of the entrepreneur Jost Stollmann as the economics minister-designate, and a publisher, Michael Naumann, as a state minister for culture in the Federal Chancellery.

It may be instructive to know that the phrase 'Neue Mitte' was used by Willy Brandt in the early 1970s in connection with the coalition between the SPD and the FDP of the 'Freiburger Thesen' (the peak of 'social-liberal' influence in the FDP). Brandt situated this Neue Mitte in the tradition of the 1848 revolution. To him, it was characterized by the combination of social rights with liberty and civic duties – ideas which sound similar to New Labour's 'third way' approach.[11] While Schroeder quoted Brandt's views in his speech at the Leipzig party convention in spring 1998, it remains to be seen whether he will succeed in fleshing out the slogan. It should be mentioned, however, that Schroeder was among the SPD's early advocates of cooperation with the Greens which he interpreted (echoing Brandt's view of the social-liberal coalition) as a strategic alliance between wage earners and the enlightened middle class (Schroeder 1985).

If a new coalition between Social Democracy and political liberalism is at the heart of the new politics of the third way (see Beer, Chapter 2, Salvati, Chapter 11), it is important to note that, in contrast to New Labour's co-operative relationship with the Liberal Democrats, there is now little possibility of the SPD forming a coalition with the German Liberal Party, the FDP. The FDP occupied a pivotal position within the German post-war party system and for many years was able to extract an extraordinary political pay-off from its pivotal, coalition-forming position. Twice, in 1969 and

1982, the Liberals effectively determined a change of government by switching coalition partners at the federal level, and no other party has enjoyed office at the federal level for such a long period of time.

However, each time the FDP changed coalition partners at the federal level, they lost a significant part of their electorate and membership. In 1969 the right-wing national liberals left the party, in 1982 the left-wing social liberals did so. As a consequence, the party became more homogenous and programmatically streamlined and less representative of different strands of liberalism. From a pivotal position in the centre, it found itself moving to a position on the neo-liberal right. This development was accentuated by the rise of the Greens which, as noted above, made the SPD a less feasible coalition partner for the FDP, and by the FDP's steady erosion of support at the state level. Participation in coalitions at the state level served for many years as a way for the FDP to avoid over-dependence upon one coalition partner and to signal its willingness to change partners. With the loss of representation in the state parliaments, however, the FDP's room for political manouevre was further restricted. In the last two decades, its *raison d'être* has increasingly come to be that of securing a centre-right majority in a coalition with the Christian Democrats.

5. The context for reform: the problem of welfare without work

Can we expect the Schroeder government to be a radical reforming government? Before we can answer this question, we need to clarify what apparently stands in need of reform and why. Here we focus specifically on the problems of the German welfare state and labour market (which, as we shall see, are closely related).

The main problem in the welfare state/labour market nexus lies in the interplay between an 'inactivity trap' and a 'productivity whip' (Hemerijck, Manow, Keesbergen 2000). Under increased competitive pressure, firms in a high-wage economy like Germany's can survive only by raising labour productivity. This can be achieved through high-quality vocational training and education, labour-saving investments and by laying off less productive, more 'expensive', mostly older workers. The latter strategy drives up social security spending and this, in turn, drives up payroll taxes (social insurance contributions), which account for most welfare state revenue in a continental welfare state. Higher non-wage labour costs in turn put renewed upward pressure on wages. In this way, a virtuous cycle of productivity growth has the potential to turn into a vicious cycle of rising labour costs, dismissal of less productive workers, stagnant or declining employment, rising social security costs, requiring further productivity increases, leading to another round of dismissals, and so on: a spiral of 'welfare without work' (Esping Andersen 1996). Moreover, if service sector wages are linked to wage growth in the high productivity tradables sector, or if a high 'reservation wage' blocks downward adjustment of wages in the service sector, job growth in the labour-intensive public and private sector services is frustrated, especially at the lower end of the labour market. Consequently, many citizens find themselves unable to gain access to the formal labour market because of the high costs of job creation, a direct consequence of the payroll financing of social security. The social security system at the same time offers numerous and generous pathways into non-employment, allowing employers and unions conveniently to externalize the costs of adjustment in the high productivity tradables sector of the economy upon the welfare state. A new cleavage between labour market insiders and outsiders is the result. In the German case, the problem is exacerbated by population ageing and the associated increase in the age-dependency ratio which will exert further upward pressure on social security spending, payroll taxes and labour costs over the long term.

What can be done in the face of these problems? To what extent can we expect the Schroeder government to offer a bold and radical response to the problem of 'welfare without work'?

6.   The difficulties of reforming the German welfare state

When the neo-liberal FDP enjoyed a sequence of successes in Länder elections in the fall of 1995 and spring of 1996, Chancellor Kohl took this as a signal to diverge from the path of incremental welfare reform that had characterized the CDU/FDP coalition for many years. The coalition introduced a bill for 'encouraging growth and employment' in April 1996, and Kohl provoked the breakdown of the 'Alliance for Jobs' talks (Bündnis für Arbeit) in which the government had sought to reach a consensus with the unions on employment and welfare issues (particularly early retirement). The proposed reform package included cuts in sick pay (from 100 to 80 per cent of the usual wage), a loosening of employment protection standards, reduced wage subsidies in the construction industry (Schlechtwettergeld), and a reduction of the old-age insurance replacement ratio from 70 to 64 per cent of net wages. The conflict over state subsidies for the coal and mining industry in early 1997, in which again the FDP pushed the Christian Democratic party to take a more radical stance, added to the impression that the Kohl government had departed from the consensual style of German policy-making.

Seizing this opportunity, the SPD led a campaign of protest. The long-standing charge that the Kohl government had embarked upon a neo-liberal attack on the German consensus model gained credibility for the first time. Consequently, the SPD election campaign promised to take back the few reforms on which the Kohl government finally had been able to agree: sick-pay reform, pension reform, the lowering of the employment protection standards and the cuts in the Schlechtwettergeld. In late 1996 the SPD overtook the CDU in the polls and the Christian Democrats never caught up again with the SPD until election day.

However, while its position on welfare reform helped the SPD to win the 1998 election, the Schroeder government now finds itself caught between its promises and the imperative of reform. The SPD campaign, which was highly successful because it sent out a contradictory message, now has to be translated into coherent policy of the red-green coalition. Efforts to this end face substantial obstacles due to the features of the party and political systems described in earlier sections of this chapter. The following points illustrate the difficulties faced by the new government:

1) *Schroeder's position as party leader*: Although Schroeder took over the position as party chairman after Lafontaine's surprise resignation in March 1999, this has not significantly improved the Chancellor's grip on his party. He may find it increasingly difficult to get support from the parliamentary party and the SPD as a whole for his policies. While Schroeder may benefit from spells of opposition weakness, it remains to be seen how strong support within the SPD is for him once his aura as a political manager gets its first scratches and once the opposition has managed to consolidate itself again.

2) *Opposition from state governments*: Where far-reaching reforms stir up electoral protest, party politicians at the state level are motivated to oppose the central government no matter what its colour. The poor results of the SPD in the EU elections of June 1999 and in the state elections in Hesse in February 1999, where a red-green coalition was voted out of office only four months after winning office in Bonn, are the first warnings that Schroeder might soon be confronted with mounting opposition from the ranks of the SPD-Länder prime ministers. Moreover, after the loss of Hesse, the majority of the SPD-Green coalition in the important second chamber (Bundesrat) was lost; the federal government now has to convince Länder governments where CDU or FDP are represented to vote for their proposals. This, however, may also improve Schroeder's room for manoeuvre since the necessity of compromise with the opposition can be used to keep the left wing of the SPD and the Greens at bay.

3) *Limited policy expertise*: Because social insurance is almost entirely the responsibility of central government, policy thinking in this area was left to the parliamentary party during the SPD's period of opposition. Here, normative maximalism often ruled supreme over political pragmatism. The major pension reform, scheduled for the second half of the government's term, will pose a much more serious challenge to the Schroeder government than the recently successfully enacted tax reform, since most resistance against the painful cuts is located within the party in the many remaining pckets of 'old Labour' orthodoxy, with its traditional plea for

184 New Labour: the Progressive Future?

massive state intervention and large-scale redistribution. In contrast to their stance on tax reform, the CDU will have no genuine interest in becoming part of an all-party coalition which would diffuse political blame for the painful adjustment of past political promises to today's realities of low growth and rapid population ageing.

4) *Weakness of the Greens*: The expertise and political weight of the Greens is still too weak in this domain to fulfil the function which the FDP at times had in the coalitions with either the Christian or Social Democrats: namely to force these two catch-all parties to engage in (sometimes painful) welfare reforms or to prevent too blatant attempts to achieve electoral success through government welfare handouts.

5) *Alliance for Jobs – an unpromising terrain for reform*: Schroeder has tried to make the 'Alliance for Jobs' talks (Bündnis für Arbeit) with the unions and employer associations, centrally coordinated by the Chancellery, the key reform platform of his government. This is, however, a risky strategy, because Schroeder, while having the opportunity of claiming credit if the alliance talks become a success, will have no chance of scapegoating if the talks are a failure. As long as unions and employers know that Schroeder needs a success in the Bündnis talks, they can blackmail him so that an agreement gets extremely costly, in fact so costly, that a 'success' will not come near to the kind of far-reaching reforms that Schroeder and with him most observers of the German political economy deem necessary.

Unions and employers have been and remain the most important beneficiaries of the generous, occupation-based and corporatistically administered German welfare state. They thus have very strong vested interests in keeping large parts, in fact the most problematic parts (like early retirement), of the current system. Given that: (1) employers have declared that they are unable to promise the creation of a fixed number of new jobs in the Alliance talks; that (2) the unions declared that they are not willing to talk about wages because this falls into the domain of bipartite collective bargaining covered by the principle of *Tarifautonomie* (autonomy of the social partners); and that (3) the Schroeder government already reversed the welfare retrenchment measures of the late Kohl government, so denying itself a major bargaining chip in the Alliance talks, it is hard to see how a major political exchange between unions, employers and the government can take place. The main issue in the talks – the establishment of joint sectoral funds that would finance generous early retirement programmes – is perfectly in line with the traditional response of the German welfare state and social partners to unfavourable economic conditions: the reduction of the supply of labour through various forms of heavily state-subsidized non-employment. But, as suggested above, these 'negative supply-side policies', as Claus Offe has termed them, are the main cause of the current economic problems (Esping-Andersen 1996, Manow/Seils 1999). They certainly do not represent their solution. It has to be emphasized, though, that the chemical workers union, the metal workers union, and the public workers union in the 1999/2000 wage round all showed a surprisingly high degree of restraint. How much this will motivate employers to reciprocate with the creation of new jobs or the training of more apprentices remains to be seen.

Thus, while the government may initially have seen the Alliance for Jobs talks as a good opportunity to circumvent the SPD and to avoid an open tussle between party 'modernizers' and 'traditionalists', there is now some recognition that the talks might also contain a quite substantial political risk. This is the main reason why efforts of the new Minister of Finance, Hans Eichel, to consolidate the budget were quickly seized upon as the prime opportunity to discipline the SPD and to push through major social-policy reforms – camouflaged as fiscal stabilization – against a reluctant parliamentary party and much protest among the party rank-and-file. After only three months in office, Hans Eichel presented an extremely ambitious consolidation programme with the aim of cutting the budget deficit by some 150 billion DM in the next 4 years (Ministry of Finance 1999). Against considerable grumbling within the party, the project of 'renewing Germany' with a 'future programme to secure employment, growth and social stability' incorporated major cuts in the domain of social policy. Since the Ministry of Labour has by far the biggest budget of all ministries, it has to contribute 12.5 billion to the 30 billion which the Minister of Finance wants to save in the 2000 budget alone.[12]

Yet, While strict fiscal discipline is valued quite highly in the German political culture, it is questionable how long the appeal to 'sound fiscal policy' as a high political priority can defuse full and proper debate about welfare reforms. After all, the immediate consequences of Eichel's 'renewal programme' for social policy are quite substantial: in a very controversial move, pensions have been temporarily linked to inflation instead of earnings growth. One of the first measures of the Schroeder government was to suspend the so-called demographic formula, introduced by the previous Kohl government, which would have ensured some downward adjustment in pension entitlements as old-age dependency ratios become more unfavourable. But having delivered on this election promise, the Schroeder government was pressed to find another way to reform the pension system, since rising social insurance contributions would sabotage the efforts of the red/green coalition to lower non-wage labour costs in order to stimulate job growth and to fight mass unemployment. Needless to say, cuts in entitlements lack popularity, especially among the SPD clientele. SPD state prime ministers like Klimmt in Saarland or Stolpe in Brandenburg, who had to stand for re-election in September 1999, were quickly alarmed by surveys which forecast that the SPD will suffer massive losses at the polls, and only the CDU scandal helped stop the downward trend – observable in Saarland and Brandenburg – in the elections in Northrhine-Westphalia and Schleswig-Holstein in spring 2000.

7.   Conclusion: the remaining absence of strategic consensus

Although pockets of 'old Labour' resistance continue to exist, the New Labour modernizers are clearly in a hegemonic position in the party that forms the British government. Whether the same holds true for the SPD is not yet certain. The SPD of the Neue Mitte government still is not a homogenous party united behind a single programme. There are still different camps that continue to exist within the party. One may loosely label them the modernizers and the traditionalists, with the conflict emerging most clearly in the areas of social and economic policy. While in the former area the traditionalists oppose all the substantial changes to the existing welfare state that the modernizers deem necessary, in the latter those advocating a Keynesian approach (lowering unemployment through expansion of aggregate demand, but through tax cuts for lower incomes rather than state spending programmes) are pitted against those who want to follow a 'supply-side policy of the left' (with the state playing the role of an 'activator' and 'facilitator' for private business, but not more).[13] But after the resignation of Lafontaine, Hombach's departure from the Chancellery,[14] and Dressler's acceptance of the post of German ambassador to Israel, the respective camps are left without their longtime respected leaders. In theory, this could be an opportunity for agreement and unification. While the heated intra-party debate about the third way paper that Blair and Schroeder prepared for the 1999 EU elections (Blair/Schroeder 1999) initially made this solution seem unlikely, prospects improved after a string of disastrous Länder election results in the summer and autumn of 1999 which made very clear the electoral consequences of party disunity. With Lafontaine having left the left wing of the party vacant, Schroeder moved to the centre, no longer putting quite as much emphasis on economic issues and starting to put the issue of 'social justice' to the fore instead. Federal aid for the ailing Holzmann construction giant was more of symbolic than substantial significance. A well-managed party convention in December 1999 reinforced the impression of regained unity, with the party eager to bury differences before the crucial Land election in North-Rhine Westphalia in spring 2000, Germany's most populous state, and a traditional SPD stronghold. Besides these internal changes, the the SPD's revival was helped by the drawn-out party finance scandal of the CDU that emerged in December 1999, paralysing the opposition completely for a couple of months and resulting in a leadership change in that party.

But if the SPD in the summer of 2000 is in a better position than a year ago, that only proves that politics is a volatile business. Nothing succeeds like success, but given its structures and traditions as we described them in this chapter, the party is still resting on shaky foundations. It remains to be seen whether it will be able to agree on a course that is acceptable to a broad majority of its membership while at the same time proving successful for the government. Given that the coalition partner, the Green Party, is occupied with a similar strategic debate (which pits those who openly claim successorship to the FDP's place in the party system against those who want to retain some degree of fundamentalist opposition even while in government), and that many of the SPD's structural problems such as a weak leadership and structural fragmentation apply at least as much to the Greens, scepticism remains about the prospects of the Neue Mitte government. Chancellor Schroeder's abilities to integrate his party and his coalition will be tested to the fullest. Only if his leadership is not even challenged in a crisis, will he really have gained command of his ship.

Notes

1 In 1982, the change in government was the result of the Liberals, the FDP, switching partners; in 1969, the SPD switched partners, albeit after an election.

2 The absence of jubilant crowds is perhaps explained by the fact that 49 per cent of Germans remained opposed to the prospect of a red-green coalition, including 27 per cent of the SPD's own voters (Forschungsgruppe Wahlen 1998).

3 This is a somewhat simplified representation for the sake of highlighting differences. For a detailed exposition of the development of the German Left see Markovits and Gorski (1997).

4 A good outline of the latter position is given in Lafontaine (1989), which not only contains a summary of Lafontaine's then position, but also a variety of reactions to them from political friends and opponents as well as trade unionists and businessmen.

5 The same is also true for many of the SPD's other political leaders. Rau, for example, as the prime minister of Northrhine-Westfalia also very much enjoyed his own power base, as did many of the other Länder prime ministers.

6 Nearly 4 million of the 1998 SPD voters had voted for the CDU and 850,000 for the FDP in 1994 (Falter 1999: 11).

7 60–70 per cent of all federal laws need the consent of the majority of the Länder.

8 This holds true at least during times in which the SPD is in opposition at the federal level, for reasons given in this section. Whether this will change after the election victory and especially after Chancellor Schroeder has also taken over the party chairmanship, remains to be seen.

9 As in any true federation, this also has fiscal consequences: the central party organization obtains only approximately 15 per cent of the members' fees, while the rest goes to the local, subregional and regional organizations. In terms of donations received, the situation is even worse: not even 5 per cent of all donations go to the central level (Lösche 1993: 42).

10 Authors' translation from SPD 1998: 13.

11 Brandt's thoughts, originally published in his 1973 book *Über den Tag hinaus*, are reprinted in Brandt (1998).

12 Further savings of 38.4, 41.9 and 49.3 billion DM are projected in 2001, 2002 and 2003 respectively; each time the Labour Ministry is supposed to contribute

the biggest share with 17.1 (44.5 %), 17 (40.6 %) and 20.3 billion DM (41.2 % of total savings) between 2001 and 2003.

13 The two respective views are best set out in Lafontaine/Mueller 1998 and Hombach 1998.

14 Hombach's departure to the post of coordinator of the EU Balkan stability pact in July 1999 was accompanied by rumours about incorrectness in the financing of his house (one cannot but smile at the parallel with the fate of New Labour's spin doctor-in-chief, Peter Mandelson). Lafontaine, in the meantime, has gone into hiding. Should be reemerge, he would have considerable power to hurt Schroeder and the modernizers were he to head the party's internal opposition.

References

Alemann, Ulrich von, 1999: Der Wahlsieg der SPD von 1998: Politische Achsenverschiebung oder glücklicher Ausreifler? In Oskar Niedermayer (ed.), *Die Parteien nach der Bundestagswahl 1998*. Opladen: Leske and Budrich, 37–62.

Blair, Tony and Gerhard Schroeder, 1999: *Europe: The Third Way / Die Neue Mitte*, London: The Labour Party.

Brandt, Willy, 1998: 'SPD und FDP in der Tradition von 1848'. In *Neue Gesellschaft / Frankfurter Hefte*, 6, 496–8.

Esping-Andersen, G., 1996: 'The Impasse of Labor Shedding and Welfare without Work in the Continental Welfare States'. In Esping-Andersen (ed.), *Welfare States in Transition*, London: Sage.

Falter, Jürgen W., 1999: 'Die zwei Wählerschaften der SPD'. In *Frankfurter Allgemeine Zeitung*, 12. Feb. 1999, p. 11.

Forschungsgruppe Wahlen, 1998: *Bundestagswahl 1998: Eine Analyse der Wahl vom 27 September 1998*. Mannheim: Forschungsgruppe Wahlen e.V.

Hombach, Bodo, 1998: *Aufbruch: Die Politik der Neuen Mitte*. München, Düsseldorf: Econ.

Hemerijck, Anton and Philip Manow, 1998: 'The Experience of Negotiated Reform in the Dutch and German Welfare State'. Paper presented at the conference on 'Varieties of Welfare Capitalism', June 1998, Max Plank Institute for the Study of Societies, Cologne.

Hemerijck, Anton, Philip Manow, and Kers van Keesbergen, 2000: 'Welfare without Work? Divergent Experiences of Reform in Germany and the Netherlands'. In Stein Kuhle (ed.), *The Survival of the European Welfare State*. London: Routledge.

Lafontaine, Oskar, 1989: *Das Lied vom Teilen: Die Debatte über Arbeit und politischen Neubeginn*. Hamburg: Hoffmann und Campe.

Lafontaine, Oskar and Christa Müller, 1998: *Keine Angst vor der Globalisierung: Wohlstand und Arbeit für alle*. Bonn: Dietz.

Lüsche, Peter, 1993: '"Lose verkoppelte Anarchie": Zur aktuellen Situation von Volksparteien am Beispiel der SPD'. In *Aus Politik und Zeitgeschichte*, B 34, 34–45.

Manow, Philip and Eric, Seils, 1999: 'Adjusting Badly: the German Welfare State, Structural Change and the Open Economy'. In Fritz W. Schmidt and Vivien A. Schmidt (eds), *From Vulnerability to Competitiveness: Welfare and Work in the Open Economy*. New York: Oxford University Press.

Markovits, Andrei S. and Philip S. Gorski, 1997: *Grün schlögt Rot: Die deutsche Linke nach 1945*. Hamburg: Rotbuch.

Michels, Robert, 1927 [1989]: *Zur Soziologie des Parteienlebens in der modernen Demokratie*. Stuttgart: Kröner.

Ministry of Finance, 1999: *Renewing Germany: Future Programme to Secure Employment, Growth and Social Stability.* http://www.bundesfinanzministerium.de/Haush99/future-programme.html

Schmidt, Manfred G., 1995: *Demokratietheorien: Eine Einführung.* Opladen: Leske and Budrich.

Schmidt, Manfred G., 1996: 'When Parties Matter: A Review of the Possibilities and Limits of Partisan Influence on Public Policy'. In *European Journal of Political Research*, 30, 155–83.

Schroeder, Gerhard, 1985: 'Das Mifltrauen praktisch überwinden: Für eine Politik der ökologischen Veränderung'. In Wolfram Bickerich, *SPD und Grüne: Das neue Bündnis?* Reinbek: Rowohlt.

SPD, 1998: *Arbeit, Innovation und Gerechtigkeit: SPD-Programm für die Bundestagswahl 1998.* Bonn: Vorstand der SPD.

14
Dutch Lessons in Social Pragmatism
Anton Hemerijck and Jelle Visser

1. A Dutch miracle?

The 'Dutch model' has become a catchphrase for progressive European politicians pondering the possibilities of a new 'third way' capitalism that reconciles employment growth with equity in an era of economic internationalization. The key proponents of the third way – Tony Blair, Bill Clinton, and more recently Gerhard Schroeder – all admire the Dutch policy mix of fiscal consolidation, wage moderation, and consensual welfare and labour-market reform which has maintained overall social security. The Netherlands, they observe, is the only EU member state to have more than halved its unemployment rate during the past decade, from over 13 per cent in 1983 to 4 per cent in 1998, while the EU average has continued to hover at around 10 per cent (OECD 1999). The average annual rate of job growth during the past decade and a half has been 1.8 per cent, accelerating to 2.2 per cent in 1997 and 1998, far above the 0.4 per cent EU average.

The Dutch experience clearly contradicts pessimistic forecasts of jobless growth, 'welfare without work' and the end of full employment. The extraordinary growth of part-time employment has facilitated the massive entry of women into the labour force, and the replacement of older workers by younger, cheaper and possibly more flexible and skilled workers. Part-time jobs account for three-quarters of the job growth since 1983. Part-time employment has surged from less than 15 per cent of employment in 1975 to 30 per cent in 1998, a share well above that of any other OECD country (OECD 1999). Just over 75 per cent of part-time jobs are held by women and almost 55 per cent of all female workers are employed part-time. The incidence of part-time work among men is, at 12.4 per cent, the highest among OECD countries (OECD 1999). The Netherlands has the highest rate of part-timers among young people in Europe (25 per cent), which suggests that entry into the labour market is commonly channelled through part-time work. With some delay, the Dutch trade unions have come around in support of these changes and taken a positive attitude towards part-time employment and labour-market flexibility.

The growth of female participation, clearly related to the part-time revolution, is surely the most dramatic development here. Female labour-force participation has historically been extremely low in the Netherlands in comparison to most OECD countries. But participation of women in the labour market increased from under 35 per cent in 1983 to almost 63 per cent in 1998, the strongest rise of any OECD country. Growth in participation is concentrated among women who are either married or cohabiting: they now represent a quarter of the active labour force. The majority of working women find employment in the service industries. The demand for a flexible workforce in the service sector coheres with a general preference among women to work part-time. As a consequence of the growth in women's employment, there is now also a growing interest in part-time work among men who wish to combine paid work with unpaid family care. It should be emphasized, however, that even with the increase in part-time work and women's participation, the average annual hours worked per worker has come down significantly since 1973. And while net labour-market participation increased from 52 per cent to almost 70 per cent between 1983 and 1998, participation in full-time equivalents is, at 50 per cent, still lower than neighbouring countries.

Dutch job growth is less associated than the US 'job machine' with sharp increases in wage dispersion and income inequality. By and large, although incomes inequality has increased over the past decade, the Dutch welfare state still ranks among the most generous. Unemployment and social assistance benefits are among the highest in the OECD area. After Belgium, the Netherlands has the lowest poverty rates. In terms of wage dispersion the Netherlands ranks behind Sweden, Denmark, Belgium and Germany. With respect to the distribution of disposable household income, measured by the Gini coefficient, the Netherlands comes again slightly below Sweden, Belgium, Denmark and Germany. The Netherlands thus contrasts with Britain and the US which display very low level of welfare benefits, high and increasing poverty rates, high levels of wage dispersion, and a comparatively inegalitarian distribution of household income (Visser and Hemerijck 1997; Hemerijck and Schludi 1999).

However, while the Dutch job miracle represents a significant departure both from the scenario of jobless growth and the scenario of job growth at the expense of equity, all that glistens is not gold. While the unemployment rate is low at just over 4 per cent, the level of structural inactivity, including all unemployed and inactive persons of working age receiving a social security benefit and persons enrolled in special job creation programmes, although declining in absolute and relative terms, remains high at 20 per cent of the current labour force (OECD 1998). As said, the bulk of new jobs are part-time, sometimes for a very limited number of hours.

Labour-force participation rates of older males (aged 55–64) is still among the lowest in Europe. Long-term unemployment (unemployment for one year or more) has started to fall, but still accounts for about 45 per cent of all unemployment. Unemployment is still two to three times the national average amongst the low-skilled. New jobs have gone predominantly to younger and better skilled recruits to the labour market. Thus, the youth unemployment rate has fallen below the national average for the first time in two decades. In short, the employment success and labour-market performance of the Netherlands is relative, and needs to be put against the background of the dismal experience of the early 1980s and the lacklustre performance of most neighbouring European countries today. There is no full employment yet and the present state of nearly full part-time employment may be judged a second-best solution only.

Does the miraculous recovery of the Dutch welfare state make it an obvious model for progressive governments elsewhere as they seek to improve employment–equity trade-offs? Perhaps. The miraculous employment performance of the Netherlands reveals a clear departure from the current unemployment malaise in the European Union. Where there are so few examples of strong job growth in western Europe, and so few signs that it is possible consensually to adjust the institutional, social and mental pattern of a passive welfare state, the Dutch example invites closer scrutiny. Although the Dutch 'miracle' has only recently attracted international attention, it has its basis in policy changes in the early 1980s. For a full explanation we must study the combination of policy problems, responses, politics and institutional capacities over the past decades in four different policy areas: macroeconomic policy, industrial relations, social security, and labour-market policy. In the next section we will trace the politics of the steady self-transformation of the Dutch welfare state in four stages: (1) the shift to a hard-currency regime and fiscal consolidation; (2) the resurgence of organized wage moderation; (3) path-breaking social security reform; and (4) new active labour-market policy.

From the outset, it should be emphasized that the institutional capacities of the Dutch political system are, unlike the Westminster model, critically constrained by the need for consensus and cooperation between coalition parties in government and parliament. Moreover, in the Netherlands policy-making authorities are often shared with non-state organized interests. This is especially true in the areas of social and economic regulation, where trade union and employer representatives participate in firmly established boards for consultation and negotiation, like the bipartite Foundation of Labour (STAR, Stichting van de Arbeid) and the tripartite Social-Economic Council (Sociaal Economische Raad, SER), often supported by statistical analyses of the independent Central Planning Bureau (Centraal Planbureau, CPB). All three institutions are products of the immediate post-war decade of economic reconstruction. The upshot of coalition politics and social partnership in the Netherlands is that policy change is critically dependent upon agreement between coalition partners in government, while relying on important measures of consensual support from the social partners. This clearly restricts the state's autonomy to respond to external shocks and societal demands and, as a consequence, encourages Dutch policy-makers to follow the more feasible path of 'negotiated change'.

In the final section we consider what lessons can be learnt from the Dutch experience, both with respect to the content of public policy and the process of negotiated policy change.

2. The gradual transformation from 'Dutch disease' to 'Dutch miracle'

2.1 Stage 1: the 'Dutch disease': unemployment, fiscal crisis and the profit squeeze

The first oil price shock of 1973 undermined any existing political consensus in the Netherlands over social and economic policy. A leftist government (1973–7), headed by the social democrat Joop den Uyl, chose to fight the first oil crisis with a Keynesian strategy of fiscal stimulation. However, given the strong commitment to trade liberalization, the Dutch independent central bank (De Nederlandsche Bank, DNB) at the same time endorsed a hard-currency policy by joining the European exchange rate stablization mechanism (the 'snake'). Under these circumstances, Keynesian reflation floundered as the unions proved unable to support the government's loose budget policy with wage moderation (Hemerijck 1995). Moderation was made difficult by the fact that private-sector wage agreements contained automatic 'price escalators'. Moreover, the minimum wage, public-sector wages and the level of social security benefits were all tied to the outcome of private-sector wage negotiations, making the government's fiscal policy a prisoner of wage bargains struck by the unions and private-sector employers. As unemployment and other demands on the public purse rose, the Den Uyl government used windfall profits from natural gas to plug the gap between revenue and expenditure. This stimulated consumer demand for goods and services, but also added to upward pressure on wages. Moreover, gas exports led to the appreciation of the guilder, putting Dutch industry at a severe competitive disadvantage.

The social democrats were followed in office by a weak coalition government of the centre-right led by the Catholic Andries Van Agt (1977–81). It too struggled unsuccessfully to get public finances and wage increases under control amidst corporate bankruptcies and rising levels of unemployment. The years between 1976 and 1982 were a protracted policy stalemate. The central bank stuck to its hard-currency policy and became ever more stubborn when it became apparent that the government had in fact lost control over wage-setting and public finance. Neither the government, nor the trade unions, and perhaps not even the president of the central bank, understood how much a hard-currency policy together with a loose budget policy without wage restraint would hurt competitiveness, engendering a vicious circle of a profit squeeze, weak investments, capital flight and rising unemployment.

2.2 Stage 2: Wassenaar and the resurgence of organized wage moderation

The switch to very high real interest rates by monetary authorities in the US, Britain and Germany in the wake of the second OPEC oil price shock (1979/80) intensified the need for wage restraint in order to meet the higher profit requirements of Dutch firms. Having failed to respond adequately to the first oil shock, the Netherlands experienced a far more severe recession than most other OECD countries. Economic growth turned negative, many sectors suffered from overcapacity, and 1 in 25 manufacturing firms went bankrupt. Unemployment soared to a record 800,000 in 1984 and its rise seemed unstoppable. The unions lost 17 per cent of their members. Union density plummeted and stood at a mere 25 per cent by 1987 compared to 35 per cent before 1980.

In this context of growing crisis, a new centre-right coalition of Christian Democrats and conservative liberals took office in 1982 under Ruud Lubbers. The Lubbers government (1982–6) made clear that it would no longer wait for the social partners to exercise wage restraint. It took the crucial step of insulating government spending from the outcomes of collective bargaining by ending the price indexation of wages and the statutory couplings between private-sector wage increases on the one hand and increases in public-sector wages and social security benefits on the other. With unemployment at a post-war record and membership declining rapidly, the unions were not in a position to resist. Employers' organizations, on the other hand, feared political interference in the form of a proposed statutory reduction of the working week. Under these intense pressures, the unions and employers finally came to an agreement in 1982 in the form of the so-called 'Wassenaar Accord'. In policy terms, the most important element of the Accord was the agreement between unions and employers that the creation of new jobs required a higher level of investment which in turn required a higher level of profitability and thus wage restraint.

The Wassenaar Accord inaugurated an almost uninterrupted period of wage restraint. Estimations of the Central Planning Bureau are that over 60 per cent of job creation in the last decade is due to this wage moderation (CPB 1995). While wage restraint in itself helps to preserve and create jobs, an additional pay-off was required to make corporatist adjustment tangible for the trade union rank and file. Over the last decade the trade unions have negotiated a cost-neutral reduction of the average working week from 40 to 37.5 hours. But a process of across-the-board labour time reduction came to halt in the mid-1980s and the emphasis shifted gradually towards part-time work as the main tool for creating jobs and redistributing employment (Visser 1999). With a brief interruption around 1990, wage constraint continued into the 1990s, helped by a reduction in taxes and by the discipline of the central bank's continuing hard-currency policy (which in turn was made more credible by continued wage moderation). Success – the recovery of profitability, strong job growth, and substantial union membership growth after a decade of decline – has fed back into greater confidence in the strategy of organized wage restraint.

The new mix of macroeconomic policy and wage-setting also changed the institutional relations and responsibilities between the social partners and the state. Since the Wassenaar Accord there has been no direct political intervention in wage-setting. The role of the national employer organizations and unions is by and large confined to redirecting sector-level bargainers towards economy-wide wage restraint. The greater the consensus at the central level, the smoother the bargaining at the sectoral level (Traxler 1990). But although the state plays a considerably less dominant role in collective bargaining, it retains an important degree of leverage over the social partners (this is what Scharpf 1993 terms the 'shadow of hierarchy'). The Minister of Social Affairs and Employment has the authority, derived from pre-war legislation, to declare collective bargaining agreements legally binding for all workers and employers in a certain branch of industry, whether they are unionized or not. This provision remains a treasured policy instrument and is crucial for securing economy-wide wage restraint. It implies the power to declare that (parts of) collective agreements are not generally binding. The Minister has the right to refuse a request for extension when the content of the agreement is not in line with public-policy interests.

2.3 Stage 3: responding to the crisis of inactivity: reform of the social security system

The Dutch social security system, as in many other EU countries, is centred on employment-related social security programmes which are geared towards income replacement and targeted at the (male) bread-winner in order to safeguard traditional family patterns (Kersbergen 1995). As the key financiers of the system (through premiums and contributions), the social partners are heavily involved in the management, administration and implementation of social security provisions. In the 1980s it became clear that the social partners were using their position in the system to externalize the costs of economic adjustment, leading to an uncontrollable growth in the volume of social security claimants. Under the tougher competitive pressures of the 1980s, Dutch firms were forced to raise labour productivity and often did so by laying off less productive, mostly older, workers. Social security contributions had to rise to cover the costs of this. But increases in social security costs made further productivity increases necessary, and thus led to subsequent rounds of lay-offs.

At the heart of the problem lay the disability benefits scheme. The rules of the scheme were idiosyncratic in four ways (Aarts and De Jong 1996). First, the scheme did not make a distinction between different causes of disability. The risk of disability was defined as a social rather than solely an occupational risk. Second, the so-called 'labor market consideration' provision stipulated that in assessing the degree of disability the diminished labour-market opportunities of partially disabled persons should be taken into account. Disability was redefined as a worker's particular incapacity to find a job similar to his former job. If the probability of not finding an 'appropriate' job was evaluated to be high then so too was the degree of disability. Third, disability and sickness benefits were closely related. A person would first receive sickness benefits for a full year and would then qualify for the disability scheme. Sickness pay is primarily financed by employers while disability benefits were entirely financed by contributions of employees. Workers' contributions were set at uniform nation-wide rates and were unrelated to the particular risk factors in different sectors of the economy. Most firms supplemented sickness benefits to cover up to 100 per cent of former earnings and many even supplemented disability benefits to a comparable level for a year or longer.

Finally, the sickness pay and disability benefit schemes were managed by Industrial Boards (Bedrijfsverenigingen) run by the social partners. They were responsible for examining the health of employees. Employers began to use the sickness and disability schemes as a convenient device for 'firing' redundant, particularly older workers without creating social friction. Paying a sickness benefit for one year and then letting the disability scheme take over was calculated as a much cheaper option than maintaining a redundant worker on the regular payroll. Medical doctors could interpret the labour-market clause of the scheme generously. Employees and the unions appreciated that the disability scheme guaranteed generous benefits until retirement.

The result was a steep rise in the number of recipients and exhaustion the scheme's resources. By 1986, those who received a disability benefit outnumbered those with a job amongst the 55–64 age group, disguising a considerable amount of unemployment. In 1987 the second centre-right Lubbers government (1986–9) reformed the social security system, trimming levels and duration of various benefits, but the reforms had little effect and by 1989 the number on disability benefit approached 1 million. Entering his third term in office, heading a centre-left coalition with the social democrat Wim Kok, Lubbers proclaimed that the Netherlands had become a sick country and that 'tough medication' was required. The government proposed radical reforms to discourage the abuse of sickness and disability benefits and to close off other options for subsidized labour shedding. In spite of the emergency and the widespread conviction that radical changes had to be made, the proposal was highly controversial, politically risky and met with stiff resistance. In 1991 nearly a million people demonstrated in the Hague against the reform in what was probably the largest protest demonstration ever. But the reforms were enacted. The duration of disability benefit was substantially shortened. Benefits for persons aged under 50 at the time of the adoption of the new legislation were reduced. Medical re-examinations of beneficiaries were undertaken on the basis of more stringent rules. Finally, a new definition of disability required beneficiaries to accept all 'normal' jobs.

The trade unions tried to circumvent the reforms by demanding supplementary benefits be included in their collective agreements with employers. As a result, the costs of sickness and disability became part and parcel of the collective bargaining process itself and this reinforced the incentives of employers to reduce absenteeism. Privatization of the sickness pay scheme in 1996 has led to a sharp drop in absenteeism.

The legitimacy of these reforms was enhanced by a parliamentary inquiry into the causes of the crisis of social security. The hearings of the Buurmeijer Commission revealed what everybody already knew: social security was being misused by individuals, employers and firms, the Industrial Boards, the unions, and local governments. Its major recommendation was that the implementation of social security ought to be monitored by a government agency that could operate independently of the social partners.

The Christian Democrats and social democrats were nevertheless punished heavily for these reforms in the elections of 1994. Ironically, however, the social democrats emerged as the largest party and, under the leadership of Wim Kok, was able to form the first government since 1918 without any confessional parties: a 'purple' coalition of social democrats, conservative liberals and reformist democrats (1994–8). Undiscouraged, this government stepped up the reform effort by an installing an independent body of control over the social security system. The second purple coalition came into power in 1998, again headed by Wim Kok, and is in the process of partially marketizing the administration of social security in an attempt to improve incentives and curb problems of moral hazard. The possibility for employers to 'opt out' of the disability system and seek private insurance is scheduled for introduction in 2000. This will allow for differentiation in contributions between sectors and firms according to occupational risks. However, it has to be stressed that the disability rate remains comparatively high.

2.4 Stage four: from fighting unemployment to increasing participation

The revived confidence in organized wage moderation, embraced by the social partners, followed by hard won social security reform, initially opposed by unions and employers, slowly but surely led to a shift in the way the problem of the Dutch welfare state is defined. In the late 1980s and early 1990s policy-makers realized that the low level of labour-market participation was the Achilles' heel of the extensive but passive Dutch system of social protection. In 1990, the Netherlands' Scientific Council for Government Policy (Wetenschappelijk Raad voor het Regeringsbeleid, WRR), an academic advisory board with a mandate to carry out future studies in areas it sees fit, proposed to break with the past and advocated a policy of maximizing the rate of labour-market participation as the single most important policy goal of any sustainable welfare state. Gradually, this lesson, though not the specific policy recommendations, was embraced by the government.

The Kok government placed 'jobs, jobs, jobs' in the centre of its social and economic policies when it came to office in 1994. The 'jobs, jobs, and more jobs' slogan is implemented through support for wage and wage cost moderation through lower taxes and social charges, made possible by improved public finances and a broader tax base through the creation of more jobs in domestic services. Additional job programmes and wage subsidies have been designed to further the participation of low-skilled workers.

The increase in labour participation of women with children has enhanced the need and created the extra income for family oriented services, jobs that are mostly taken up by women. Since these services are historically underdeveloped in the public sector, low-cost personnel services have gained importance in the private sector. The popularity of part-time work in the Netherlands is supported by the presence of a basic pension system which makes part-time work more attractive than in countries where pensions are strictly earnings-related. Coverage for social insurance, healthcare and additional pension schemes is now readily available for part-time workers. The new Labour Time Act of 1996 obliges employers to take into consideration the care duties of the employee. At time of writing, there is also a new initiative afoot to create a legal right to work part time.

Labour-market flexibility has become an integral part of the Dutch employment strategy. This should not be mistaken for labour-market deregulation. The Dutch approach is best characterized as geared towards 'flexicurity': matching flexibility with decent levels of social protection for part-time and temporary ('temp') workers. With the liberalization of the employment service in 1990 and 1996, job placement and related services are now provided by the Public Employment Service and commercial agencies, often in cooperation with social insurance organizations and municipalities. The growth of employment through temporary work agencies from virtually nothing in the late 1960s to over 200,000 person years in 1997 has created a large market for temp agencies. Temp agencies are increasingly involved in the management of subsidies and job placement. In 1995 unions and employers signed the first proper collective agreements for temporary workers, introducing a right of continued employment and pension insurance after 24 months of service. This agreement formed the basis for an agreement between the central organizations of unions and employers on 'Flexibility and Security', concluded in May 1996. This central agreement paved the way for an overhaul of Dutch dismissal protection law in January 1999. A relaxation of statutory dismissal protection for regular employment contracts (i.e., a longer probation period, more possibilities for negotiated termination-of-employment, but with the possibility of legal appeal) is exchanged for an improvement of the rights of temporary workers (e.g., continued employment after two years, pension contributions and social security rights).

3. Lessons from the Dutch experience

At the end of the twentieth century there is much anxiety over the future of the welfare state in Europe. Critics point out that European welfare capitalism has accumulated a vast array of labour-market rigidities, impeding flexible adjustment, blocking technological innovation and hampering necessary economic and employment growth (OECD 1994). From this perspective, the recipe is to scale down social protection and deregulate the European labour markets. The Dutch experience shows that it is possible to adjust successfully to the demands of economic internationalization without dismantling the welfare state.

In this paper we have shown that the self-transformation of the Dutch welfare state has its basis in policy change across four different policy areas and how – over time – these changes created the conditions and the demand for one another, and that none on its own could have sufficed in managing the crisis of the Dutch economy and welfare state from the 1970s to the 1990s. Most but not all of these sequentially related policy changes have resulted from lengthy processes of (re-)negotiation between coalition parties and the social partners. In the sequential modernization of the Dutch welfare state there has not at any point in time been a grand design or master plan from which successful policy responses ensued. The Dutch trajectory of adjustment and reform was paved with many contingencies, such as two major recessions, multiple policy failures, a change in the balance of power between capital and labour, a spiralling crisis of social security, and changes in the political landscape from left to right and back again. Likewise, there is no constant 'Dutch culture' of consensual decision-making which only has to be mobilized in times of crisis. Economic adjustment and welfare reform required hard-won changes and slow learning processes, and success was not assured. Moreover, it was not always possible to break policy deadlocks without a significant departure from the prevailing rules of negotiated decision-making. *In short, the Dutch experience of the past fifteen years does not add up to a model of 'third-way' political economy for other countries to emulate. It is best judged as a dynamic, path-dependent and politically contingent learning process* (Visser and Hemerijck 1997).

But this is *not* to say that there are no general lessons to be learnt from the Dutch experience of negotiated reform. In this final section we allow ourselves to speculate, on the basis of the Dutch experience, about the policy options for an employment-friendly and equitable welfare state, which we believe should be at the heart of any discussion of the 'third way'. In the following, we distinguish between two sets of lessons in Dutch social pragmatism: one concerning the content of policy; the second concerning the institutional pros and cons of negotiated change.

3.1 Lessons for policy content

The Dutch experience shows that a stable macroeconomic policy is an important precondition for high levels of economic and employment growth. High inflation and large public deficits are in the long run not compatible with globalized financial markets. There is ample evidence that protracted wage restraint produced an enormous boost to employment, especially in the sheltered sectors. Over time, wage restraint allowed for a rather smooth interplay between wage-setting, monetary, fiscal and tax policy, stimulating economic growth while keeping inflation low. Moreover, the Dutch two-level wage bargaining system has been quite successful in combining moderate wage increases with a high level of flexibility at the micro level. Finally, from the perspective of equity, organized wage restraint seems to have curtailed wage dispersion by putting the brakes on the growth of higher earnings. Moreover, the statutory minimum wage has continued to reduce earning differentials between men and women and between firms and sectors, and to limit the exploitation of low-skilled workers.

The crisis of inactivity in the Netherlands revealed how much the (continental) welfare state model really depends on high levels of employment. Wage moderation, after a first phase of boosting competitiveness in the exposed sector of the economy, can help to create jobs in domestic services. This diminishes the number of people on social security benefits, which in turn allows governments to reduce the tax wedge at or near the minimum wage to get more low-skilled workers into jobs. It is possible to reverse the vicious circle of 'welfare without work' (in which rising labour costs reduce employment which raises social security costs which in turn raises labour costs ...). But it is important that there is 'light at the end of the tunnel': the 'jobs, jobs, and more jobs' strategy is vital, and the promise of these jobs has to be realistic when social programmes, such as the sickness and disability programme in the Netherlands, are drastically curtailed. In this sense, the Wassenaar Accord of 1982 laid the foundation for economic recovery and rediscovery of a job-intensive growth path, which in turn created the political conditions for welfare reform.

Labour-market policies have clearly moved out of the periphery of Dutch social and economic policy-making. Dutch labour-market policy and regulation is in the process of adapting to the new realities of post-industrial working life and family relations. The surge of part-time work, the revolutionary increase in female participation and the rapid expansion of the service sector have, next to wage moderation, contributed enormously to employment growth. If it is true that voluntary part-time work is important for job growth, then raising the status of part-time work through legislation is of the utmost importance.

3.2 Lessons in policy-making: institutional capacities

In general, these policy lessons have more relevance for countries like Belgium, Germany, France and Italy, whose social and economic policy repertoires resemble the Dutch format, than for Britain under New Labour. The exception here, however, may be the 'flexicurity' approach to the labour market, from which New Labour may have something to learn.

Britain, like other Anglo-Saxon welfare states, lacks a tradition of shared and negotiated policy-making. This, we believe, is both the strength and the weakness of the British political system, where single-party majorities and executive power concentration allow for bold political reform efforts. In the Netherlands, it is true, disagreement among and between coalition parties and the social partners can block policy change. However, the Dutch experience also shows that the institutions of negotiated policy-making persuade policy actors to think again, seek a second opinion, manage spill-over effects between different policy areas, and take the social costs of bold reforms into consideration, so as to organize a strong social support base for staying on course. In the rhetoric of the 'third way', civil society and social capital are increasingly singled out as particularly relevant to shaping the new social-policy agenda. Our advice for New Labour would be to suit policy to the word and help to strengthen the institutional capacities of civil society by way of public policy and thus rebuild what was lost during the Thatcher era.

What the Dutch experience of negotiated change shows is that, in order to realize combinations of wage restraint *and* wage flexibility, labour-market flexibility *and* social protection, a smooth interplay between macroeconomic policy, wage-setting, social security and labour-market policy is required. This is more likely to be forthcoming if the government is able to consult and negotiate with robust, nationally organized interest associations with the capacity and willingness to learn and take account of the interests and insights of others. Shared policy authorities can encourage the development of a responsive style of joint problem-solving and conflict resolution, which in turn is likely to reinforce voluntary compliance on the part of the rank and file. It is this type of policy harmonization which experienced a second youth in the Netherlands after 1982 when it moved away from redistributive incomes policy measures towards a focus on the joint improvement of supply-side conditions.

Responsive policy-making is critically dependent on a number of institutional preconditions. First of all, the availability of a good infrastructure of trustworthy information and policy analysis, which supplies all parties with agreed facts and sometimes enables them to see policy problems in a new light. In the Netherlands the CPB and the WRR have proven their worth in this respect. Second, bi- and tripartite institutional structures like the SER and the Foundation of Labour, bringing together the social partners and state officials, allow these parties to draw up common responses in the face of urgent problems. For cooperation to be possible, however, parties have to be prepared to seek long-term mutual gain on the basis of agreed diagnoses of these problems. Repeated encounters within these institutions faciliates cooperation in so far as repetition allows unfair outcomes to be corrected in successive rounds of negotiations.

But negotiated change is no *passe-partout*; the 'problem-solving style' of decision-making which it can help produce is inherently unstable and fragile. Coalition politics and social partnership easily produce political gridlock and policy immobility. State support for private interest government is conditional upon substantive outcomes. The general point is that the procedures and outcomes of shared policy-making are not beyond critique. In democracies, governments must answer, ultimately, to parliaments and voters. Effective policy coordination needs a strong democracy and a state that is willing and able to take final responsibility.

References

Aarts, L. and P. De Jong (eds) (1996), *Curing the Dutch Disease*, Aldershot: Avebury.
CPB (1995), *Centraal Economische Plan 1995*, The Hague: SDU.
Esping-Andersen, G. (1996), 'Welfare States Without Work: the Impasse of Labour Shedding and Familialism in Continental European Social Policy', in *idem* (ed.), *Welfare States in Transition: National Adaptations in Global Economies*, London: Sage.
Hemerijck, A. C. (1995), 'Corporatist Immobility in the Netherlands', in C. Crouch, C. Traxter and F. Traxler (eds), *Organized Industrial Relations: What Future?*, Aldershot: Averbury.
Hemerijck, A. and M. Schludi (1999), *Policy Adjustment under International Constraints: Sequences of Challenges and Responses*, Max Planck Institute for the Study of Societies, Cologne.
Kersbergen, K. van (1995), *Social Capitalism: a Study of Christian Democracy and the Welfare State*, London/New York: Routledge.

OECD (various years), *OECD Economic Surveys* 1971–98, Netherlands, Paris: OECD.

OECD (various years), *OECD Employment Outlook*, 1994–9, Paris: OECD.

OECD (1994), *OECD Jobs Study*, Paris: OECD.

Scharpf, F. W. (1993), 'Coordination in Hierarchies and Networks', in Scharpf (ed.), *Games in Hierarchies and Networks: Analytical and Empirical Approaches to the Study of Governance Institutions*, Frankfurt am Main: Campus.

Scharpf, F. W. (1997), *The Games Real Actors Play: Actor-Centered Institutionalism in Policy Research*, Boulder Colo.: Westview Press.

Traxler, F. (1990), 'Farewell to Labour Market Assocications? Organized versus Disorganized as a Map for Industrial Relations', in C. Crouch and F.Traxler (eds), *Organized Industrial Relations in Europe: What Future?*, Avebury: Aldershot.

Visser, J. (1999), 'The First Part-Time Economy in the World: Does it Work?', Paper presented at Euro-Japan Symposium on the Development of Atypical Employment and Transformation of Labour Markets, Japan Productivity Centre for Socio-Economic Development, Tokyo, 24–5 March 1999.

Visser, J. and A. Hemerijck (1997), *A Dutch Miracle: Job Growth, Welfare Reform and Corporatism in the Netherlands*, Amsterdam: Amsterdam University Press.

15
Pluralism and the Future of the French Left

Laurent Bouvet and Frédéric Michel

1. Introduction

The French left has rediscovered its self-confidence. Almost twenty years after François Mitterrand emerged from the wilderness of opposition to announce a 'break with capitalism' located between traditional social democracy and Soviet socialism, the French left is once again renewing its commitment to progressive reform. Throughout this period the French left has always tried to remain faithful to its core values: equality, liberty and social justice. But it has often been cautious about the means to deliver change. Lionel Jospin's government has exhibited no such conservatism. It has used an impressive variety of policies and instruments to further its programme – different both from its predecessors and from its current European partners. Whether in its legislation to reduce working time, the use of privatization to recast the role of the French state, or the development of a constructive dialogue with employers, the Jospin government has shown itself willing to confound textbook accounts of how left politics should be conducted.

It is not just the nature of policy instruments that has changed in France – it is also the parties and political groupings that make up the left. The current French experiment with coalition politics, the *gauche plurielle*, which emerged following the left's victory at the legislative elections in 1997, reflects a major rupture in recent French political history. It is the first time during the Fifth Republic that five parties of the left – the Socialist Party (PS), the Communist Party (PC), the Greens (Les Verts), the Citizens' Movement (Mouvement Des Citoyens) and the Radical Party (Parti Radical de Gauche) – are part of the same majority in parliament and government. Lionel Jospin took it for granted that this unique coalition – *la majorité plurielle* – would require a new mode of governance: that the new left government would have to accept the diversity of its membership and seek to accommodate important aspects of the agendas of its partners. The differences within the coalition mean that policy has emerged as a result of a very intense process of debate, consultation and compromise. If this ongoing negotiation sometimes results in indecision, it none the less seems to be a valuable means of implementing effective economic, social and cultural reform. Pluralism, with its particular political rules, is at the heart of Jospin's statecraft and seems to be capable of generating landslide support. The impressive mix of political pluralism and strong economic performance makes France a very interesting policy laboratory for the European left.

2. The new pluralism

In order to understand the nature of the contemporary left in France it is necessary to consider the different positions or political 'families' that make up the French left. The way in which these groups have responded to structural social and economic change reveals the extent to which left politics in France has been redefined. The issues are familiar: the challenge that further European integration poses for national sovereignty; the need to articulate a left-of-centre response to neo-liberalism; the idea of 'French exceptionalism' and the response to American cultural dominance; the rise of individualist and post-materialist values; and the demise of class-based solidarities.

The first group is the 'social liberals', which developed out of the 'second left' of the 1960s and 1970s. The *deuxième gauche* rejected statist socialism in favour of less interventionist forms of economic regulation. It gained prominence through its opposition to the 'first left', founded by François Mitterrand, which was associated with the extension of public ownership. The social liberals are now the group closest to the third way position advocated by Tony Blair.

By the end of 1995 the social liberal group was fully committed to a modernizing agenda and in particular to the implementation of new social policies. It argued that the welfare state should not be subject to the dogmas of either the 'left' or 'right' agendas. The pragmatic case that the welfare state had to cope with the realities of the new economic environment was used to oppose traditional ideological arguments. The debate on welfare reform reflected a wider social liberal argument that French society had to adapt its statist structures to make them more efficient, and cultivate a market economy as the most effective means of ensuring economic efficiency.

Meanwhile globalization was portrayed not as a threat but as an opportunity, or at worst an unavoidable force with potentially beneficial effects. This type of thinking was welcomed by the business communities of the right and left and is now highly influential inside parts of the current government. However, it has brought social liberalism into direct conflict with the traditional anti-reformist position of the French left. Indeed, the social liberal group's support for the Euro and the independence of the European Central Bank, its questioning of the role of public provision, and its scepticism of many traditional forms of economic regulation, has contributed to the group's marginalization within the wider left.

The second group on the left comprises those whose principal concern is what they see as the defence of 'the Nation and the Republic'. The combined challenges of European integration and American cultural and political hegemony have placed the question of national sovereignty at the heart of contemporary French politics. The former Home Affairs Minister and leading figure in the Citizens' Movement (MDC), Jean-Pierre Chevènement, has called for the 'preservation at all costs' of national sovereignty. The idea of 'French exceptionalism' is popular amongst the French left. The Communist Party and some parts of the extreme left also oppose European integration because of Economic and Monetary Union, and they harbour a distrust of American foreign policy. The origins of this wave of 'exceptionalism' can be traced to the early 1990s when there were objections to the intervention against Iraq during the Gulf War and to the Maastricht Treaty during the 1992 referendum. Resentment flared up during the ratification of the Amsterdam Treaty and NATO intervention in Kosovo.

This political agenda shares much with the French right. Indeed, a number of left intellectuals show no hesitation in taking part in meetings organized by the political right to defend their common values. Gaullism, or the variant concerned with the 'defence of French specificity', offers an ideal bridge across the political divide. Amongst the republican left this is currently reflected in the belief that the European debate will force French political parties to take stronger stances on the future of European integration. Significantly, the Socialist Party used the term 'Federation of Nation States' in its June 1999 European manifesto, demonstrating its reluctance to present a federal model to a public still perceived to be keen on republican notions of sovereignty. The difficulty for the Communist Party and the MDC, however, is that they are part of a government responsible for setting up the Euro and negotiating with the European Central Bank. By voting with the government they have had to betray their own Euro-sceptic agendas.

Third, there is the section of the left associated with the 'new social movements', whose principal target is globalization. It includes on the one hand radical intellectuals such as Pierre Bourdieu and Vivianne Forester (author of the recent bestseller *The Economic Horror*) and social movements such as ATTAC (which opposes the Multilateral Agreement on Investment and supports a tax on currency speculation), who are highly critical of the growing influence of international financial markets; and on the other, groups such as employees of state-owned companies opposed to their privatization. For this section of the left, globalization is a shorthand for all the negative consequences of neo-liberalism on French society. They seek what they call a 'pluralist economy', which would entail further reductions of working time and the development of a vibrant 'third sector' of socially owned enterprises.

The intellectual origins of this movement come from Bourdieu, the leading sociologist on the French radical left. Yet the ambiguity of his agenda helps to explain why it has failed to gain significant representation. On the one hand, he articulates the leftist case for civic republicanism, while on the other he seeks to popularize the identity aspirations of the new 'social movements': feminists, gay activists and ethnic minorities. From the point of view of the radical left, attitudes towards these social groupings have come to represent the new fissure in French politics, separating a 'real' left approach, embracing all excluded groups, from the government's pursuit of the comfortable middle classes, with its accompanying betrayal (as they see it) of radical ideals and values.

Located at the fulcrum of these three groupings is the fourth and politically most significant, the 'neo-Keynesians' or 'modern socialists', who include Lionel Jospin and most of the hierarchy of the French Socialist Party. Their position is encapsulated in the slogan 'yes to the market economy, no to the market society'. As Jospin has written in his recent Fabian pamphlet: 'though the market produces wealth in itself, it generates neither solidarity nor values, neither objectives nor meaning'. At a policy level the result is a blend of pragmatism and idealism best illustrated by the government's two flagship policies: the most ambitious programme of privatization carried out by any French government and the simultaneous introduction of the 35-hour working week. From a comparative European perspective, however, what really distinguishes the mainstream left French position is that, despite its willingness to reign back the role of the state in some areas, there continues to be concerted public intervention throughout key sectors of the economy. This arises from its concept of 'economic government': the belief that market regulation is both socially desirable and capable of generating greater efficiency.

At a political level Jospin's success is due in large part to a combination of rhetoric and pragmatic policy able to satisfy the often divergent positions of the *gauche plurielle*. His government has learnt how to convert the systemic constraints of coalition into political advantage. It has provided a discourse under which different components of the left can unite and share in the collective achievements of the government. Whether it is the Communists with privatization, the Citizens' Movement with the Euro, or the Greens with energy policy: each partner has been able, most of the time, to support the government's agenda.

3. Labour-market reform and the unions

Over the last two decades reforms which have sought to ensure either a higher degree of government intervention or a higher level of social protection have faced virtually insuperable institutional obstacles. The power of inertia has proved formidable, while any serious clash with entrenched vested interests has been presented by both right and left as the dismantling of the welfare state, an idea which remains deeply unpopular. It is in this difficult context that the new left government has been required to advance its reform agenda. Three interrelated projects have been central to its programme: the introduction of the 35-hour week; the reshaping of the role of the state in economic and industrial policy; and development of a new social policy.

Labour-market politics goes to the heart of the Jospin project. No other left-of-centre government in Europe has attached so much political significance to efforts to reform existing patterns of work. Indeed, it is at the very moment when conventional wisdom maintains that nation-states should be deregulating their labour markets that the Jospin government is seeking to orchestrate, via the legislative process, an ambitious legislated reduction in working time. The Aubry Law, named after the former Minister for Employment, is by some way the most interventionist employment policy now being attempted in Europe – and has been widely dismissed, both in France and elsewhere, for precisely this reason.

The 35-hour week is in fact somewhat misnamed, since the law requires firms to implement only an average week of this length over a year's employment. The result so far – to the surprise of some – has been to introduce a considerable amount of flexibility in working patterns. Though business organizations continue to complain that the law will impose substantial extra costs and will reduce their competitiveness, this does appear to have led to productivity gains as well. The government moreover argues that the 35-hour week has succeeded in increasing employment (as it was intended to do): by the summer of 1999, its claim (though it is disputed by others) is that 120,000 jobs have been safeguarded or created by the new law.

Concerns with working time have been a recurrent theme of left politics in France. They have been renewed now as a result of the failure of the left's previous attempts to solve the long-standing deficiencies of the French labour market. During the Mitterrand Presidency (1981–95) the left was on the one hand committed to levels and forms of social benefits which in practice diminished work incentives, and on the other proved itself unwilling to reform the cumbersome system of collective bargaining. The failure of this traditional approach towards employment regulation led to scepticism about the capacity of public-policy initiatives to tackle this issue (and indeed others). Each set of attempted reforms seemed merely to create its own array of perverse incentives. This encouraged a shift, even on the left, towards a more laissez-faire approach. One effect of this was to distract attention from the need to update the main safeguard for employees – the Labour Code (*Code du Travail*) – to better reflect the contemporary labour market: large parts of the Code have become increasingly irrelevant to the needs of part-time and short-term workers.

A key issue in this area is the role of the trade unions, for a long time key players in the French left. Like every other government of the left in Europe, the Jospin administration has been trying to restore long-term employment growth by involving the different 'social partners' (trade unions, other employee organizations and business representatives) in the policy process. Nevertheless, the debate on the 35-hour week has had the effect of eroding the formerly pre-eminent role of French unions. By focusing narrowly on specific conflicts with employers at a national level, the union movement lost the opportunity in the first phase of the reform to engage in the wider questions of flexibility, holidays, training and wages which the 35-hour week opens up at the workplace level. More recently the large general unions such as the CGT and CFDT have started to put the reduction of working time at the forefront of their activities, seeking to ensure that the process of achieving working time reductions is driven at a grass-roots level. But the issue has exposed the low level of union membership in much of the private sector. This has forced the government to introduce the concept of the 'mandated worker' with responsibility for implementation of the 35-hour week at the level of the firm. With the mandated worker being appointed by the employer, this system is not supported by the unions; but the proposal shows up more generally the failure of the union movement to play a full and active role in the modernization of industrial relations.

If reductions in working time can indeed help to stimulate employment, they represent a real opportunity for the unions to define a new partnership with the state and trigger a new culture of collective bargaining. Contrary to received wisdom in the rest of Europe, French corporatist structures are far from being 'old-fashioned' or symbols of an 'old way'. They have the potential to be revived as a modern instrument for forging consensus across a key range of policies, from employee share ownership to pensions reform. But this will take new thinking within the unions as well as within the government.

4. The left and the future role of the state

Debate about globalization rages on the French left, fuelled by a sweeping process of adjustment taking place in key sectors of the economy, from banking to energy. In a country where the state has always been pre-eminent and where its economic presence has been felt more than in most other Western democratic societies, the current transformation is even more striking. Confronted not just with wider economic globalization but with the specific emergence of the single currency, the issue is how the French nation-state can and should respond to the challenge of an apparently shrinking role. The different sides of the debate were represented clearly during recent conflicts in the banking industry. On the one hand neo-liberals accused the government of an anachronistic 'Colbertism' – a reference to Louis XIV's protectionist economic and finance minister. On the other, critics on the left denounced the state for its passivity in the face of the destabilizing diktats of the market. Too slowly for some, too quickly for others, the French state is being forced to adjust to the pressures of globalization.

France still has one of the strongest traditions of centralized government in Europe. The state has long maintained monopolies in public services such as rail transport and the postal service. State-owned companies dominate industries such as coal mining, aerospace and nuclear energy. There are also a variety of quasi-public companies in which the state is one of several shareholders. In addition to its role as owner, the government has played an important part in French industry in other ways, arranging takeovers and mergers to improve performance and international competitiveness and providing financial support for sectors or companies in difficulty.

Much of this remains; but there has been a notable shift in government policy over the past two years. Amongst the most visible is the continuation of the previous government's programme of privatization. In early 1998 the government began to liberalize the telecommunications sector; then in October 1998 the timetable for the long-awaited privatization of Crédit Lyonnais was announced. The government has since begun (albeit behind schedule) to deregulate the electricity sector, as required by an EU directive. In effect, this will end the monopoly role of Electricité de France (EDF) in supplying power to 450 large enterprises which together represent about 26 per cent of total electricity consumption.

Privatization is being accompanied by the development of new forms of 'public–private partnership'. Some such partnerships exist already, most commonly the *société d'économie mixte* or 'mixed public–private company'. These companies are public–private joint ventures that provide services at both the local and central government levels. The French government is now forming public–private partnerships in the area of research, setting up alliance networks of public laboratories and private enterprises. The number of these hybrid arrangements looks set to increase. In addition the government is increasingly selective in its aid to industry, shifting from ailing industries to growth sectors, especially those engaged in cutting-edge technologies. Direct subsidies have given way to tax credits for research and development, investment incentives and regional development grants. There is an increased public recognition of the need to create an environment that fosters internationally competitive industries.

At the same time, other constraints are forcing the Jospin government to reassess the size and functioning of the state administration itself. Most notable has been the paramount need for budget discipline. In order to meet the Maastricht convergence criteria, the government has tightened fiscal policy, forcing departments to reduce their spending. This budgetary pressure is expected to continue into the next century as a result of the enforcement procedures of the EU's stability and growth pact. Rising expectations of government services among citizens are also helping to drive reform. And, as in other countries, decentralization has become one of the core defences of national government to challenges to its role. Although France remains highly centralized, the government has been gradually ceding more power to the lower administrative levels. It is now conceivable that the government will consider removing one of these levels – most likely the *département*, putting more power in the hands of the regions. All these reforms reflect the growing acceptance by the French left that the state must change in response to changing circumstances.

5. The social question

For most of the French left the most urgent crisis in French society is that of poverty and social exclusion, with unemployment in particular continuing at high levels among certain 'excluded' groups in society. The Jospin government has made this a strong priority, passing a high-profile 'law against social exclusion' incorporating its key measures. Considerable public spending has been pumped into the programme to tackle youth unemployment, involving subsidized employment in the private sector and major public works schemes in municipal government.

But the most serious controversies have arisen over welfare reform, in particular in the field of pensions. There is widespread recognition in French society today that the welfare state needs reform: it is widely thought to entrench and legitimize inequalities. But the practicalities of carrying out such reform are highly complex. On pensions, it is accepted that as the population ages the current funded system, set up in the post-war period, will collapse without reform early in the twenty-first century. But there is considerable opposition to the introduction of private pensions invested in the financial markets – at time of writing, both the Green and Communist Party coalition partners have rejected the government's proposals, and the reform package has been twice postponed. There are potential opportunities here to extend industrial ownership by giving employees control over the pensions funds invested in their name. But there remains considerable work to be done to persuade the unions of the full significance of this. As in other countries, the implementation of the modernization programme will prove a searching test for the government's political skills.

6. Conclusion: the 'new alliance'

A few years ago Laurent Fabius, the former prime minister (now leader of the parliament), famously described the modernization of the left as a 'degrading job' which had to be done but brought little reward. This is no longer the case. So far at least, the new French government's modernization programme has not merely delivered faster economic growth and reversed economic decline, it has also won electoral success. The government has not been slow to claim credit.

The basis of the government's appeal lies partly in the diversity of political positions represented in the *gauche plurielle*. But it is also based on a new appeal across social classes. Jospin has used the concept of a 'new alliance' to describe the coalition of support he is attempting to build: from the long-term unemployed and the socially excluded to the comfortable middle classes. His task now is to consolidate this. Having placed considerable emphasis on the low paid and excluded in his first two years, the priority now is to recognize the 'legitimate aspirations' of the wage-earning middle-income groups. To this end Jospin promised, in what might be described as a rather New Labourish way, a cut in income tax aimed at the middle classes. Where once the left was founded on its working-class base, Jospin has recognized that social change today makes middle-class support the central pillar of electoral success. In this, inevitably, he is not so different from Blair or Schroeder.

Bibliography

Bouvet, Laurent, 'Tony Blair est-il exportable?', *Politique Etrangère*, 80, Summer 1998.

Bouvet, Laurent, 'Quartre, elles sont quatre', *Le Monde*, 8 Oct. 1999.

Bouvet, Laurent and Michel, Frédéric, 'Le blairisme est-il un socialisme?', *La Revue Socialiste*, 1, Spring 1999.

Bouvet, Laurent and Michel, Frédéric, 'Paris, Bonn, Rome: a Continental Way?', in Ian Hargreaves, ed., *Tomorrow's Politics: the Third Way and Beyond*, London: Demos, 1998.

Bouvet, Laurent and Michel, Frédéric, 'La Troisième Voie', introductory chapter to the French publication in one volume of Tony Blair, *New Politics for the New Century* and Anthony Giddens, *The Renewal of Social Democracy*, Paris: Seuil, 2000.

Crouch, C., *Social Change in Western Europe*, Oxford: Oxford University Press, 1999.

Lazar, M. 'La social-démocratie européenne à l'épreuve de la réforme', *Esprit*, March–April 1999.

Marian, M., 'Lionel Jospin, le socialisme et la réforme', *Esprit*, March–April 1999.

Rhodes, M., 'The Political Economy of Social Pacts: "Competitive Corporatism" and European Welfare Reform', in P. Pierson, ed., *The New Politics of the Welfare State*, Oxford: Oxford University Press, 2000.

Rosanvallon, Pierre and Fitoussi, Jean-Paul, eds, *Le Nouvel age des inégalités*, Paris: Seuil, 1996.

16
Conclusion: New Labour and the Uncertain Future of Progressive Politics

Stuart White and Susan Giaimo

> The crisis consists ... in the fact that the old is dying and the new cannot be born; in this interregnum, a great variety of morbid symptoms appear.[1]

This book has addressed two questions: Does New Labour offer a genuine future for progressive politics? Is there a new and coherent model of progressive governance emerging in the advanced capitalist world which New Labour shares with social democrats elsewhere in Europe and with liberals in the US? Let us now try to draw together some provisional conclusions from the foregoing discussion.

1) In broad terms, it seems clear that the New Labour phenomenon reflects a broader, international trend to re-prioritize 'liberal' values and practices within social democracy, in particular to make social democracy more market-friendly (see especially Chapters 1, 2, 11, 12). Moreover, it would in our view be wrong to dismiss this turn to liberalism as necessarily a mere capitulation to free-market ideas. First, the 'social liberalism' in question here does not seek to reduce income redistribution and social insurance to a minimum. It affirms a significant role for the state in tempering the inequality in earnings that results from market-driven employment growth, and in pooling resources to meet risks and, for example, some of the costs associated with parenting and other carer responsibilities. Secondly, this social liberalism notably affirms a much larger role for the state in regulating the distribution of assets (skills, capital, etc.) that citizens bring to the market. Public policy must seek actively to *build* assets (financial, human, and social capital) amongst the asset-poor and to *spread* assets around. Such 'social investment' is seen as not only good for equity but as a source of efficiency gains. Thirdly, while more receptive to neo-liberal worries about state failure than traditional social democracy, the social liberal perspective also stresses the potential for market failure. Neither market nor state instruments are privileged; they

have to be pragmatically balanced and integrated with non-state, non-profit instruments in the voluntary and mutual sectors (see Chapters 4 and 5).

2) Nor need social liberalism involve a dilution of the left's traditional egalitarian values. A number of economists and political theorists have recently begun to explore the possibilities of 'asset-based egalitarianism' as a way of improving the equity–efficiency trade-off in liberal market economies, and their ideas give a clear sense of what a robustly egalitarian social liberalism might consist in.[1] One recurring proposal is to introduce a scheme of sizeable universal capital endowments, financed from wealth or inheritance taxes or from public investment in the stock market.[2] Citizen's Income is another variant on this basic idea. However, the kind and level of equality at which progressives ought ideally to aim remains a source of uncertainty amongst contemporary progressives (see especially Chapter 12, also Chapters 1, 6). To some extent, of course, this has always been the case, but the ambiguity is perhaps greater today than in the past. Critics on the left worry that the greater receptivity to market mechanisms is accompanied by a rightward revision of values, a shift towards a more meritocratic understanding of 'equal opportunity'. There is some evidence for this in the official 'third way' literature (see Chapter 1). But, as the proposals of Ackerman and Alstott and others show (see note 1), social liberalism is compatible with strong egalitarianism. There is still a profound debate about values to be had under this rubric.

3) New Labour's record in social and economic policy does to some extent exemplify a progressive social liberalism. In particular, New Labour has appreciably increased the level and expanded the scope of in-work benefits to tackle the problem of working poverty (see Chapters 5 and 6), and introduced a Minimum Income Guarantee for pensioners the level of which will rise with growth in average earnings (Chapter 5). There have also been important moves towards a more family-friendly work regime: the Childcare Tax Credit for low/middle-income households and new legal rights to (unpaid) parental leave are perhaps the two most noteworthy examples (see Chapters 6 and 9). There is also a strong policy orientation towards asset-building and asset-spreading. This is reflected in a range of policies from the nascent Individual Learning Accounts (ILAs), the New Deals, new initiatives for those in the 16–18 age group such as the piloted Education Maintenance Allowance, to long-term programmes focused on infant development such as Sure Start (see especially Chapters 4 and 6). Also noteworthy here are the government's initiatives on second pensions, as described by Paul Johnson in Chapter 5, the introduction of a new tax-privileged savings vehicle (Individual Savings Accounts), and efforts to promote wider access to Credit Unions. Last and certainly not least is the expansion in public spending on education and healthcare, particularly following the budget of March 2000.[3]

These policies will produce clear and undeniable benefits for some of Britain's most disadvantaged citizens. The independent evaluation by the Institute for Fiscal Studies of the distributive impact of the New Labour budgets up to and including that of March 2000 shows that the gains from tax-benefit changes have been concentrated on lower income groups. Those in the bottom wealth decile, for example, have seen a roughly 9 per cent increase in their weekly income as a result of these changes, while those in the upper deciles have seen no increase or a slight reduction.[4]

4) Nevertheless, New Labour's policy record can be criticized from a progressive standpoint for at least three reasons.

a) *The modesty of New Labour's social liberalism.* The foregoing policies are thought by many, including some contributors to this book, only to represent a start in getting to grips with the problems of social exclusion and economic insecurity allegedly afflicting the country. Even sympathetic critics typically argue that more must be done, e.g., to help disadvantaged workers out of entrapment in poor-quality jobs (Chapter 6), implying the commitment of further resources. There is, however, a tension between New Labour's social and economic strategy, which demands a high level of 'social investment' along the lines just laid out, and its political tactics, which require an avoidance of visible increases in taxation on high- and middle-income groups. Prior to the 1997 general election, Labour pledged that it would not raise rates of income tax above the levels inherited from the Conservatives for the lifetime of the parliament. This pledge, which has been met, may well have helped Labour win the election as convincingly as it did,[5] but has obviously limited the scope for increasing public spending. Thus far, the government has sought to increase its room for manoeuvre by adopting a policy that commentators have labelled 'redistribution by stealth' – finding less visible ways of increasing the tax take from middle- and high-income households to finance initiatives aimed at low-income groups. But there are undoubted limits to the strategy both in that it is becoming more difficult to find new 'invisible' taxes to increase or introduce and because initially invisible tax increases tend to become more visible over time.[6] Strong macroeconomic performance has provided additional room for manoeuvre in the form of a projected budget surplus over the next few years.[7] But the basic tension between social investment and a tax/spending economy stands as a fundamental feature of the New Labour 'project' (see also Chapter 4).

b) *The unevenness of New Labour's social liberalism.* For all the talk of New Labour's 'liberalism' (on which see especially Chap. 2), New Labour cannot be said to have acted consistently from a recognizably liberal public philosophy. In certain areas, such as devolution, its liberalism is hesitant and uncertain (see Chapter 8, and also, for a related argument, Anna Coote's discussion of New Labour's ambivalent feminism in Chapter 9). In other areas, such as freedom of information and the proposed reforms to the right to trial by jury,[8] the prevailing approach is widely seen as the reverse of what a liberal approach would be. New Labour thinking and rhetoric, in common with much third way/radical centre thinking and rhetoric elsewhere, stresses the importance of civic responsibility. But the confusion between 'liberal' and 'communitarian' conceptions of civic responsibility (see Chapter 1) remains, and has perhaps facilitated the adoption of policy initiatives which many see as illiberal. Perhaps here there is some truth in the thesis that New Labour is not essentially interested in developing and acting from a coherent public philosophy at all but is, rather, a simple centrism or populism (see Chapter 3).

c) *The potential weaknesses of social liberalism itself.* In one extreme form, social liberalism approximates to what one might call 'Left Thatcherism': an ideology which says that we should try to assure citizens roughly equal initial endowments of marketable assets and then let the free market rip. This approach can be criticized for ignoring or understating the potential gains, both to equity and efficiency, from old-fashioned forms of state intervention and non-market coordination. A 'Left Thatcherite' will, for example, seek to dismantle 'corporatist' modes of wage bargaining as a barrier to the operation of market forces. But a lack of centralized coordination between labour and capital can make it more difficult for these collective actors to solve, to their mutual advantage, a host of collective action problems, from wage restraint in a buoyant economy to effective cooperation on the making and enacting of education and training policy (see Chapter 7 and the conclusion to Chapter 14).[9]

5) In considering the move towards social liberalism in other advanced capitalist countries, and the likely degree of convergence with New Labour, we must allow for the fact that other progressive governments face very different institutional inheritances which will constrain and shape the extent to which, and the way in which, social liberal ideas are developed and enacted. An interesting comparison, which brings out this point, is with Germany (see Chapter 13).

The German economy suffers from a problem of inactivity. High labour costs – the result of high wages and a welfare state financed primarily from payroll taxes – price out labour in sheltered services and encourage labour-shedding in manufacturing. Inactivity, in turn, feeds into the second problem: growing fiscal strain on the welfare state. Low levels of labour-force participation mean an insufficient funding base for social provision even as a growing number of people depend on it. Many analysts argue that Germany stands in need of higher levels of employment which, in turn, will require greater wage dispersion and a shift in the tax base of the welfare state from payroll taxes to eco-taxes. The effects of increased wage dispersion can be mitigated, it is argued, through wage/earnings supplements to low-wage workers.[10]

This is classic social liberal thinking. However, successful policy change cannot be imposed. In the German context, it must be negotiated with the unions and employer associations, the 'social partners', through the 'Alliance for Jobs'. And one or other of the social partners may find grounds to disagree with the government's proposals. In addition, while New Labour can try to claim credit for repairing the social fabric damaged by Conservative predecessors, to effect reform Schroeder must reduce or withdraw some of the accustomed entitlements from powerful Social Democratic constituencies even as he seeks to articulate a new social contract. And he must do so with a party that has yet to undertake a programmatic renewal and in coalition with another, quite independent political party. Notwithstanding some commonality in analysis and rhetoric, we should therefore not expect Germany's 'Neue Mitte' to end up looking very similar to New Labour's 'third way'. There is even less expectation of convergence in the French case, though the practice of the French 'Gauche Plurielle' may in some areas, such as the cultivation of public–private partnerships, have more in common with New Labour than might be thought (see Chapter 15).

6) These differences aside, progressive governments in the advanced capitalist countries do face a common challenge. If they are to avoid the inequality associated with liberal market economies like Britain and the USA, and the high levels of inactivity associated with some of the 'coordinated' market economies like Germany, they must find a way to combine flexibility in the labour market with equity objectives (what Visser and Hemerijck in Chap. 14 call 'flexicurity'). But this is difficult, to say the least. As we have just noted, in the case of economies like Germany and France, 'flexibility' and related welfare state reform provoke the opposition of powerful institutional actors who are well-placed to veto proposed changes. At the same time, as we have noted in regard to New Labour, doubts arise as to whether progressive governments in liberal market economies will commit themselves to sufficient social investment.

The US case, discussed by Margaret Weir in Chapter 10, is particularly instructive in this latter respect. The main achievements of the Clinton years have been the expansion in the level of the Earned Income Tax Credit as a corrective to working poverty and the maintenance of rapid aggregate economic and employment growth. But against this we have to set the 1996 welfare reform, one of the centrepieces of Clinton's legacy. The work obligations it places on citizens far outweigh reciprocal government commitments to provide training. As a result, the reform is likely to increase the insecurity of those at the bottom of the labour market, as former welfare recipients join the ranks of those in contingent, low-wage employment. The act does little, moreover, to ensure that those in such jobs have access to adequate pensions and health insurance.[11] Thus, while the poor may end up gainfully employed, the problems of social exclusion and inequality bred through the deregulated labour market are likely to remain. The Clinton case shows what can happen when, with progressives seemingly impotent to shift the basic frame of policy debate, a social liberal agenda is diluted to the point where it becomes, across many policy domains, little more than cosmetic.

At the other end of the scale, the Netherlands looks like a relative success story (see Chapter 14). Coordinated wage restraint has produced rapid job growth, enabling increased participation by women and youths in particular (albeit substantially in part-time sheltered services and temporary work). But employment growth has not come at the expense of working poverty or a significant increase in income inequality. The state has underwritten social insurance contributions for the low-paid and has extended social rights to cover workers in contingent employment. Universal programmes like healthcare and citizens' pensions alleviate fears of illness and insecurity in old age and for the low-paid and temporary workers. Flexibility is combined with security and, as a result, at least a modicum of equity. Particularly interesting, we think, is the way the Netherlands seems to have pioneered a new system of social solidarity which, basing itself on a serious but carer-friendly 'participation ethic', avoids both the high inactivity of the German model and the narrow productivist focus of the US welfare system in which income security tends to be tightly conditioned on paid employment to the neglect of care work.

7) Progressives have no alternative but periodically to revise their programmes because capitalism changes over time and, in doing so, poses the challenge of reconciling equity and efficiency in new ways. But revisionism always carries with it a risk of excessive accommodation to changed circumstances, reflected in a stretching or dilution of core values and the abandonment of a distinctive long-term vision. This book, we believe, provides a series of selective snap-shots of a left, in Britain and elsewhere, currently working through the trials of necessary revisionism. For this reason alone we should expect the picture to be a mixed one featuring renewed efficacy in some areas alongside some basic confusion of goals and identity. Looking at the situation from an engaged progressive standpoint, and focusing specifically on Britain, we think there are three key areas – more closely related than they perhaps appear at first sight – in which work remains to be done.

a) *Public philosophy.* Progressive politics, as represented by New Labour, currently lacks a clear and attractive public philosophy. In the 1980s, just as many progressive politicians began to think about how to make their defeated parties re-electable, many academic political theorists became engaged in the task of 'rethinking socialism' in response to the energetic critique provided by intellectuals of the New Right. At the end of the 1990s, a rough and ready consensus had begun to emerge amongst a number of the leading theorists. At the institutional level, the consensus favours some form of market egalitarianism: James Meade's model of a 'partnership economy', featuring 'labour–capital partnerships', inheritance taxes and a universal social dividend, is in many ways the template here.[12] This institutional vision is typically grounded in some variant of the liberal egalitarian political philosophy of which John Rawls is the classic exponent (see also Chapter 12).[13] This egalitarian social liberalism, in many ways a rigorous development of the 'New Liberalism' of the early years of the century, and of the broader background tradition of democratic and social republicanism stretching back to Thomas Paine, offers a rich vein of material for developing a more coherent and attractive progressive public philosophy. Philosophically, this egalitarian social liberalism *is* the third way between free market liberalism and 'state socialism' that New Labour claims to be interested in. Much of the philosophical, 'big picture' thinking around New Labour has ignored or dismissed this theoretical work, however. New Labour thinkers have made the mistake of thinking that the 'third way' is something that they have to *invent*, instead of seeing it in terms of the reappropriation of a long-standing philosophical tradition which has itself already undergone considerable refinement and development in recent years.

b) *Public spending.* Much depends, in the British case, on how New Labour slowly resolves the tension between its social investment and taxation commitments. The budget of March 2000 was significant in this respect in that it saw the New Labour government choose to use its strong fiscal position primarily to boost spending in core public services (notably healthcare) rather than to make further cuts in rates of income tax. Looking to the longer term, adopting one of the ideas of James Meade, New Labour might explore the possibility of collective asset accumulation as a means of establishing a revenue base for the welfare state that is independent of the taxation of labour incomes.[14] But above all, British progressives need to think of how, over the longer term, government can cultivate and deepen the sentiments of solidarity on which redistributive, opportunity-spreading taxation rests. This is in fact one aspect of a larger problem of building and maintaining civic commitment.

c) *Civic commitment.* Progressive politics presupposes citizens with a high level of civic commitment: commitment to participate in politics, to bear a fair share of the costs of providing public goods and substantial opportunity for all, and to provide a range of complementary goods through forms of collective self-help that are independent of the state. Today, however, progressives cannot take civic commitment as a given; more than ever, building such commitment has to be the conscious objective of policy. Ideas for Citizens' Service schemes, and for the wider use of Citizens' Juries to assist decision-making in local government and the social services, may offer some pointers here. Devolution may also help in some respects (see Chapter 8). Also important, however, as Margaret Weir implies in Chapter 10, is the form of progressive politics itself. At time of writing, there is much comment on New Labour's apparent inability to enthuse and mobilize its natural supporters, resulting in low turn-out at elections and an increase in the electoral credibility of the Conservative Party. There are doubtless many factors behind this. But the lack of widespread enthusiasm for New Labour, the perceived failure of voters to see 'what we have done', may in part bear out Weir's point – that a successful, lasting progressive politics must ultimately be a politics *of* the people, and not merely something that clever and well-meaning politicians do *to* or *for* them.

An appropriate historical reference point here might be the 'Popular Liberalism' of late nineteenth-century Britain, with its strong roots in working-class civil society (the trade union, the chapel, the friendly society, the working men's club). This civil society, and the wider civic commitment it promoted, offered invaluable support for Liberal party politicians in the late nineteenth and early twentieth centuries. Over time, however, the civil society of progressivism has been slowly hollowed out. It is not obvious how the challenge this implies can be met. But if the next century is indeed to be the 'Progressive Century' of which Tony Blair speaks, the challenge of rebuilding a supportive civil society, of cultivating a truly popular social liberalism, is one that progressives will need to do their best to meet.

Notes

1 See, in particular, Bruce Ackerman and Anne Alstott, *The Stakeholder Society* (New Haven: Yale University Press, 1999), Samuel Bowles and Herbert Gintis, *Recasting Egalitarianism* (London: Verso, 1998), and Joel Rogers and Robert Freeman, *The New Inequality* (Boston: Beacon Press, 1999).

2 See Ackerman and Alstott, *Stakeholder Society*, and for a more modest variant on the idea, David Nissan and Julian Le Grand, *A Capital Idea: Start-Up Grants for Young People* (London: Fabian Society, 2000).

3 The Chancellor, Gordon Brown, announced a real increase in spending on the National Health Service of roughly 6 per cent per annum for the four years starting 2000/1.

4 See Howard Reed, 'Post-Budget Analysis: Personal Tax and Benefit Issues', <http://www1.ifs.org.uk/gbfiles/distribution>.

5 At the 1992 election 43 per cent of the electorate supported the 'status quo' in taxation and spending (no increases, no cuts) but Labour only secured the support of 26 per cent of voters in this key middle group. At the 1997 election, Labour won the support of 57 per cent of this key middle group. See Paul Whitely, 'Tax Aversion Therapy', *The Guardian*, 4 Feb. 2000.

6 A good example of the redistribution by stealth strategy is the decision, taken in the government's first budget in 1997, to end the system whereby pension funds could reclaim Advanced Corporation Tax on the dividends from their share

holdings. This raised a handy £5bn but was not immediately visible to the middle and higher income groups most significantly affected by it. More visible have been the decisions to phase out mortgage interest tax relief and the married couple's tax allowance (completing a process begun under the previous Conservative government). Overall, the tax burden (tax revenue as a share of national income) has risen modestly under New Labour. The UK Treasury's official figures, as announced in the budget of March 2000, describe a rise from 36.5 per cent in 1997/8 to 37.4 per cent in 1998/9 followed by a projected fall back to 37 per cent for 1999/2000, a further fall to 36.8 per cent in 2000/1, and a projected rise to 37.2 per cent in 2001/2. See Michael White, 'Labour Admits Tax Rises', *The Guardian*, 15 March 2000.

7 According to the Institute for Fiscal Studies the government was due, prior to the budget of March 2000, to run a surplus (on current spending) of almost £13bn for the financial year 1999/2000. The surplus was set to rise to around £20bn per year for the next four years (or over 1.5 per cent of national income). See Lucy Channells, Andrew Dilnot and Carl Emmerson, *The IFS Green Budget* (London: Institute for Fiscal Studies, 2000), esp. tables 3.7, 3.8, pp. 25–6. The authors stress, however, the very large margins of error involved in making such forecasts.

8 The proposals, announced in 1999, would reduce the range of alleged offences for which citizens can insist on a jury trial. Given notable differences in acquittal rates between magistrate and jury trials, the proposals have excited considerable alarm amongst civil liberties groups in Britain.

9 For further relevant discussion, see Andrew Glyn and Stewart Wood, 'New Labour's Economic Policy', in Andrew Glyn, ed., *Social Democracy and Economic Policy* (Oxford: Oxford University Press, 2000).

10 Fritz W. Scharpf, *Employment and the Welfare State: a Continental Dilemma*, MPIFG Working Paper 97/7, July 1997, Cologne: Max Planck Institute for the Study of Societies. The Green Party has championed eco-taxes as a way to stabilize and reduce pension contributions across all sectors, and the Schroeder government introduced them in 1999.

11 The federal welfare reform law requires no more than transitional health insurance for a specified time period. Given the lack of universal health insurance or compulsory second-tier pensions, most employees rely on fringe benefits offered voluntarily by their employers. Such benefits, however, are least likely to extend to those in contingent and low-wage jobs.

12 In addition to the works cited in note 1, and James Meade, *Agathatopia: the Economics of Partnership* (Aberdeen: University of Aberdeen, 1989), see Paul Hirst, *Associative Democracy* (Cambridge: Polity, 1994), David Miller, *Market, State and Community* (Oxford: Oxford University Press, 1989), John Roemer, *Equal Shares* (London: Verso, 1998), and Philippe Van Parijs, *Real Freedom for All* (Oxford: Oxford University Press, 1995).

13 See especially John Rawls, *A Theory of Justice* (Oxford: Oxford University Press, 1972).

14 Gerald Holtham envisages using proceeds from reformed inheritance and capital gains taxes to establish over a 10-year period a Community Fund of £50bn invested on behalf of the state in the stock market. If the rate of return on the Fund is 6 per cent, and the Fund is left to grow at 3 per cent per annum, the Fund would then offer the rather modest sum of £1.5bn for public spending in its first year of operation. But over the longer run the Fund would continue to

accumulate and would thus eventually offer a much larger annual sum for spending purposes. See Gerald Holtham, 'Ownership and Social Democracy', in Andrew Gamble and Tony Wright, eds, *The New Social Democracy* (Oxford: Blackwell, 1999), pp. 53–68.

Index

232 *Index*